T0185389

Technical Animation in
Video Games

This book provides a comprehensive overview of video game technical animation, covering the next generation pipelines that industry developers utilise to create their games. It covers the technical animation workflow from start to finish, looking at both software and hardware, as well as the industry standard processes that all technical animators need to know.

Written to be an accessible technical animation resource, this book combines easy-to-understand principles with educational use cases on how to combine the principles and tools taught within. Example test scripts, animation files, and rig assets are provided as tangible examples that can be modified and taken apart to deepen your understanding. It covers the end-to-end pipeline of technical animation, from the very first steps of placing joints in Autodesk's Maya to breathe life into your static characters, through tools and automation development, all the way to Unreal Engine 5 integration and optimisation.

Additional resources are available on the book's GitHub repository. From this resource, you will find example files for Maya and Python scripts that will help with your own work and demonstrations featured throughout this book.

This book is essential reading for early-career game technical animators as well as those studying game animation courses. It will also appeal to technical animators working in the film industry.

Technical Animation in Video Games

Matthew Lake

CRC Press
Taylor & Francis Group
Boca Raton London New York

CRC Press is an imprint of the
Taylor & Francis Group, an **informa** business

Designed cover image: Robert Green

First edition published [2024]
by CRC Press
2385 Executive Center Drive, Suite 320, Boca Raton, FL 33431

and by CRC Press
4 Park Square, Milton Park, Abingdon, Oxon, OX14 4RN

CRC Press is an imprint of Taylor & Francis Group, LLC

© 2024 Matthew Lake

Library of Congress Cataloging-in-Publication Data

Names: Lake, Matthew (Animator), author.
Title: Technical animation in video games / Matthew Lake.
Description: 1st edition. | Boca Raton : CRC Press, 2024. | Includes bibliographical references and index. | Contents: Technical animator -- Introduction to software -- Introduction to motion capture technology -- A technical understanding -- Introduction to Maya -- Introduction to Python -- Python for Maya -- Maya building a skeleton -- Maya building a control rig -- Introduction to Unreal Engine -- Unreal : skeleton setup -- Unreal : the animation blueprint -- Unreal : the control rig blueprint -- Unreal : physics assets -- Unreal : sequencer cinematics -- Unreal : cloth dynamics -- Unreal : optimisation -- Evaluation.
Identifiers: LCCN 2023029887 (print) | LCCN 2023029888 (ebook) | ISBN 9781032203409 (hardback) | ISBN 9781032203270 (paperback) | ISBN 9781003263258 (ebook)
Subjects: LCSH: Computer animation | Video games--Design. | Video games--Programming.
Classification: LCC TR897.7 .L35 2024 (print) | LCC TR897.7 (ebook) |
DDC 777/.7--dc23/eng/20230926
LC record available at https://lccn.loc.gov/2023029887
LC ebook record available at https://lccn.loc.gov/2023029888

ISBN: 9781032203409 (hbk)
ISBN: 9781032203270 (pbk)
ISBN: 9781003263258 (ebk)

DOI: 10.1201/9781003263258

Typeset in Times LT Std
by KnowledgeWorks Global Ltd.

Support material available at https://github.com/MattLakeTA/TechnicalAnimationInVideoGames

For Ian Hitchen

Contents

About the Author

Matthew Lake is a technical animator working in the video game industry. He started his career producing short movies in the early days of YouTube, leading on to work with the online entertainment network Machinima. Matthew has spent more than a decade working on content creation, and after finding a love for interactive storytelling, he pursued a career in video game development. After acquiring a Bachelor of Arts degree in computer games animation, Matthew worked on the multiplayer game Destruction AllStars, a PlayStation 5 exclusive launch title. He most recently worked as the lead technical animator on Fort Solis, a single-player narrative game also for the PlayStation 5.

1

Technical Animator

1.1 What Is a Technical Animator?

A technical animator (TA), as the name may suggest, is an animator who is technically minded or focused on technical animation-related tasks for the production of a video game. It is a partial support role due to supporting animators with tools and pipelines, as well as an active production role producing game content such as skeleton rigs, state machines and simulations. While an animator may focus on the creative expression of animation by posing a character to convey an emotion or an action, a TA will build the means for the animator to achieve that goal by building the skeleton, rigs or even the tools and pipelines required to bring that character to life. By nature, a TA should be instrumental in gelling a studio's animation department, focusing keenly on being orderly and efficient in all aspects of development. They must ensure project assets and files are neatly organised and named according to studio conventions and also identify inefficiencies within a pipeline and remedy them.

When comparing the TA role to other roles within a studio, it is in effect a combination of an animator, a rigger and an technical artist all rolled up into a single job role. Some studios may refer to TAs as character technical artists or even technical directors, the latter of which is a term more commonly used within the visual effects industry to describe a rigger or TA.

TAs sit in the middle of the pipeline (Figure 1.1); they will communicate in both directions to not only support the needs of animators and designers but will also talk to concept artists and

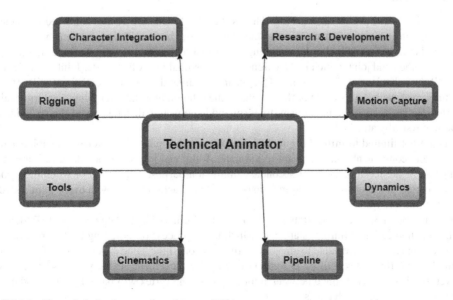

FIGURE 1.1 The technical animator role and responsibilities.

DOI: 10.1201/9781003263258-1

modellers to ensure the best possible work can be developed for a character. Discussions with the concept artists and art director are often done to flag any potential issues that can cause problems later in the pipeline or even to offer suggestions on how the animation team can be more involved to improve the work.

TAs are lucky enough to have two audiences when developing a game—first, the audience that all game developers have, the customers purchasing the end product, and second, their team around them. TAs are likely to create control rigs and tools that will be released to the team more frequently since they are a TA's immediate client, so the work produced will have to be tailored for that demographic.

1.1.1 Responsibilities

The responsibilities that a TA can take onboard vary drastically between studio and even project— often this is determined simply by the unique makeup of said studio. In some studios, several TAs may spread the workload, while in other studios, an individual TA may support an entire studio. As a rule of thumb, the smaller the studio, the more responsibilities will be expected. While there is not a definitive checklist of responsibilities a TA will always complete, they can range from, but are not limited to, character skeleton rigging, control rig setup, game engine integration, state machines, animation, development of tools and pipelines, motion capture support, run-time and offline simulations such as cloth and ragdoll, or even more artist-oriented tasks such as materials and shader work.

Ultimately, no matter the quantity of responsibility at a given studio, the core principles of what makes a technical animator a technical animator stay the same. They are a bridge between animators, artists, programmers, game designers and the engine. Their primary role is to focus on the technical aspects of a studio's animation department by ensuring that creatives like animators can animate, be that through building smooth and efficient pipelines, removing technical roadblocks or building rigs that can allow a creative's vision to come to life.

1.1.2 Rigging

1.1.2.1 Skeleton Rig

Every character starts with a skeleton rig. This is the core foundation of any animated character or object, consisting of a series of positions named "joints" or "bones." These positions are connected to one another in a hierarchical order matching bones in a real skeleton, with the forearm joint being the parent of the hand joint, which is the parent of the proximal index finger, etc. Joints in a hierarchy inherit all the behaviour of their parents. This means anything done to a parent's joint will affect all their children as well. An example of this would be the rotation of a shoulder joint in an arm chain— when the rotation occurs, the upper arm, forearm and hand would all rotate about the shoulder as if they were physically attached.

Joints are not limited to mimicking movement joints from a real-world skeleton, as joints can be added for any component you may want to animate. Additional joints can be added to improve the deformation of the mesh or even for secondary animation purposes like cloth or wobbling armour. It's best to think of a skeleton rig as akin to making a digital action figure, with every joint added for an area that moves.

Joints sit inside a 3D model at strategic positions to deform and articulate the model. To deform a model, a method called skinning is applied, which is the process of assigning each vertex on a 3D mesh a percentage influence value to any joint in the skeleton. If the value on a vertex is 100% skinned to a single joint, the vertex will be moved entirely by the movement of that joint, as if glued to it. However, if it is partially skinned between multiple joints, the vertex will partially move and deform to the sum of all skinned influences.

1.1.2.2 Control Rig

A control rig is a set of animation-friendly controls that sit on top of a skeleton rig that allows for easy pose manipulation for the animators. While animating directly with a skeleton is possible, it is not particularly user-friendly and can be very painful to work with to achieve simple results. Animation in development is stored on the control rig and is only baked or transferred to the skeleton for importing into the game engine. Control rigs feature functionality such as inverse kinematics and forward kinematics switching, animation spaces and much more—we will delve into the details of these functionalities later. In a marionette analogy, the skeleton would be our puppet, whereas the control rig would be the cross-brace control.

The control rig is what the animators use every day. It must be intuitive and simple to use, and it must be constantly checked to ensure that it is effective for its intended purpose. The control rig should not be a roadblock to creativity; it should empower animators to fulfil their dreams. While the implementation of lots of complex features and the latest technology may seem like a good idea, if the playback frame rate is poor and the animator needs to playblast their Digital Content Creation software (DCC) to preview an animation, then your rig is bad. Complexity does not always mean quality.

Unlike the skeleton, the control rig itself doesn't end up in the video game but is a tool and an important step in the pipeline to ensure animators can create animations with ease.

1.1.3 Engine Integration

Engine integration is the task of implementing assets into the game engine, setting up and connecting all the appropriate content so that it works as intended at runtime. This includes, but is not limited to, animation state machines, simulations, gameplay systems, logic and even cutscenes.

An animation state machine is a behaviour tree model that controls the run-time animation of a skeleton rig by moving from one state to another, triggered by gameplay input variables such as an event or action. An example of this would be a character that can idle and walk forward—this would be controlled by two states. The first state is idle or stationary, and the second state is walking. Transitions can be set up to interconnect states with conditional factors that trigger the active state to transition to another state. The conditional factor, in this case, would be joystick input from the player. When the player is not pushing in any direction on the joystick, the state machine would transition to an idle state, whereas if the player is pushing forward on their joystick, the state machine would transition to a walking state. State machines are the core building blocks of complex animation functionality and behaviour in games. Depending on the game engine that is being used, some offer intuitive visual node-based animation state machine-building tools, while others may be code-reliant.

A cutscene is a non-interactive animation sequence in a game, akin to a movie or an animated film. Integration of cutscene assets may be necessary depending on the project; this would include collating all the cutscene animation data into the engine, such as character animation, camera animation with properties such as focal length, f-stop and focus plane, as well as any additional props, visual effects or environments, to work in unison as the animators intended.

Run-time simulations vary from setting up physical animation setups such as ragdolls, cloth dynamics, or hair dynamics to secondary animation dynamics such as spring constraints—these are a method of applying procedural animation to characters and objects without the need to bake any data. For a character, this may include using spring dynamics to create an earring that moves in the game, setting up a cloth simulation on a character's cape or even creating a rigid body ragdoll simulation that will cause the character to fall over when they die.

While typically the job of a specialised technical artist, shader development or support may be required if animation integration is necessary. Shaders in games determine how the surface of an object is rendered, or how it is "shaded," which is where the name derives from. The visual output of the shader is determined by the various inputs that can be provided to it. Input data can consist of geometry, texture colours, the world position of an object, variables and many more. It is, in effect, several math operations that determine how an object looks or reacts to the game world around them. Some game engines may have user-friendly and intuitive shader graphs that allow you to visually construct your shaders through node connections, akin to Unreal or Unity engine's shader graphs, while others may require shaders to be written directly in a shading language such as Direct3D's High-Level Shading Language (HLSL). As a TA, you may need to involve yourself in the development of shaders if animation needs to drive any property in the shader. If the art of the character requires an animated material or textures to fade in on command, such as adding wrinkle maps to a face or even changing a sprite sheet number, you may need to add integration between the animation and the shader.

1.1.4 Tools

Tools are custom-developed programmes, plugins or extensions designed to improve development workflows through new functionality, efficiency improvements or automation to make work easier and faster to complete. Many existing applications have custom programming languages that allow developers to build scripts to modify or expand software capabilities, such as Autodesk's Maya has MEL (Maya Embedded Language), Autodesk's 3D Studio Max has MaxScript, or a universal programming language like Python. While each programming language has its own unique formatting style, the principles of how to construct it are very similar. This is comparable to animating in different software; the principles are the same, but the buttons you press are different.

Tools that speed up workflows or automate repeatable tasks are invaluable in game development studios, as iteration is key. Why waste time doing the same task repeatedly when it can be automated? If a task takes 2 weeks to do and you do it 6 times, that is 8 weeks of production time that could be saved. Not only will your production schedule benefit, but you will also prevent human errors from appearing in the automated work; a misclick, a typo or the wrong connection can be prevented by a singular automated process that is the same every single time.

1.1.5 Motion Capture

Motion capture is the process of recording the movements of objects within the real world into a format that can be used for animation purposes. There are many different methods of capturing motion, from high-end, warehouse-sized motion capture studios with optical camera sensors to lo-fi equipment such as a repurposed Xbox Kinect depth sensor. Each method has pros and cons, and some provide objectively better data but at a much higher cost.

Depending on the game studio and project, the ownership of motion capture may vary vastly. In smaller-scale projects, you may be responsible for the entire motion capture process, from the hardware setup and data capture to animation retargeting and modification into an appropriate format for your work. On the other hand, bigger-scale projects may be the opposite. While working with dedicated motion capture companies, they will be responsible for a significant portion of the pipeline, including retargeting the recorded data onto your skeletons, but you will be required to liaise with the studio and fulfil their requirements, typically providing them with character skeletons and aiding with a real-time engine stream setup if applicable.

Some studios may be entirely keyframe animation-based, so motion capture won't be necessary.

1.1.6 Pipeline Research and Development

Pipeline research and development refers to the research of new technologies, techniques and processes that can be implemented into your game development pipeline. As the game industry is ever-evolving, it's always wise to allocate time to researching and developing new processes or even overhauling existing processes that can speed up workflows or bring work to a higher quality than before. While sticking with what works may seem like a safe mentality, it's always important to move forward with technology and not be left behind. Old ways of doing things can lead to inefficiencies or unnecessary expenses at the cost of time, money or performance in your game.

While researching new technologies and processes may not be the number one priority while developing a game, ironing out a pipeline process to ensure it is a rock-solid process to get from A to B with minimal fuss for developers is paramount.

1.1.7 Animation

Depending on the studio and the time available, you may have the opportunity to do some animation tasks. At a small studio, you may be the one-stop shop for character work, so you'll have to dip your toes into all aspects, including animation. At a bigger studio, you will be working with animators who will be responsible for this task instead.

Whether you are animating or not, it is still important to understand animation and its principles, as they will feed directly into your work. How will you be able to make good control rigs or tools if you don't know what the animators need? Understanding the language of animation will allow you to communicate with your animators better.

1.2 Character Traits

It is often said that certain people are born to play certain roles, and the video game industry is no exception. Game development attracts a certain creative mentality, and technical-oriented roles like TAs can thrive when their traits enhance the requirements of their role.

1.2.1 Every Day Is a School Day

The video game industry is forever evolving, with new processes constantly being built just as fast as they are deconstructed and replaced with even newer processes. In the process of writing this book, I, myself, have had to learn various new processes and tools to achieve ever-changing and moving goalposts. Being open to change and learning is not only essential for growth as an individual but also to enhance your contribution to your role, which will, in turn, benefit those around you. You and your team don't want to be stuck utilising dated processes when there are better ways to do things—new processes that can make work of higher quality or more efficiently achieve the same goal in less time—and as a TA, you may even make tools and pioneer processes that your team will have to learn.

While the tools you use may change frequently, having a strong foundation of what, why and how will always keep you focused on the task. The buttons you press in different software may change, but the action you want to achieve is the same. Animating is still animating, no matter where you do it.

If learning isn't your strong suit, learning how to learn may become one of the most valuable skills you can develop.

1.2.2 Tidy Outliner, Tidy Mind

Being clean and orderly is paramount in game development across all disciplines, but more so as a TA as you'll be dealing with hundreds, potentially thousands of files for your game. Being a stickler for correct naming conventions and appropriate folder structures will benefit you and the project in the long run, and maintaining tidy work prevents mess and miscommunication.

1.2.3 Identify Inefficiencies

Identifying efficiency problems is a pivotal skill to have. If you find yourself doing repeatable tasks over and over again, why not automate the task so it's completed in a fraction of the time, allowing you to spend more time on more pressing tasks that will benefit the production of your game? It is important to identify when the appropriate time for automation is, as sometimes it can be faster to do a task manually. Ultimately, the mentality is about allocating your time wisely, choosing the correct battles to pick and working smarter, not harder.

1.2.4 Thick Skin and Constructive Mentality

As a TA, you'll be embedded deeply into the inner workings of a game—meaning you will be touching many facets and working with many disciplines at a studio. This means your work will be frequently in the hands of others, and in the same way, you'll be utilising others' work to achieve your goals, such as an artist's model to rig. Go into the development process expecting work on both sides to be criticised. Don't be upset or defensive when your work is criticised or potentially used in ways you never intended or expected, which could highlight faults in the work. Use this as a fantastic opportunity to learn and improve your work by fixing any issues or increasing the compatibility of your work with different workflows that you had not previously thought of. On the flip side, you'll have to develop appropriate conduct for criticising others' work. In instances like rigging, you'll be going over almost every vertex of an artist's asset; there is potential to find issues in their work, and being able to communicate feedback professionally and constructively is paramount.

Be patient with one another when giving or receiving feedback; in order to learn, the criticism needs to be fully understood—the flinch reaction to criticism can be to shut off. Even if it becomes an uncomfortable situation, it is important to ask the right questions to understand the feedback being given. Don't walk away until you fully understand their point of view; sometimes people may not fully articulate their point unless they are asked to elaborate.

Ultimately, everyone on a team is facing the same direction and wants the same thing; support one another by bringing each other up with valid criticism, and everyone's work and relationships will be better for it.

1.2.5 Problem Decomposition—The What and Why?

In development, it is inevitable that problems will arise, but they are only a problem when they become a roadblock stopping other people from being able to do their jobs. This can hold up project schedules and release dates, or even worse, cause cuts in content or delays. Problems within games can be incredibly complex, with a mammoth list of intertwining systems that are co-dependent and also influence one another. Having a good problem decomposition process that allows you to effectively break down an issue, removing possible causes from the equation one by one until you find the culprit, is a great character skill to have as a TA, as a good chunk of your role is efficiently firefighting any development issues that may arise. Do not try to brute-force fixes through trial and error! The last thing you want to do is resort to redoing work that then fixes an issue by fluke. You will learn nothing from stumbling into a fix with this method. You can't replicate or deconstruct the problem, so you never grasp an understanding of what caused that issue to prevent it from happening again or fix it in the future if the issue returns. Redoing a whole piece of work to fix an issue is not an acceptable workflow.

This decomposition extends to more than just debugging; a peer may approach you with a specific request, and rather than fulfilling their request one-to-one, breaking down the what and why of what they want to achieve can allow you to approach the request with a lot more grace and an informed answer.

1.2.6 It's a Process

It's good to keep in mind that game development is a process; the first implementation of work typically isn't perfect, and it's only through iteration that the quality of work improves. While development is the sum of the best possible work done in a set amount of time, submitting work at the last possible moment before a deadline should be avoided at all costs. Get work in the game early and get eyes on the work in context—give it time to breathe, time for feedback and time to act on that feedback. Otherwise, this will lead to bugs and a distinct lack of polish in the work. "Fail early, fail often, but always fail forward" (John C. Maxwell, Failing Forward, 2000). Get the work in the engine and viewed in the context of the game as soon as possible, and allow your peers to review it with you. This will allow for easier identification of the flaws in the work and areas that can be improved.

1.2.7 Out of Sight, Not Out of Reach

With the field being ever-evolving, there will inevitably be new processes or pipelines that you may want to dip your toe into trying to improve your work; some of these may be completely outside your wheelhouse with a new piece of software or something fundamentally different from what you do. No matter what it is, just give it a try. While this new process may seem out of reach, it's usually within reach if you give it a try. At some point, every single person was bad at something until they started doing it.

The worst-case scenario is that even if you do fail at trying the new process, at least you learn that it's not a viable avenue rather than wondering what if. You could even end up rewarding yourself with some transferable skills back to your own discipline—for example, delving into some 3D modelling could help you articulate or even give examples to modellers on how you want to receive your models to rig in the future. If you do succeed in giving it a try, then excellent! Either way, you will have learnt a lot by doing so.

1.2.8 Reference, Reference, Reference!

As the old saying goes, "knowledge itself is power" (Sir Frances Bacon, Meditationes Sacrae, 1597), and for anyone wanting to improve their knowledge base, the best resource is to understand the world around them—reference is king! When building any work that is supposed to mimic real life, do not just copy what you see; deconstruct what and why it works or feels correct and then you'll be able to apply that understanding to your work. If you can't find the reference for what you need, you can always try to get up and do it yourself.

Refer to other people's work; watch their talks; see how they process and approach challenges and the solutions they've come up with; Rip apart and dissect any and all free samples that are provided by developers—learn what they do and stand on their shoulders, so to speak. This doesn't mean plagiarising; this means don't spend time reinventing the wheel. Research processes are standard practices that work; use them, then build off what you need to support your project, workflow and team.

1.2.9 Being Human

Finally, if you are going to pursue a career in technical animation or games in general, it's always good to put your best foot forward and strive to output the best you can in the time you have. However, don't let this compromise your life. Don't get lost within the role; it's important to be human.

Film, games and animation are all becoming increasingly desirable career paths, with more courses in colleges and universities than ever before, more game studios around the world than ever before, and in 2020, the video game industry surpassed revenue for movies and music combined. Games can provide escapism beyond imagination and can be a lifeline for some people. It's easy to see why people pursue it as a career.

However, it is imperative to set boundaries between yourself and work, with clear working hours. If your work has a communication application such as Slack, make sure it's muted between out-of-hours times to give yourself a rest. With the work-from-home situation becoming more prevalent since the global COVID-19 pandemic, it's more important than ever to set boundaries. Depending on your living situation, this can be difficult, such as if you're living in a studio apartment where you physically cannot close the door on work when your hours are up. If you do not set healthy boundaries, there can be a variety of consequences worse than one may think, such as burnout or making yourself sick with psychological and physiological ailments.

Be human, go out and have fun—don't spend all your energy behind a desk working, even if it is a hobby. Putting distance between yourself and work will allow you to come back recharged and ready to tackle your next challenge.

2

Introduction to Software

In game development, you will use many different types of software applications for a range of different purposes. The two distinct sides of software that you will be expected to utilise are Digital Content Creation (DCC) and Game Engines. These co-exist and fulfil different purposes within the game development pipeline.

When beginning any project, choosing what software is right for you, your team and your project is an important factor to weigh. Development pipelines and processes will be built around the chosen packages. You are not always beholden to your chosen software for the entirety of a project, especially regarding DCCs. In some cases, different departments or individuals on a project may use different DCCs to produce content. Some may use many packages to get their end result, while others may only use one. Produced content is mostly interchangeable between packages, as ultimately, the work that matters most at the end of the day is the produced content, not the tool that got the job done. At the end of the day, the animation is data on joints, just as models are polygons in any package.

2.1 Digital Content Creation

Digital Content Creation is software designed for creators to bring digital content to life, be that images, 3D models, or even animations. The content created in these packages is typically the first step in the pipeline and is exported upon completion into a game engine. As a TA, DCCs will be where the rigging and skinning of model assets will be performed, as well as creating tools and pipelines for animators and the larger team to utilise.

There are many different DCC packages available, from paid monthly subscriptions such as Autodesk Maya to free open-source software such as Blender. Some packages excel in particular areas, and some are jack of all trades—but each one has its pros, cons, unique quirks and unique workflows; fundamentally, they are all 3D computer graphics applications for creating 3D content within. Each DCC typically has its own proprietary file format—meaning you cannot load one DCC's files in another; however, there are several format files that most, if not all, DCCs allow for exporting, such as FBX, which can be used to move data between packages.

One of the primary and most consistent differences between most DCCs is their 3D coordinate systems. Not all software has a universal consensus of which axis goes where and in which direction; some software uses the Z-axis as the altitude and X and Y as right and forward, which may make sense if you consider an architectural mindset for making blueprints—that X and Y will be flat on the piece of paper like a typical XY graph, then the Z would be the additional floors. However, some software utilises Y as altitude, then X as right, and Z as forward. This makes sense if you think of a computer screen—if you display a 2D graph on your screen X will be going right, Y will be going up, and Z will be depth into the screen, causing the Y to be the altitude.

To complicate matters further, there is direction involved in 3D coordinates. This is typically referred to as a left- or right-handed coordinate system, with left-handed coordinate systems having their positive rotations go clockwise and right-handed going anti-clockwise. This direction harkens

DOI: 10.1201/9781003263258-2

FIGURE 2.1   3D packages and their axis alignments.

back to how 3D renderers decided which side of a polygon was the front side or the backside—if you have a triangle to render, you needed a way to know if the front or the back of the triangle was visible, so the front could be rendered and the back could be culled. The 3D direction decided which direction was the front of the triangle, and not every software came up with the same answer, hence the differences. This can cause the same axis between differing software to go in different directions, so 40 X in one software may be −40 X in another.

3D software scatters among left-handed with Y up, left-handed with Z up, right-handed with Y up and right-handed with Z up (as demonstrated in Figure 2.1). These differences are vital to consider when rigging and replicating packages. Fortunately, on the content data side, no matter the package, conversion to formats like FBX does the intelligent math operations on export to convert 3D content into a consistent 3D coordinate system to move between packages with ease.

2.1.1 Autodesk Maya

Autodesk Maya was originally released in 1998 by Alias as Maya 1.0, advertised as an animation, modelling and visual effects package. Over the years, the package has had many owners, from Wavefront Technologies to Silicon Graphics, and it is currently owned by Autodesk, which purchased Maya in 2005 and rolled it into their portfolio of 3D applications. Typically recognised for its debut in Disney's movie Dinosaurs, it has since been utilised in many pioneering computer generated imagery (CGI) movies of the early 2000s, including Spider-Man, Lord of the Rings and even the prequel Star Wars movies. Maya is a market leader and industry standard piece of software within video games, from AAA to indie and film, alongside its sibling software, 3D Studio Max, which is also owned by Autodesk.

On a fundamental level, Maya is built upon a scripting language called MEL, which means every action, button and command are executing a MEL script—this means every command of the software is highly modifiable, customisable and expandable, which is a huge benefit over its competitors, which typically have their commands compiled so they are unreadable and unmodifiable. Maya offers a "Listener" tool; after every input a user presses in Maya, the corresponding MEL command appears in the logs—allowing beginners a huge degree of accessibility to begin developing their own scripts. Whether you are making a simple script or a complex pipeline automation tool, the breadth of exposure to scripting that Maya has is exceptional. Maya also supports the Python language, with almost the entire suite of MEL commands exposed to it if you prefer to use Python.

Maya sports the right-handed with Y up coordinate system.

2.1.2 Autodesk 3D Studio Max

Autodesk 3D Studio Max was originally released in 1990 for MS-DOS operating systems under the name 3D Studio. While initially developed by the Yost Group, it was published by Autodesk until 1996, when Autodesk fully purchased the package and rolled it into their suite of 3D packages. The name has gone through several iterations since its inception, with a rebrand to 3D Studio Max to coincide with their update from MS-DOS to Windows NT systems, followed by 3Ds Studio Max later in its life. Akin to Maya, Max has had vast success within the 3D realm, not only being a market leader and industry standard for architectural and engineering design, Max has been utilised to make countless video games and movies, from Avatar and Mission Impossible to Harry Potter.

In games, Max is renowned for its accessible, fuss-free modelling and animation toolkits. On the animation front, Max offers an incredibly flexible, feature-rich tool called Biped, which is a character control rig system. Bundled with every tool you would need for production, from animation saving and loading to pose library tools and a great inverse/forward kinematic-based limb workflow that removes the complication of juggling multiple versions of the same limb that is typical of most control rigs. This as a tool allows for highly flexible iterative workflows out of the box without any custom setup being required. However, its greatest strength is its own worst enemy—Biped isn't particularly extendable except for components offered directly in the tool. Biped is also quaternion based, rather than Euler, which we will discuss at length later in this book, but this means features that animators typically expect, such as curves, are represented very differently through a Tension, Continuity and Bias system (TCB).

3D Studio Max's axis uses Z up and a right-handed coordinate system.

2.1.3 Autodesk MotionBuilder

Autodesk Mobu was originally released under the label FiLMBOX and was developed by Kaydara in 1994. Kaydara and FiLMBOX were acquired by Alias in 2004, followed by Autodesk in 2006, when it was rebranded to Mobu. Mobu is the origin of the now industry-standard FBX file format, as it was the native format for the software's files, stemming from its name, FiLMBOX. Unlike Maya and 3DS Studio Max, Mobu is a dedicated animation package—not a general 3D package; its emphasis is entirely around building motion, be that for keyframing, motion capture or cinematics. Due to this, Mobu has found itself as one of the industry standards for animation, motion capture and virtual production, finding its way into movies such as Avatar, Tintin and Rise of the Planet of the Apes.

Mobu is superb at handling scenes with lots of character and dense data without the performance impact that is typical of other 3D packages. It hosts a suite of animation-centric tools, one of which is a full-body inverse kinematic control rig and animation retargeting system called HumanIK. The tool itself allows for easy character posing through full-body IK, pinning, auxiliary effectors and manipulation modes, as well as easy quality-of-life animation tools like full-body or limb keying. The retargeting system allows for the mapping of animation data between different characters of different sizes, build or even skeleton rig differences—all with a suite of parameters to control to retarget with fine-tuning.

Mobu's axis uses Y up and a right-handed coordinate system.

2.2 Game Engines

A game engine is the heart of the game; like in a car, the engine is what runs everything. They are not only the collection of all the functionality that the player experiences in the game but also the suite of tools that developers use to create the game. Game engines include tools for 3D rendering, physics, animation, networking, etc.

There are dozens of engines utilised in games today; most bigger studios will have their own proprietary game engine that is bespoke to their own studios, such as Ubisoft's SnowDrop or Guerilla's Decima engine. Some game development studios may license their in-house engines out to other studios, such as Epic Games' Unreal Engine. There are even dedicated companies that make their engines solely for licensing but don't produce in-house games, such as Unity Technologies' Unity engine or YoYoGames' Game Maker Studio engine.

All engines have their advantages and disadvantages, and it's always important to weigh up what's best for the project, team and target platform for the game. Unless you work at a studio with a proprietary engine, the Unreal or Unity engines are the current go-to for 3D work due to their openness, vast amount of documentation and generous licensing.

2.2.1 Unreal Engine

Unreal Engine is a game engine developed and released by Epic Games. The first game to utilise the engine was a first-person shooter called Unreal in 1998, from which the engine derives its name. The software itself has gone through five main versions over its history, with the latest version being Unreal Engine 5 in 2020.

In the past, Epic offered to license the engine to external companies until the fourth version of the software, when they switched to royalties system meaning you could use the software for free and pay Epic a 5% royalty once your game was earning more than $3,000 per calendar quarter. This was later rectified with the announcement of Unreal 5, where you only pay royalties once you exceed $1 million in revenue for all games made with Unreal. Unreal is an industry leader in the field of game engines and is praised for its high visual fidelity output, which has led it to become frequently used in film and virtual production.

Unreal is known for its flexibility in empowering artists to achieve their creative vision, no matter what the type of project may be. There is a significant breadth of features and tools Unreal comes bundled with out of the box to satisfy almost every department in a game studio; the software is expandable through plugins and an active online marketplace to purchase extensions, asset packs, etc.; and the best part of the software is that source code is modifiable, allowing you to customise the engine entirely to your specifications. At the heart of the Unreal engine, is a visual scripting system called Blueprint, which is a node-based flow connection graph that allows artists and non-coders to access functionality typically only available to programmers. Blueprint is incredibly useful for artists, designers and even animators.

In the Unreal 5 release, Epic is pioneering some cutting-edge technologies with Nanite and Lumen—the former being a new way to render polygons in incredible quantities, and the latter being a high-fidelity real-time global illumination and reflection system. As the engine has continued to evolve, it has become commonplace in many TV or film productions.

The breadth of animation tools that are updated and grow with every release will satisfy any animator, technical or otherwise. Out of the box, it offers a variety of animation-focused tools, such as a highly flexible animation state machine which is connected to its Blueprinting system called AnimBlueprints, physics simulations such as ragdoll, physics-driven ragdoll and cloth simulations, run-time animation data retargeting systems and cinematic building tools called Sequencer, and even the ability to build control rigs directly within Unreal for animating entirely in the package.

2.2.2 Unity Engine

The Unity Engine is developed by Unity Technologies. Initially released in 2005 as a Mac OS X-exclusive game engine, it has since grown to become multi-platform, supporting a wide range of target platforms from consoles to mobile devices.

Originally sold as a perpetual licence until 2016, Unity has since adopted a subscription licence with two options—free and pro. Users qualify for the free option if they make less than $100,000 annually from products made with Unity. The pro would require developers who did not qualify for free to pay royalties on their produced products. This model has since been changed again to a four-tier system of Personal, Plus, Pro and Enterprise. In this model, more or fewer features are available to you depending on your tier, such as access to engine source code, which is not available for the first two tiers.

Unity is known for its low overhead when compared to its competitors, as stock Unity can be stripped back to the barebones to where it's almost just a renderer—this low overhead makes it favourable for target platforms with limited hardware specifications, such as mobile devices. This focus on being lightweight is a double-edged sword, as those wishing to strive for high visual fidelity will need to create or install a lot of additional features that would be absent out of the box. Unity has a history of being code-reliant, but Unity Technologies continues to make impressive strides to reduce the barrier to entry for artists, such as introducing a visual scripting system and shader graph editors to prevent the dependency on code knowledge or a programmer for art or design tasks.

Unity offers a suite of animation tools called Mecanim, which will aid in achieving your animation goals. These include an animation state machine system, an avatar system for retargeting animation data, as well as simulation tools for ragdolls, dynamics and cloth. Unity offers several free packages to expand the animation functionality in the editor, such as the animation rigging package or Cinemachine. The former is a series of tools that allow for the runtime modification of animation data for dynamics, constraints or layering systems on top, such as inverse kinematics or aiming. The latter is a camera and cinematics tool for building cutscenes in Unity.

2.3 Third-Party Plugins, Extensions and Tools

Most software's feature scope isn't always limited by what its developer provides out of the box. The functionality available can be enhanced through the use of plugins, extensions or third-party toolsets to include features in the software that are not available in the vanilla package. The game and digital film industries have been around for decades at this point, and there are a plethora of tools developed by individual developers, teams or even studios. These tools come in a selection of licences from royalty-free to non-commercial to commercial—when picking a third-party tool, ensure you get the correct licence for your project!

There are several advantages to utilising third-party tools, with the primary advantage being the development time—the time it would take you and your team to create tools with similar functionality has been shaved off the production time by using third-party tools. The knowledge you gain from these toolkits is also transferable between studios. You are not beholden to learning bespoke tools that you will lose access to when you leave a studio, the skills and the tools can transfer with you. From a recruitment perspective, using tools that are available to everyone could potentially ease a new member into the team, as they will already know the tools rather than needing to adjust to a new workflow and toolkit.

Their use does not come without some downsides. While they can be distinctly beneficial for time efficiencies, there is something to be said about building your house in someone else's garden. If any of these tools fail, it is much harder to remedy the issue in a timely manner, as no one in-house developed the toolkit, so it can be even harder to track down and remedy the issue. In some situations, plugins can be a black box where the internal workings are hidden or inaccessible, which may be due to the code being precompiled or obfuscated. In this case, you will not be able to fix anything yourself—you and your project are at the mercy of the third party that provides the tool. If any of these issues arise in the long run, the time-saving benefits may become invalid. Finally, if the plugin is in a black box state, this also means you cannot improve or develop the tool further to fully integrate it with your workflow and tools.

Third-party plugins, extensions and tools are available for most DCCs and engines to help with a variety of your game development tasks. For a TA, tools to aid in rigging and animation would be most useful. Some examples of TA-focused plugins include AnimBot, a suite of animation tools, Studio Library, a pose library tool; and a variety of rigging tools such as Advanced Skeleton, mGear, or RapidRig. Unreal and Unity both offer online marketplaces, Unreal Marketplace and Unity Asset Store, respectively, with free and paid content to help you fulfil your engine-side development needs.

2.4 Technology Choice

The decision of which technology to use for yourself, your team, and your project is critical because it will be the foundation of the entire project. These options include selecting your DCC, engine, SDKs, APIs, plugins, hardware and any other tooling you may require.

Conduct thorough research on each package, as well as research on what you hope to achieve in each package. Check to see if your goals are achievable, and ensure that your choice has the best tools, flexibility, and cross-package compatibility to get the job done. Choose what is best for you. Everyone can easily become trapped in decision paralysis, deciding which software is better than the other when they all have their advantages and disadvantages and, for the most part, are all capable of producing the same results in different ways.

Check that your packages will not have a negative impact on you in the long run. For example, prior to 2022, Autodesk products only supported Python 2, a deprecated version of Python, which means that when you upgrade to 2023 or later, Python 2 is no longer supported, requiring you to convert your Python content to Python 3. This deprecation of Python 2 was an industry-wide mandate. As part of the VFX Reference Platform (https://vfxplatform.com/), be sure to evaluate this platform to see if there are any shared resources or libraries that may affect you.

As a general rule, do not change technology choices in the middle of a project. This can lead to a slew of development issues and, potentially, a disaster for your project. Changing technology should be restricted to the period between projects or during the pre-production phase.

If you're wanting to hit the ground running with minimal setup, I'd recommend Autodesk 3ds Max because the out-of-the-box animation tools in Biped are second to none and are all included in the vanilla version. It's great to get started quickly with animation content, but it comes with the trade-off that you have little control over those systems. If you want to get into the weeds of development, I would recommend Autodesk Maya. This will require you to build a lot of systems and tools from the ground up, but you will have comprehensive control over them. If your project is a student project or hobbyist endeavour, tailor your technology choices while considering what you will enjoy and learn the most from them, or tailor them towards potential career aspirations if that is your end goal. Maybe find a studio you really admire or aspire to work for, look at their job applications and see what software they use—tailor yourself accordingly.

2.4.1 Technology Chosen

With these considerations in mind, we will focus on Autodesk Maya as our DCC of choice and Epic Games' Unreal Engine 5 as our game engine. With our choices, keep note of the fundamental difference between our DCC and engine in that they do not share the same direction coordinate system; Unreal is Z up and left-handed, while Maya is Y up and right-handed. Keep in mind that these processes and practices are not specific to any one package; these lessons are universal between packages; all that may change is where the buttons you press are.

2.4.2 Additional Resources

Make sure to download, inspect and learn from the additional resources available on the Technical Animation In Video Games GitHub repository. From this resource, you will find example files for Maya and Python scripts that will help with your own work and demonstrations featured throughout this book.

Find the repository at https://github.com/MattLakeTA/TechnicalAnimationInVideoGames

3

Introduction to Motion Capture Technology

Motion capture, commonly referred to as mocap or performance capture, is a process that involves the digitalisation of positional and/or rotational values of objects, animals or humans. The outputted data can be used in a variety of industries, from video games and film to military, robotics, simulation, medical and even biomechanical analysis. Motion capture is incredibly popular in video games, as it allows animators to capture real-life movements and performances into a 3D digital form very quickly compared to keyframing those actions from scratch. If animation is the illusion of life, what better way to allude to life than to capture life itself?

Motion capture is an incredibly powerful tool, but it is not the silver bullet for animation. There is a common misconception that the moment the recording stops, shippable data is ready to go. This couldn't be further from the truth; there is still a considerable amount of work to do to get the data into a shippable state. This is akin to when an artist is texturing a wall in 3D if they take a digital photograph of a real wall, there is still a considerable amount of work to be done to the image of the wall to make it usable as a wall texture. For example, 3D-lighting information needs to be removed, it needs to be tiled and various other textures need to be generated from the colour.

There are several unique approaches to capturing motion data, all of which require unique hardware to accomplish. Each approach to motion capture comes with advantages and disadvantages, but what is viable for your project is key to weighing up when choosing a motion capture solution. Each type of data capture solution has varying degrees of precision, ranging from sub-millimetre accuracy to dozens of centimetres of inaccuracy, but typically more accuracy means a larger price tag to acquire.

3.1 Optical Marker

Optical marker solutions are the quintessential association for motion capture when the subject is brought up—it's the poster child for the technology as it's the most accurate equipment you can use to date. If you have seen an actor in a skintight suit with shiny ping-pong balls on such as in Figure 3.1 or 3.2, that is an optical marker solution. Optical markers come in two flavours: passive and active.

3.1.1 Passive

Firstly passive is a process that involves the use of retroreflective markers attached to a subject. The subject is then placed in an area that allows for recording from several static infrared cameras; they not only emit infrared light but also only capture infrared information. When the infrared cameras emit electromagnetic radiation in the direction of the subject, these wavelengths of light hit the retroreflective markers and bounce directly back to the camera, which captures them as a white dot. It is imperative for the use of retroreflective markers and not reflective markers—since the camera is the emitter and the sensor, the retroreflective markers

DOI: 10.1201/9781003263258-3

FIGURE 3.1   Roger Clark in a motion capture suit in 2021 for Fort Solis.

are used to bounce the infrared back to the source rather than reflect it away like a mirror as demonstrated in Figure 3.3.

The markers are placed at strategic locations on the subject to ensure clean, accurate data can be extracted from their positions later—this means placement in areas that will maintain rigidity with the least amount of wiggle for the appropriate component the marker is tracking.

Several cameras work in unison, tracking all markers in the scene, then collating all the captured video data together—through triangulation of all the marker dots, it is possible to extrapolate a position within 3D space for each marker. With each marker extrapolated into 3D space, the data is now in the format of a point cloud—several animated positions representing where the markers are in 3D space shown in Figure 3.4. Clusters of positional markers from each limb can be utilised to generate rotation values of yaw, pitch and roll; with these rotation values, they can be mapped onto any 3D object, such as a limb on a skeleton.

Since the received video feed is binary (white or black), there is room for error in how the markers are identified. A common issue experienced is called marking swapping, which is when the identifier

FIGURE 3.2   Julia Brown in a motion capture suit in 2021 for Fort Solis.

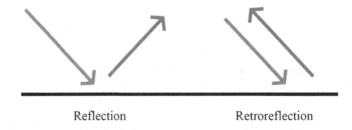

Reflection   Retroreflection

FIGURE 3.3   Diagram of the differing nature of reflection versus retroreflection.

FIGURE 3.4 Visualisation of how the motion capture sensors view the markers.

for a marker is swapped with another marker. This can happen for a variety of reasons, but it will need to be addressed when post-processing the data, either manually or by attempting to automate it as much as possible.

3.1.2 Active

Active is a very similar process, but it removes the three-step transaction of infrared light communication from the camera, to the marker and back to the camera. Instead, the markers are electronically powered to emit infrared wavelengths of light directly to the camera sensors.

One unique merit of active compared to passive is that they have a unique way of solving the marker swapping issue—one approach to this is to shift the wavelength of infrared light, so different markers have unique colours, resulting in marker swapping being removed in the capturing process—which optical marker passive methods can suffer from due to all markers registering as the same.

While both optical marker methods are sub-millimetre accurate and the resulting data is exceptional, the technology is very expensive to buy or rent, so it may not be within every studio's budget to accommodate motion capture. While purchasing the equipment may have a fixed fee, you need to have a large space to record in and account for the additional man-hours required to clean up the data yourself. Renting the equipment or working with a motion capture studio may be a more viable option; the cost will be significantly cheaper than purchasing, but this cost comes with some conditions as it is usually split into two distinct bills. The first is the cost of renting the studio—this is normally a fixed price per day per equipment. The second cost is the data cleanup; many studios charge per second of animation data for the body and an additional rate per second for face data too.

3.2 Optical Markless

When compared to optical markers, optical markless is a more generalised method of recording motion through optical means, except without any marker to use as a measuring method. Optical markless comes in several different flavours, from software video tracking, video depth data analysis or AI/Machine learning algorithms that can analyse video data.

3.2.1 Depth Tracking

Depth tracking is the process of analysing sequential point clouds and extracting animation from the information. Depth is computed through LIDAR (light detection and ranging) and is commonly used for scanning real-world objects, environments or characters for use within games, giving a one-to-one 3D representation of their real-world counterpart. This, however, is only for static objects in a single depth scan—sequential depth can be processed to extract animation. This technique has found its way to the forefront of budget motion capture solutions.

An accessible and cost-effective version of depth tracking technology came in the form of the Xbox's motion sensor device, the Kinect, as the produced depth data, shown in Figure 3.5, could be analysed to produce animation data. There are a handful of software available, such as Brekel or iPiSoft, which can utilise the Kinect to record and output bipedal, facial or even finger animation data. Developed by PrimeSense, which licensed the technology to Microsoft, the Kinect came in two iterations. The first was for the Xbox 360 in 2010, followed by Kinect 2.0 in 2013 for the Xbox One. The original version had a 30FPS 640x480 depth camera, while its successor had a 30FPS 512x424. While it has a lower resolution, the second iteration operates through a time of flight system, which measures distances by the time the emitted infrared light takes to bounce back from the scene to the sensor, whereas the predecessor measured through a pattern projection, a process that involved projecting an infrared pattern into a scene, then the sensor records the distortion of the pattern into the scene, which is used to calculate depth. Both approaches have the same end result of evaluating the depth of the scene.

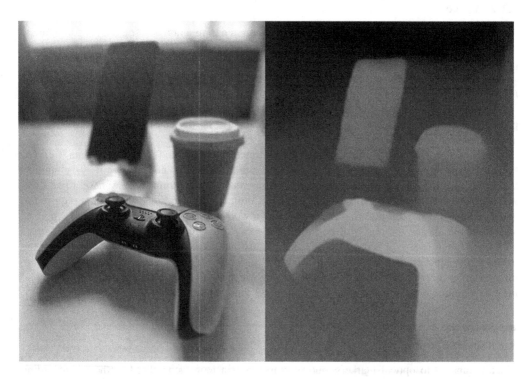

FIGURE 3.5   Depth visualisation from an iPhone 14.

While the Kinect was discontinued by Xbox, the technology lives on another platform. In 2013, PrimeSense was purchased by Apple, which integrated the depth perception hardware into their iPhone and iPad family of devices. On the stock device level, this technology is utilised for making animated emojis driven by human faces, but several developers have created applications on the app store to capture depth data for 3D scanning or even animation purposes, including Epic Games' Live Link Face App for capturing facial animation. This accessibility and low cost of the iPhone have led it to be popular for homebrew or previsualisation facial motion capture.

3.2.2 Pixel Tracking

Pixel tracking or motion tracking, is the process of analysing pixels within a video and extracting positional values into a usable format. Pixel tracking is commonly used within visual effects when compositing CG elements into live-action footage. Several tracked locations can be used to extrapolate 3D positions or rotations. There are many motion analysis software products that combine pixel tracking with intelligent AI systems that understand the movements of biomechanics and anatomy that can capture bipedal animation from a video clip. While these types of solutions are inexpensive and accessible, akin to inertial setups, the animation fidelity accuracy, that is, the accuracy produced, is low and susceptible to noise and jitter.

3.3 Inertial Systems

Inertial motion capture solutions record animation through physical sensors called inertial measurement units. There are many types of inertial measurement units, such as an accelerometer, gyroscope and magnetometer—all of which are commonplace in your mobile phone. As their names suggest, accelerometers measure acceleration, magnetometers measure magnetic fields and gyroscopes measure orientation and angular velocity. These sensors have various applications in many fields, but within animation, these sensors can be used to record animation data if the recorded data is used sequentially. Sensors can be placed in strategic positions over a subject, such as their limbs, to capture and record their orientation and movement.

There are several examples of inertial-based motion capture suits available on the market, the most prevalent being the MVN suits provided by XSens or the Perception Neuron suit by Noitom. These two suits both work from a combined gyroscopic, accelerometer and magnetometer inertial measurement units. In comparison to optical marker solutions, these suits are affordable for hobbyists and indie studios alike, which is why their usage has become so widespread. The technology does come with several caveats, but the most significant is that what is saved financially is sacrificed in terms of the fidelity of the data that the hardware is capable of recording. The way rotations are extrapolated from the sensor's data requires each sensor movement to be relative to its parent sensor. While stationary and grounded, this isn't an issue, but when movements that have nobody part grounded to the floor, such as a jump, the technology has difficulties knowing you have left the ground plane and where you are relative, causing the data to fall apart. The inertia sensors are subject to external interference, which may cause noise in the data, or occurrences like magnetic interference may cause the magnetometer to incorrectly report data.

Some solutions on the market combine inertial suits with other measurement devices, such as the Gypsy 7 mechanical motion capture suit shown in Figure 3.6. The suit itself works with a combined inertial and potentiometer sensor and visually looks like an exoskeleton suit. Potentiometers are another form of measurement sensor that can measure translation on a single axis. While these suits have the same advantages as the inertial systems previously mentioned, they suffer from limited mobility for the user.

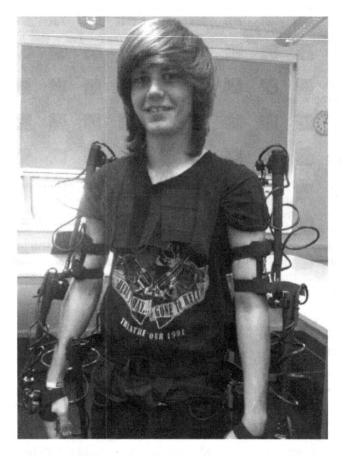

FIGURE 3.6   A young Matthew Lake wearing a Gypsy motion capture suit (2013).

4

A Technical Understanding

While technical animation encompasses a wide range of responsibilities, each one falls into one of three categories: DCC, Engine or Programming. In the following chapters, we will learn about the fundamental tools and processes available in each category, as well as how and where to use them effectively, using follow-along examples and use cases. But first, we need to understand a range of technical concepts that will propagate through everything we study and inform every decision we make as a technical animator (TA).

4.1 Meshes, Polygons and the Dreaded NGon

Meshes are the modular building blocks of a character; as a TA, you will inspect every facet of a mesh when rigging, so it's wise to understand what is a good mesh and what is a bad mesh. Meshes are built with a series of 3D shapes called Polygons. Not all shapes can be polygons, as polygons are closed shapes that are constructed of straight lines, so you cannot have a circle polygon. Polygons are defined by a set of points known as vertices (singular; vertex) that exist in 3D space. Each vertex has its own X, Y and Z values, which correspond to the Cartesian system, which uses horizontal, vertical and depth positions to represent a location. Edges connect vertices together, and three edges can form a triangle polygon shape.

There are other methods of creating and representing 3D shapes, including NURBs (Non-Uniform Rational Basis Splines), which are created through curves and splines rather than edges and triangles. NURBs are widely used in the computer aided design (CAD) industry but can also be used to create game art.

A "polygon" is the umbrella term for any 3D n-sided geometry. They can have an infinite number of sides, but under the bonnet, they are always constructed from several triangle shapes to form the entire shape (Figure 4.1). Even a Quad, a four-sided polygon, is still made up of triangles—two triangles, to be precise.

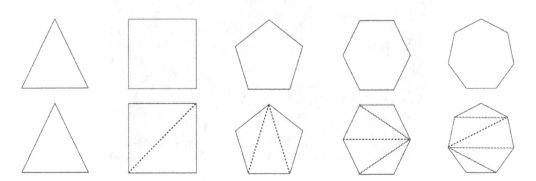

FIGURE 4.1 Multiple triangles are combined to render different-sided polygons.

DOI: 10.1201/9781003263258-4

Within Maya, you can display triangles on any n-sided polygon by:

1. **Select the geometry** you desire to see the triangles for.
2. Open the **Attribute Editor** (**Ctrl+A** cycles between Channel Box and Attribute Editor).
3. Select the relevant shape tab at the top of the **Attribute Editor**.
4. Navigate to the **Mesh Component Display** category.
5. Enable **Display Triangles**.

It is recommended that models be created with a quad polygon-based workflow, as they provide clean geometry that can be easily sub-divided with no visual artefacts, edge flow selection that would be broken by triangulated or NGon-riddled models, and most importantly, they provide a good baseline topology for skin weighting and deformations, as you will not have to triangulate shapes or sharp edges protruding with a clean quadded mesh. This workflow does not have a super strict policy of every polygon being required to be a quad, as unnecessary quadification of a mesh can lead to increased polycounts and unnecessary geometry. Meshes can be tidied up and organised as demonstrated in Figure 4.2 to still hold the same amount of detail and maintain most of the quad polygons.

When you import a polygon into your engine, it is transformed into a triangle regardless of how many sides it has. This is an automatic conversion procedure that will go unnoticed in most circumstances, but it has the potential to cause rendering and deformation issues if the direction of the automated triangulation is done incorrectly. As demonstrated in Figure 4.3, the quad polygon may appear fine when viewed, but once triangulated, it can assign the split edge in one of two alternate directions to triangulate the polygon, resulting in drastically different surfaces. The scale of the polygon drastically impacts the perception of this change.

The source of this issue stems from the fact that polygons containing four or more sides can become convex or concave—this occurs when all four vertices do not exist in a single plane. A convex shape is one in which the polygon appears to curve outwards, whereas a concave shape is the opposite, easily remembered as being a shape that "caves" in. With each of the shape vertices being able to be positioned anywhere, there is a chance this can occur. If the quad polygon was completely flat, with all vertices existing on a single plane, this would not be an issue. While it is recommended to have the model consistent with quads, in cases like this, it is acceptable to triangulate the polygon to ensure you achieve the intended final look if you are unable to define a quad plane.

While the automated triangulation can cause issues with convex or concave quads, it can only appear in one of two ways; however, this issue is exacerbated by polygons with more edges than

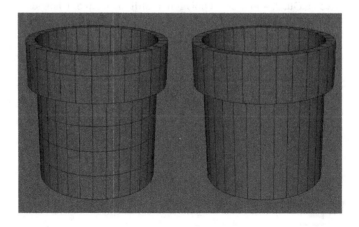

FIGURE 4.2 A simple example demonstrating unnecessary topology on a mesh that does not contribute to geometry detail.

FIGURE 4.3 Visualisation of how a surface can cut differently on concave surfaces.

four since there are many more variants of how each vertex can connect up showcased in Figure 4.4. Polygons with five sides or more are referred to as NGons, and these should be avoided in models. Beyond just the triangulation direction issue present, NGons can cause a range of shading rendering problems and are particularly troublesome for any object that needs to deform.

Polygon rendering on meshes that deform, such as characters, is more expensive to render than the polygons on a static environment due to the deformation technology. Skinning has to compute every frame on the mesh, which will bend and deform the model into the desired shape based on its skeleton rig, whereas static models are just that—static. This is why triangle counts on skinned objects are more strict than triangle counts on static meshes.

You may have heard of the term 'polygon count' as a determining factor of a model's performance cost. However, it is vital to note that this is not an accurate measure because, for the reasons we just described, a polygon, big or small, is always made up of triangles. An eight-sided polygon would

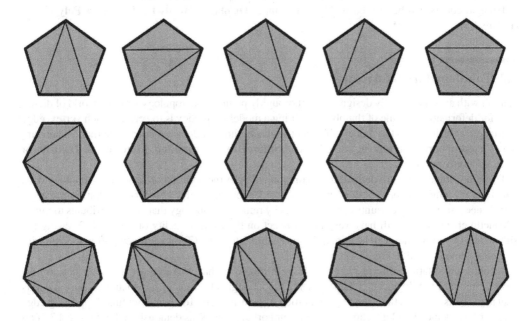

FIGURE 4.4 Random results for automated triangulation across different shapes.

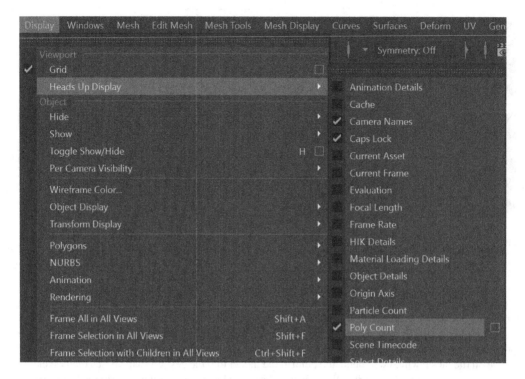

FIGURE 4.5   Maya interface option to enable triangle count preview in the viewport.

register in a polygon count as one polygon when there would be six triangles, and a quad polygon would count as one polygon when there are two triangles. Instead of the polygon count, always refer to the triangle count for a genuine measure of the model's performance impact.

Triangle counts can be viewed within Maya under **Display > Heads Up Display > Poly Count** (Figure 4.5).

4.2 Topology for Deformation

A mesh with an appropriately designed and thoroughly planned-out topology makes a world of difference for deformation. A rule of thumb for auditing a model's topology is to verify if each vertex, edge or triangle contributes to the model—if it contributes nothing, it does not need to be there. There are only a handful of reasons topology should exist: **Silhouette**, **Deformation**, **Materials & Textures** or **Vertex Colour** purposes.

The silhouette criteria are defined by a situation where if the addition or removal of topology does not affect the silhouette of a mesh, even after viewing from all angles, then that topology is unnecessary. If necessary, triangle counts can be reduced by removing topology that only contributes to minor silhouette changes; this will have very little impact on the overall fidelity of the mesh. Viewing the silhouettes of your models can be as painless as enabling lighting (**7**) on your viewport in a scene with no lights demonstrated in Figure 4.6.

Second, deformation criteria refer to adding a topology that will support the deformation of a model. Standard topology can collapse when a model begins to transform, which can cause hideous visual artefacts and ruin the volume preservation of your models. To counteract this, supporting edge loops or kite-shaped topology can be added to support any bends, as demonstrated in Figure 4.7. If an area of a model won't deform, then that area does not have extra supporting geometry.

FIGURE 4.6 A 3D model with unnecessary topology as it does not contribute to the silhouette.

FIGURE 4.7 Example of topology designed to improve deformation.

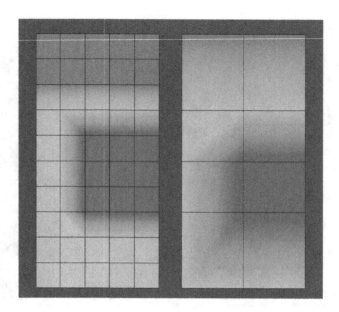

FIGURE 4.8 An example of vertex colours applied to geometry with differing topology counts greatly affects the vertex paint distribution.

Third, the materials and texture criteria are an umbrella category for any topology that is added to support the visual rendering of the asset. Since materials are assigned on a per-polygon basis, there may be some situations where the art of the character may require a different material assignment without an edge between polygons to accommodate this. In such situations, topology additions would be acceptable to add to achieve the intended look. This same criteria applies if the mesh requires a UV seam in a particular place.

The fourth criteria is to support vertex colour systems—for those not familiar, vertex colour is a system that allows you to apply colour information to each vertex of a model; this data can then be used in a variety of ways at runtime in shaders. Vertex colour is commonly used in environment art to layer different materials on top of one another. By assigning different colours to vertices, each colour can represent a particular material—for example, applying 50% red, green and blue will blend three materials equally or if a vertex is assigned 100% red, it will be a singular material. Use cases of this include adding variance onto walls, such as layering in moss or stains. This process can also be applied to characters and is commonly applied to damage or impact zones. Now, how can topology affect this process? Since colours blend linearly between each vertex, with too little topology the spread of colour can appear very inaccurate compared to that of a consistent topology. As demonstrated in Figure 4.8, both objects share the same assignments, but the colour assignment in a small area can spread across the object if the topology is too simplified. If you plan to use vertex colour assignments on your deforming meshes, it would be ideal to decide on a maximum spread size for your colours and ensure no polygon is larger than that size.

Ultimately, whether a model is created by an artist or by you, we must ensure that it is fit and ready to be moved into the pipeline before we begin any rigging, as this will have an impact on you later on.

4.3 Bind Pose—The T-Pose and A-Pose

A bind pose, also known as a reference pose, is the position and pose of a mesh prior to the skin being applied. Character models should have a natural bind position that is the middle ground of a common range of motions so that the topology of the character looks its best for the majority of the time. Some

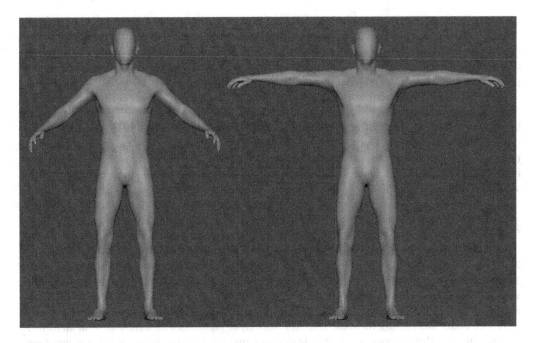

FIGURE 4.9   A character in the T-Pose and the A-Pose.

extremes will inevitably break the topology's fidelity, so it is best to find a bind pose that is the best middle ground.

You may be familiar with the terms "T-Pose" and "A-Pose." These are examples of commonly used bipedal bind poses. A T-pose is a character bind pose that looks like a T, with legs straight and arms up horizontally at 90 degrees. An A-Pose, on the other hand, has the upper arm at 45 degrees and a 45-degree bend in the forearms—sometimes there is no bend or a minor bend. T-Poses align the limbs with the axes of the world, so the arms appear in a straight line, which can make modelling much easier compared to modelling in an orientation like the A-Pose. While it may make modelling easier, it has some disadvantages when the character begins to move. The topology of the character will not deform pleasantly when the arms are in a rest pose, which is what a character will spend most of its time in. From T-Pose, it needs to travel and deform 90 degrees, while from A-Pose, it only needs to travel half that distance. This is why a T-Pose isn't as effective as an A-Pose, since the A-Pose resides in a much more natural pose that the arms will spend the majority of their time in. For best results, it is recommended that you have your characters in an A-Pose before beginning rigging. Both poses are demonstrated in Figure 4.9.

T-Poses aren't completely totally out of the running, though. They are extremely useful in the calibration of animation retarget systems in order to determine a baseline pose between characters. This is used in systems such as HumanIK in Mobu and Maya.

4.4 Engine-Friendly Content

The concept of engine-friendly content is an important technical limitation that you must adhere to within game production. In your DCC, almost anything is possible. The highest-fidelity techniques that are used to render all big-budget movies' computer-generated imagery (CGI) stem from these DCCs. These techniques in your DCC are referred to as offline techniques—offline means they are pre-calculated, sometimes taking up to several hours of computation time to calculate a single frame. Because of the unrestricted nature of the time taken to produce results, anything is possible. On the flip side, real-time content must operate in real-time—meaning it is computing the operation multiple times a second. Video game frame rates are commonly between 30 and 120 frames per second; rendering and computation techniques must function at this frequency. Some offline techniques can be converted into an engine-safe format by caching their end result, such as baking offline cloth simulations to a geometry cache, which is effectively a flipbook of 3D models that can be played back like an animation. However, this real-time requirement is a limitation and throws many offline techniques out the window, rendering them inaccessible in the engine. As technology improves, many offline techniques are becoming more accessible in real-time; their calculations improve and methods of achieving the same goal become more achievable in real-time, but for some, they are out of reach.

To be engine-ready, most DCC character work has to be boiled down to joints, linear skinned geometry, blend shapes and curves. Some engines will accept nothing but joints as the basis for all transforms and pivots in a character, but some do accept animated meshes or even locators that will be used as transforms. It is always best to keep joints consistent across the board. Standard linear skinning or blend shapes-wise, very little is operated except for standard linear skinning. Engine-side skinning also has limitations compared to its DCC counterpart, with vertices having a maximum influence count, so if you perceive the skinning in your DCC not matching the engine skinning, there is the potential that the model is exceeding the engine's influence count and culling the data. Unreal offers eight influences as standard, with an unlimited option for offline purposes, but mobile or older engines are limited to much lower numbers. For most other DCC mesh deformers, a conversion process through a geometry cache file type such as Alembic or OBJ Sequence, or even resampling the results into linear skinning or blend shapes, would be required.

4.5 Forward Kinematics and Inverse Kinematics

Forward kinematics (FK) and inverse kinematics (IK) both refer to the direction of manipulation an animator must perform on a bone chain to influence it. FK, as the name suggests, requires forward manipulation of a chain from root to tip—in a leg, you would be required to rotate the thigh, then the calf, then the foot, to pose the limb. IK operates in the opposite direction, but instead of rotating the joints sequentially, the entire chain's orientations are calculated from positions—the foot's position drives the rotation of the calf and thigh, then the twist of the calf and thigh is determined by a second position called a pole vector. IK comes in many forms, with its most common uses being rotated plane IK or IK spline solutions.

A rotate plane solution is frequently used on bipedal characters for their limbs. They are based on three positions: the root, an end effector and a pole vector. The root is the start of the chain. The position of the end effector is used to calculate where the chain should reach or if it should bend. The end joint attempts to be in the same position as the end effector, except when the distance from the base joint to the end effector exceeds the length of the fully extended chain, then the end joint cannot reach the end effector. The third position is a pole vector, while an end effector controls how much the chain will bend, the pole vector determines the direction of the bend points. The end effector, pole vector and root positions define a 2D plane within 3D space that the IK will orientate the chain—this is why it is referred to as a rotate plane IK.

The applications of both FK and IK have their place in animation, with each system having utility to make your required animations faster—FK use is great for achieving arcs but is poor at allowing limbs to be planted in space, such as a feet contacts on a floor, which is where the use of IK comes into play. To get the best of both worlds, rigs can be set up to use both solutions on limbs and allow blending between the two, which we will cover in our control rig setup chapter.

4.6 Euler and Quaternions

The basis of rotation in most 3D packages is built upon one of two spatial rotation systems—Euler or quaternion. Both Euler and quaternions are different methods of representing spatial orientations, with the former being the most commonly understood method of rotation because of its intuitive nature, but they do not come without drawbacks.

Euler rotation, named after its author Leonhard Euler, consists of three angles of rotation: X, Y and Z. Each angle value is successively stacked to create a total rotation in 3D space. The X, Y and Z angles correspond to the roll, pitch and yaw of an object. To determine the final rotation with a rotation order of X Y Z, it is rolled first, pitched second and then finally yawed. Euler does support modifying the rotation order, so it could go Z Y X, so it could yaw first, then pitch, then roll last—but this will have a different final destination orientation than the X Y Z order.

But why would we want to change the order of rotation? Unfortunately, Euler rotation suffers from an inherent limitation that can cause the visual loss of one axis of rotation, meaning when you rotate all three axes, only two of those axes will appear to change, but one of those two will rotate twice, causing a loss of input data—this limitation is called gimbal lock. In an XYZ configuration, the Y-axis only has to be rotated 90 degrees to achieve a gimbal between the X and Z axes, meaning if you change X or Z, the same result will occur. This is shown in Figure 4.10 with the X and Z. Not only can a gimbal lock limit animation control of an object, but it can also cause a singularity flip to occur when the first and third axes align and then exceed one another. The second axis will correct itself by rotating 180 degrees instantly to achieve the desired orientation. This can cause disastrous visual artefacts when animated skeletons spin their joints and meshes around.

Changing your rotation order can reduce the likelihood of a gimbal lock occurring by prioritising the rotations you will most frequently use for the animation at hand. Rotation orders should be set

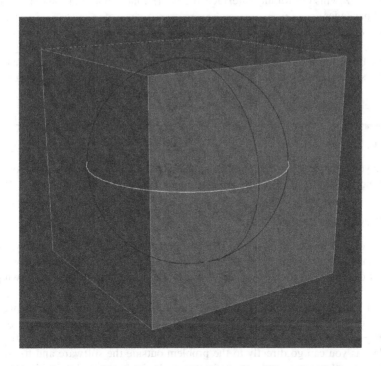

FIGURE 4.10   This rotation is now gimbaled, as demonstrated by the Z and X rotations aligning.

up prior to animating, as changing the order mid-animation will change the orientations you have previously animated, which can destroy your animation unless you have a tool to fix it! Consider your animations ahead and set the appropriate rotation order before animating; different animations will benefit from different rotation orders—you will benefit in the long run.

Quaternions are a four-dimensional rotation system, developed by Sir William Rowan Hamilton in 1843, calculated using four values, X, Y, Z and W—unlike Euler, these values are not a series of sequential rotations with a fourth layer to the system. Instead, the XYZ components are a unit vector that describes the axis of the desired rotation, and W is the amount of rotation around the XYZ component. A quaternion is written as follows:

$$Q = W + X\,i + Y\,j + Z\,k$$

As shown, Q is the total sum of the preceding equation, with the W, X, Y and Z components being real numbers, while the i, j and k components are complex numbers that are used to calculate the quaternion. The math calculations involved in a quaternion can get quite complicated, so do not worry if the concept does not entirely sink in; their use case within DCCs or engines typically has the underlying math done for you.

Quaternions have the benefit of not suffering from limitations such as gimbal lock or singularity flips, making their use a go-to for reliable rotations when compared to Euler. This makes blending between quaternions much more reliable than that of Euler. There are many problematic instances with Euler where the shortest rotation to blend between a rotation of 175, and −175, values which are 10 degrees in separation, is to go the long way of 350 degrees, resulting in bad blends. Quaternions do not suffer this issue and can reliably blend accurately between rotations through linear interpolation (LERP) or spherical linear interpolation (SLERP). Given these benefits, quaternions have a major disadvantage that you may have already identified—they are far less intuitive than Euler. Quaternions are difficult to represent and comprehend on paper, which is why Euler's XYZ wins out for any interface and is the common animation curve interface you will see in all packages.

Quaternions and Euler both have their place in game development despite their differences, quaternions are best used behind the scenes when a user does not need to engage with them, otherwise, use Euler for an intuitive experience for a user. It is important to note that you are not stuck with one system or the other—rotations can be transferred and converted between types if needed.

4.7 What Is Data?

Everything on your computer is made up of data. From the operating system to the programmes and down to each individual text file. It is all data, but not all data is created equal.

4.7.1 ASCII vs Binary Data

Different types of data will come in one of two flavours: ASCII or Binary. Ultimately, both contain the same information but are very different in how they save and store it. Certain software offers the ability for their data to be saved in either ASCII or Binary format, including Maya's own proprietary file format (Maya ASCII (.ma) or Maya Binary (.mb)).

Maya ASCII files can be opened within a text editor external to the Maya software, and the entire contents of the file are readable—every model, joint, attribute and keyframe is all there to see and modify, clear as day. This editable nature of the file is fantastic for debugging broken or corrupted files, as you can go directly to the problem outside the software and fix it, preserving your data. However, this comes at the cost of a larger file size compared to its binary counterpart.

ASCII files have the benefit of being able to be "diff'd," a process where you can compare the differences between multiple versions of the same file to see the exact changes, which is an invaluable tool for debugging. Binary files, on the other hand, are fully compressed data and are unreadable externally, so if the file corrupts, it's gone for good. The trade-off with binary is that it has a much smaller file size.

I would recommend using ASCII files, particularly for Maya files; your future self will thank you if something goes wrong! Some file formats unfortunately do not offer ASCII formats, so utilise them whenever possible. In Maya, you can easily switch to Maya ASCII by clicking Save As, then selecting the file type dropdown and changing to. MA Maya ASCII. This can be set as a default if you click the options box next to "Save Scene As," change to Maya ASCII, then click file save settings on the dialogue window.

4.7.2 What Makes Data Tick

Understanding what data is, be that DCC data, exported FBX data, or data in the engine, it's good to know what that data is and how it's working so that you can manipulate or take advantage of it in interesting and creative ways. It's easy to forget what a system is doing under the hood when the process has been automated. While there are benefits to automation, there are disadvantages to you as a user not knowing what's making it tick.

Positions within 3D space are built upon groups of three numbers, called a vector3, and in this case, those three numbers are X, Y and Z. Rotations are a vector3, and scale is also a vector3—it's all just sets of numbers. You may have noticed the colours of these XYZ axes correspond to a similar vector3 group, RGB, with X being red, Y being green and Z being blue. You may notice similarities with textures where every pixel can be represented by a vector3—they can also support an additional channel of Alpha, where RGBA, a vector4 comes into play. Each entry in a vector typically contains float values for transformations and integers between 0 and 255 for colours. The combination of the integers in a colour determines the output colour—so (255,0,0) would be bright red, (0,255,0) would be bright green and (0,0,255) would be bright blue. The result of every pixel in every channel creates the visual texture—it's all just numbers and more numbers! Even the UVW unwrap for your 3D mesh is a vector3, although UV is only used in texturing and the W is used for the understanding of 3D space, such as for volumetrics. It's all just numbers! Animation is just a series of all those previous numbers changing over time; it's a set of numeric numbers of positions, rotations and scales, but they have a driving force—that may be the time that drives the animation playback or an outside force. It's all just numbers!

Since it's all just numbers, manipulate them accordingly. Consider the data you are working with, and use it effectively—for example, if you have separate occlusion, roughness and metallic textures, the data we require from each texture is merely black-to-white information. We can channel pack these together in a single texture, with occlusion in the R channel, roughness in G and metallic in B. This reduces our texture assets but maintains the exact amount of data. Do you need more texture information but can't use an additional texture? How about using half a channel's space to act like a full channel? Rather than 0–255, use 0–127 and 128–255 to store different information in the same texture space. Is your animation file too large? It is just a series of numbers—maybe remove every other frame to reduce file size, or even remove unnecessary data channels such as transformation from joints where it's not needed.

4.8 Preparing Your Workspace

Before we dive headfirst into production, we must plan and prepare for our future endeavours. Forward-thinking will preempt problems long before they arrive, and it will go a long way to maximising efficiency and orderliness.

4.8.1 Folder Structure

Planning begins with your folder structure. This will determine the organisation of your entire project for both source and engine content. You must be organised. Don't spread your files across multiple directories or on your desktop. Properly organise yourself so you know where all your files are located. Losing a file is detrimental to yourself, and if you're working within a team, detrimental to the production of the whole project. Your structure should be organised sensibly so users can intuitively find content where they would expect to find it.

Engine content should be kept separate from working and export files for a multitude of reasons. First Unreal does not acknowledge non-UAsset files inside the editor, so visually you will have a discrepancy between files visible in the editor and in the file explorer. Second, not all users will want the working files; for example, a programmer—why would they want your animation source files? They don't need it. So organise in a format that allows users to get the files specific to them without taking up their hard drive space. With this in mind, source files should also be organised in a departmental fashion, so an environmental artist doesn't need to download the animation team assets. It is also wise to keep the engine content's structure matching the structure of the source assets' structure wherever possible, so users only have to learn a single structure.

The project structure is not a one-shoe-size-fits-all; what works for one project and team may not work for others—so communicate with your team and collectively decide on what is the best approach.

4.8.2 Naming Conventions

Once you have defined the folder structure for your project, your next step is to decide on naming conventions. This convention determines how all assets will be named, and it can be approached in a variety of ways, but ultimately, as long as everything is consistent, you can approach it in whichever way you prefer.

The first choice is the case of your name formatting—do you prefer PascalCase, CamelCase or Snake_Case for your files? PascalCase capitalises every word and removes all spaces, such as CharacterProp or PropGun. CamelCase, on the other hand is similar, but the first word is always lowercase and the proceeding words are uppercase, such as characterProp or propGun. Snake_Case, on the other hand, has no requirement for capitalisation; it can be upper or lowercase, but all spaces are replaced with an underscore, such as Character_Prop or prop_gun. For assets, I recommend using Snake_Case, as it is the most readable.

Prefixing your file name is an effective way to easily communicate the contents of the file with anyone who reads it; without it, you could have multiple files of the same name with different purposes, and it would be difficult to understand their purposes at face value. Within Table 4.1 are a variety of

TABLE 4.1

File Type Prefix Examples for Unreal Assets

File Type	Prefix
Animation Sequence	A_
Blendspace	BS_
AnimBlueprint	ABP_
Skeleton	SKEL_
Skeletal Mesh	SK_
Physics Asset	PHYS_

An extensive naming convention system for Unreal is available (https://github.com/Allar/ue5-style-guide).

examples of animation-focused prefixes; while not exhaustive, they give an indication of how they can be structured.

When creating new source assets, consider their target file type inside of the engine and name the source file accordingly for consistency—so if you are working on a character skeleton file, the engine prefix should be SK_, so consistently name the Maya and FBX files so they are associated correctly but can still be distinguished by their file type extension (SK_Character.ma, SK_Character. fbx, SK_Character.uasset).

Having unique file names with their asset type prefixes can also aid in debugging and tracking down issues. If a log reports an asset has an error, if there are multiple files with the same name, fixing the issue can take longer than necessary. It is also recommended to avoid illegal characters from across software, so spaces and colons are illegal characters in Maya, and Windows generally does not function well with full stops, forward or backslashes, question marks, or asterisks within their names, so keep away from them as a general rule. If there is the potential for multiple variants of the same file, such as various walk cycles, utilise a double-digit suffix at the end starting at 00 and increment up with each file.

In any game's development, things change a lot. If you're making a game with characters, at the beginning of the project that character may have one name, but throughout the production lifespan it may switch several times and end up with a completely different name. This can cause issues with filenames, as at the beginning of production, all the files could correspond to X name, files from the middle of production correspond to Y name, and files from later in production correspond to Z name. Three different file name labels that all correspond to the same character. This could get very confusing. One way to counteract this would be to use a fixed development codename for the asset, maybe an acronym, or just a consistent name that sticks regardless of the name change.

With all these considerations, here are some examples of file names for developing a bipedal character called Matt (see Table 4.2).

The earlier you implement a naming convention in a project, the fewer headaches will arise later when files need to be adapted to this convention.

TABLE 4.2

File Name Examples for Source and Unreal Assets

File Type	Prefix
Animation Sequence	A_Matt_Walk_Forward_00.ma
	A_Matt_Walk_Forward_00.fbx
	A_Matt_Walk_Forward_00.uasset
Blendspace	BS_Matt_Walk_00.uasset
AnimBlueprint	ABP_Matt.uasset
Skeleton	SKEL_Human.uasset
Skeletal Mesh	SK_Matt.ma
	SK_Matt.fbx
	SK_Matt.uasset
Physics Asset	PHYS_Matt.uasset

5

Introduction to Maya

With our technology chosen and fundamental considerations understood, it's time to learn all about tools! As a TA, tools are your best friend—but it is important to understand what tools you have at your disposal and how they work on a fundamental level. You can't use a tool you are not aware of; in the same way, you can't use the tool to its full potential if you don't know how it works! Autodesk's Maya (Figure 5.1) will serve as our main tool bench for the creation of all our non-engine-authored content, which includes our skeleton rigs, control rigs and animations, as well as any tools we create to help with the development of any of the former items. For those familiar with Maya already, the following chapter will be familiar ground to most, but for the sake of clarity, let's cover some of the interfaces and tools at our disposal.

5.1 Interface

5.1.1 Toolbar Menu Sets

The first thing you'll notice about Maya is that not all menu options are available simultaneously; there are menu sets that you must switch between to display different categories of options (Figure 5.2) Since Maya is such a comprehensive package, its tools are organised into categories for each discipline.

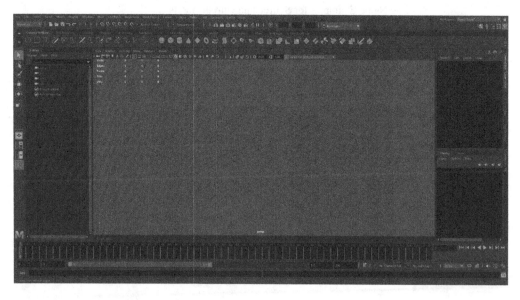

FIGURE 5.1   The interface for Autodesk Maya.

DOI: 10.1201/9781003263258-5

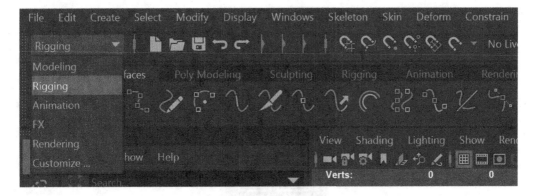

FIGURE 5.2 The menu sets are accessible via the toolbar.

FIGURE 5.3 The shelves interface in Maya.

5.1.2 Shelves

Below the toolbar are the shelves (Figure 5.3)—these are tabs that feature quick-access buttons for the most common tools for each category of work. There are unique shelves for modelling, sculpting, rigging, animation, etc. You can even add custom shelves, to which you can add buttons for shortcuts to an existing tool, or even your very own scripts.

To add a custom shelf:

1. Select the COG icon (🔘) on the left-hand side of the shelves interface.
2. Select **New Shelf.**
3. Enter a name into the dialogue box for your new shelf, then press OK.

To add a quick-access shelf button for an existing Maya tool, simply hold **Shift + Ctrl then select the menu button** for the tool.

5.1.3 Viewport

Front and centre of the interface is the viewport—this is your window into your 3D scene. While the viewport is self-explanatory, here are a few useful tips to get the most out of your viewport experience. On the left-hand side of the interface are the panel layout buttons (Figure 5.4); when pressed, they will alter the viewport panel layout from one to four views. Alternatively, press the Space key to toggle between your current viewport panel layout and four panels. Under the **panel** dropdown, you can "tear off a panel copy," which will create a duplicate floating window of the viewport.

Along the viewport toolbar (Figure 5.5), there are a variety of quick access shortcuts, ▬▬▬▬ which will each change the rendering style of the viewport, including wireframe, shaded, textured models and enabled lighting. The 🔲 icon will isolate the selected objects in the viewport to help focus work. The 🔲 X-Ray icon will allow you to see through meshes, and the 🔲 X-Ray joints icon will layer joint rendering on top of all meshes.

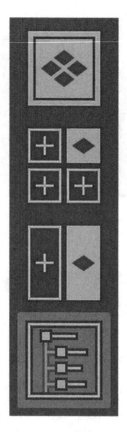

FIGURE 5.4 The quick layout buttons for viewport alterations.

FIGURE 5.5 The viewport toolbar.

5.1.4 Scene Outliner

On the left-hand side of the interface is the Outliner (Figure 5.6). This panel acts like a browser for all the scene contents, and each node of the scene listed. Each node is presented hierarchically, with the + icon next to each node will expand the structure to showcase any children the node has.

By default, the outliner does not show everything within the scene. There is a distinction between certain nodes; all nodes fall under the DG (dependency graph) nodes category, but a subset of nodes are referred to as DAG (Directed Acyclic Graph) nodes. DAG are the nodes you will commonly work with within the viewport, such as meshes, joints, lights or locators, as a DAG is defined by the node having a transform (position, rotation and scale). It is possible to view all nodes within the outliner by unchecking the **DAG Nodes Only** checkbox from the **display** dropdown. Each animation, material or even plugin node has DG nodes that are hidden in the scene.

5.1.5 Channel Box

The channel box, located on the right side of the interface (shown in Figure 5.7), is a selection and time-context-sensitive tool that allows the user to easily modify, lock or even mute attributes on a

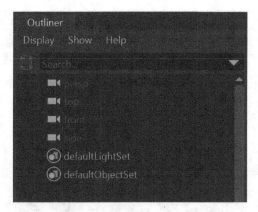

FIGURE 5.6   The scene outliner window panel.

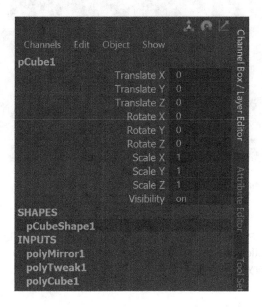

FIGURE 5.7   The channel box window panel.

selected node. The channel box does not display an exhaustive list of all attributes for a node, but it showcases all attributes that are flagged to be quickly accessible in the channel box; these are commonly the typical transform attributes, visibility and any user-generated attributes.

Not only does the channel box display attributes and their current values, but it also shows all relevant construction history for the selected node at the bottom of the interface; additional connected nodes, such as shapes or nodes that are inputted into this node, are also shown for quick access to modify those nodes.

5.1.6 Attribute Editor

The attribute editor is a comprehensive list of all a node's attributes, with access to all other connected nodes to the currently selected node. The attribute editor can be accessed via the attribute editor button at the top-right corner of the screen, or by pressing **Ctrl+A**.

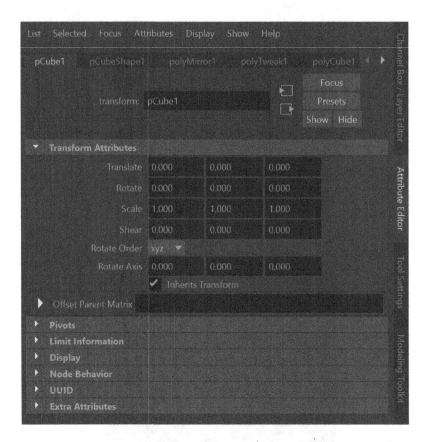

FIGURE 5.8   The attribute editor.

The interface shown in Figure 5.8 allows for the visualisation and modification of all attributes in a nice, compact window; along the top are several tabs that will showcase any connected input nodes, such as construction history or the shape nodes.

5.1.7 Node Editor

Maya's node editor (shown in Figure 5.9) is a node-based DG that can be used to display all the interconnections between nodes within your scenes in a visual form, showing which node's attribute connects to another node's attribute. The node editor is an incredibly powerful tool for rigging.

5.1.8 Workspaces

Finally, Maya also includes Workspaces—these are presets that determine the interface's layout as well as what panels are enabled and docked where. These workspaces are available from the drop-down in the top right corner of the interface; switching between workspaces will automatically update the interface layout. Maya offers several presets, but you can even add your own workspace layout as a preset.

If you ever find yourself accidentally modifying your user interface, you can lock your workspace from being modified by pressing the padlock icon next to the workspace dropdown.

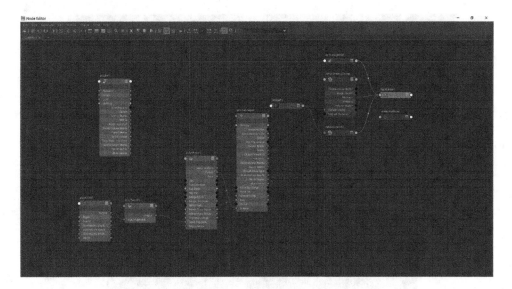

FIGURE 5.9 The node editor.

5.2 Scene Setup

When creating a new scene, you will need to ensure that the scene settings are appropriately applied for your project; otherwise, it could have some unintended consequences later.

5.2.1 Working Units

Maya's default units of measurement are metric, with 1 Maya unit equaling 1 metre. This metric matches the units utilised within Unreal, which will keep the units identical between packages.

If you do require to change your units of measurement for team, project or personal reasons, you are able to change your settings (**Windows > Settings/Preferences > Preferences > Settings Category > Working Units; Linear**).

5.2.2 Frame Rate

You must set your frame rate relative to your project's needs; for most, a 30 FPS is great, even if the game project's target FPS is 60 or 120. This is because while the animation file may be authored at 30, playback in the engine will interpolate between those frames up to 60 or 120 FPS as required. Previous generations of games were sometimes animated at 15 FPS, which would then interpolate up to 30 FPS. The higher the frame rate of your animation scenes, the larger the file size for animation data will be; a 60 FPS animation has double the data of a 30 FPS animation.

It's easy to change the scene's current frame rate via the frame rate drop-down in the lower right corner of the interface (Figure 5.10). Alternatively, you can also modify this setting in the preferences (**Windows > Settings/Preferences > Preferences > Settings Category > Working Units; Time**).

5.2.3 New Scene Defaults

To save you time from re-applying the scene settings every time you create a new file, you can customise your new scene default settings. Inside the New Scene Options (Figure 5.11—**Maya Menu > File > New Scene > ❐**) you can set your new scene preferences, including frame rate and starting frame.

FIGURE 5.10   The timeline dropdown that controls the frames per second of the scene.

FIGURE 5.11   The Maya menu's file dropdown.

5.3 Rigging Tools

Switching to the **Rigging Menu (F3)** via the Toolbar Menu Sets will expose the rigging toolkits; new menu options for Skeleton, Skin, Deform, Constrain and Control will appear under this set. When working on rigging, you will predominantly find yourself living in this menu. The skeleton menu is where you find tools for dealing with joints, whether that's creating, mirroring or labelling. The skin menu contains all tools required to utilise the skin technology to weigh our geometry to a skeleton rig. The deform menu includes a variety of tools to deform geometry, such as via blend shapes or lattices; a lot of the tools in this menu are not engine-safe and are primarily for offline purposes. Excluding the blend shapes tool, not many of these tools will be touched on. The constraint menu exposes all the constraint tools. These are powerful tools that allow relationships to be built between nodes, such as one node following another's position or rotation or even aiming at the other. We will dive into these tools more shortly, as they are essential for any rigger. The control menu includes tools that will be utilised for building a Control Rig setup. We can tag controllers via this menu. As we progress through the chapters, we will use several of the tools found in these menus to rig and skin our characters.

5.3.1 Constraints

Constraints are tools that allow you to create a one-way relationship between the properties of two or more objects; the first object in the constraint is the destination of the properties, and the second object (or more) would be the source of the relationship; this source is what drives the properties of the destination object. There can be multiple source objects driving a constraint, which results in the driven property being averaged from the source objects. Constraints offer a "**maintain offset**" functionality that allows the destination object to preserve its property state prior to the constraint being applied— this causes the constraint to have an offset to the source object's properties rather than follow directly.

There are a variety of types of constraints, all of which bring their own feature set to the table. In combination with one another, they are extremely powerful tools that empower the automation of animation, measurements of 3D space, or even the transfer of data between objects.

Constraints are standard across all DCCs, from 3DS Max to Maya—some are even replicable at runtime within a game engine as they are cheap computational operations, such as a point, orient or look-at constraint. Unfortunately, some types of constraints are computationally expensive, so they cannot be replicated like their DCC counterparts.

5.3.1.1 The Point, Orientation and Scale Constraints

These three types of constraints are all relationships that drive one of three of the 3D transformation matrix components—translation, rotation and scale. With a point constraint having positional influence, an orientation having rotational influence and scale having scale influence. These three constraints control the full transform matrix of an object. While rigging, these constraints are useful for copying information from one joint to another or linking two objects together so that when one rotates, the other rotates with it, even if they are in different parts of the skeleton hierarchy.

An example of an orientation constraint is with a shoulder pad—you could source the upper arm joint, then orientation constraint it to the destination shoulder pad joint; this would cause the shoulder pad joint to rotate one-to-one with what the upper arm does, but it would rotate from another pivot point. This is useful to apply if you want to prevent mesh intersections.

If a single source object is used, the constraint will cause the destination object to follow the property directly, so positional, rotational and scale values will follow one-to-one. If there are multiple source objects used, the destination object will have the average result of the source objects.

5.3.1.2 Parent Constraint

Parent constraints drive a destination object to behave like it is a child object hierarchically of the target object; it inherits both translation and rotation properties.

It is important to note that this constraint's behaviour differs from having both a point and orientation constraint applied. While the latter two may influence the destination object with matching behaviour, parent constraints will move relative to the distance between the sources and the destination. If the objects are at different locations and the source object rotates, instead of the destination object rotating on the spot like it would with an orientation constraint, the object would swing like it was a child object.

Parent constraints are particularly useful when rigging control rigs—in some cases, you may want some objects to behave as if they are the children of a different hierarchy; the parent constraint is perfect for that.

5.3.1.3 Look-At/Aim Constraint

A look-at constraint, sometimes referred to as an aim constraint, drives the orientation of a destination object so that it always aims at another source object in a specified axis direction.

Look-ats are useful in cases such as simplifying the animation process of eyes on a character. Rather than independently animating each eye, a look-at constraint would only require a single target to be animated and both eyes would look around. Look-ats are useful even within mechanical rigging for pistons, they can be used to maintain the piston in the correct orientation as the gear spins around.

The aim axis direction is defined by the user, as well as the up axis direction, which defines upwards relative to the aim. It is important to note that if the destination object aims in the direction of the up axis, it will cause the object to flip. To remedy this, Look-ats offer a mode where the up axis can also specify an up object, so no longer will the destination object's up aim at a world axis; it will aim the up axis towards another object, so moving any one of the three objects within this constraint relationship will cause rotations to occur on the destination object.

5.3.1.4 Rivet Constraint

A rivet constraint allows you to attach a destination object to a specific point on a deforming mesh. There are several approaches to a rivet constraint; the most flexible approach attaches to a single or many vertex positions and then receives orientation input from the normal of that vertex. Alternative approaches attach the relative UV position to its 3D counterpart position, however, this can cause issues with models with UVs that are stacked on top of one another. These two approaches cannot be replicated in real-time in an engine due to the render pipeline order of video games, in which the calculation for the rendering of the polygons is after the calculation for any animation calculations, so the values are not available.

While these approaches cannot be replicated in the engine, there is a third approach that can be. In the first approach, the rivet is acquiring the transformation values from the vertices, those vertices have skin weighting values from joint influences, which cause the mesh to deform when the joints move. On a fundamental level, the way skinning is calculated is equivalent to parent constraints applied to each and every vertex, which means we can use these skin weight values in a parent constraint to behave like a rivet. This approach removes the middleman from the first approach and directly drives the destination object with the skinning values that would drive the vertex. We will cover how to replicate this in Unreal in Section 13.3.4.1 in Chapter 13.

While rigging, rivets can be useful for attaching rigid objects to deforming surfaces such as a badge riveted to a shirt.

5.3.2 Transformation Limits

Transformation attributes for translation, rotation and scale can be set to stay within a particular range through the use of limits. With a minimum and maximum value, objects such as joints can be set to stay within boundaries if you so wish. In Maya, these can be set in the **Attribute Editor > Limit Information**.

The use of limits can be useful in situations where you want to prevent any movement in a particular axis, such as on a human elbow, in which rotation in a single axis is all that is desired. The twist and roll axes can be limited to 0, and then additional limits can be applied to the bend axis to keep the rotations within a range that prevents them from rotating the wrong way, which will break the elbow or cause excessive rotation of the elbow into the upper arm.

5.3.3 Attribute Connections—Direct/Math/Curve

An attribute connection is a one-way relationship between two attributes, a driver attribute and a driven attribute, rather than entire objects influencing one another like a constraint, these are limited to a single attribute sending and receiving information.

A direct connection between two attributes is the simplest, when the driver attribute changes, the driven attribute changes with it one-to-one. This is as simple as connecting translate X to rotate Y; when translate X changes the rotate Y will equal it exactly. This can be useful for the transfer of information between two objects that need to act identically; rather than changing both objects, if one drives the other, only one will need to be changed. Attribute connections can have intermediate operations between the two connections, whether that's a math operation to multiply the value, invert it, clamp it or even use a lookup curve to find the correct output value. With a driven key, an input value is checked with a curve to output the Y value from the curve (Figure 5.12). Attributes can be

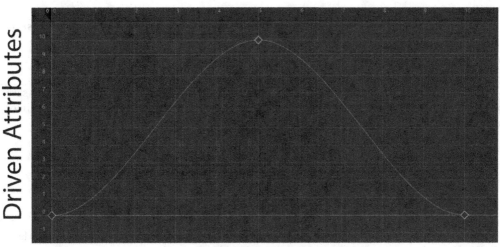

Driver Attributes

FIGURE 5.12 A curve representing how driver attributes can influence driven attributes.

connected via the node editor in Maya. This curve allows for a lot of user-controlled freedom for the output to equal a particular output value compared to math or one-to-one connections. In Maya, the lookup curve technique is called a Driven Key which can be found under **Animation > Key > Set Driven Key.**

5.3.4 Animation Expressions

Animation expressions are mathematical formulas or codes that can be executed at defined time intervals, whether that is every frame or on demand. They can be used to automate animation from scratch with optional random or formulaic properties, or even drive an object with the animated behaviour of another object. Expressions can even contain mathematical curves such as sine, cosine or tangent, which are extremely powerful for procedural animation. In Maya, expressions can be set in Windows > Animation Editors > Expression Editor.

A practical use case of an animation expression is the automation of wheel rotation on a vehicle when it travels through space. The animated translation of the vehicle's body can be connected to the rotation of the wheels, and the rotation will dynamically update if the animation ever changes, which will prevent an animator from being required to reanimate the wheels as well—saving time and money!

5.4 Useful Maya Settings and Tips

Here are a handful of useful settings and tips to get the most out of your Maya experience.

5.4.1 AutoSave and Incremental Saves

Backing up your work is vital, and Maya offers a handful of options to ensure your work is perpetually backed up—your future self will appreciate you enabling both of these options in case anything goes wrong.

AutoSave:
1. Open Preferences Window (**Maya Menu: Windows > Settings / Preferences > Preferences**).
2. Select **Files/Projects** from the **Categories**.
3. **AutoSave > Enabled**.

When enabled, new settings will be visible. These options will allow you to automatically save on a specific time interval, which, at intervals of 15 minutes, will back up your work four times an hour.

Incremental Save:
1. Open Save Scene Options Dialogue (**Maya Menu: File > Save Scene As []**).
2. Enable **Incremental Saves** checkbox.
3. Customise the maximum amount of incremental saves you wish to store.

Incremental saves can also be manually iterated by pressing Save and Increment on the Maya Menu File dropdown.

5.4.2 OS-Native File Browser

By default, Maya has its own type of file browser, but you may opt out of this to use the standard native OS-Native file browser, such as File Explorer in Windows.

1. Open Preferences Window (**Maya Menu: Windows > Settings/Preferences > Preferences**).
2. Select **Files/Projects** from the **Categories**.
3. Scroll to the **File Dialog** section, and select the **OS native** option to activate.

5.4.3 Infinite Undo

Maya comes with the fine-tuned ability to control the number of undo operations that are remembered; the more undos you have, the larger the performance cost. If you have a high-specification machine, then set the option to Infinite; it may save you.

1. Open Preferences Window (**Maya Menu: Windows > Settings / Preferences > Preferences**.
2. Select **Undo** from the **Categories**.
3. Enable the **Queue > Infinite**.

5.4.4 Hotkey Editor

Shortcuts will be your best friend when navigating any software, while learning a shortcut may only save seconds, the frequency of pressing commands over years of development soon adds up! Maya offers an extensive shortcut editor, so you can customise it to your heart's content, including the ability to assign scripts to hotkeys. **Maya Menu: Windows > Settings / Preferences > Hotkey Editor**

5.4.5 Floating Menus

If you find yourself frequently navigating to the same dropdown or sub-menu then detach it! If you hit the highlightable bar at the top of all dropdown menus, you can turn the window into a floating menu for quicker access!

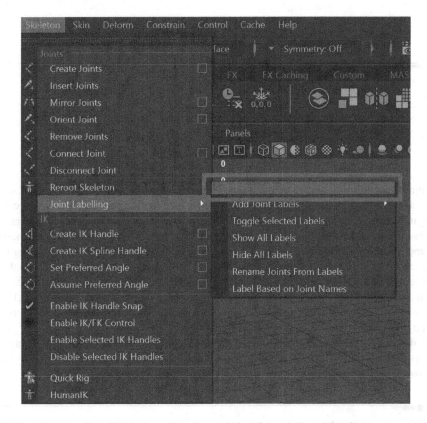

FIGURE 5.13   The button that will detach any drop-down windows into a dedicated interface.

5.4.6 Documentation

The ultimate source of help in Maya is the accompanying documentation (**Help > Maya Help** or **F1**). Whether you are looking for an explanation of how a feature works or a command for a Python script, Maya's documentation is comprehensive and is updated with each subsequent release and feature. Always refer to it!

6

Introduction to Python

Programming in an offline package that supports languages such as Python, MEL, or even MAXScript can be used to automate processes and speed up your workflow, saving time and resources so you can spend time doing more creative and fun tasks instead of the repetitive and tedious ones. Learning a language like Python is one of the best skills you can learn as a TA since it's a transferable language between most DCCs and even engines, Maya, 3DS Max, MotionBuilder, and even Unreal all support Python as a language.

Python can be used to build toolkits on top of the existing software functionality, bespoke interfaces to automate repeatable tasks and audit your scenes for errors, or if you're working in a team, you could even create and deploy tools to the rest of the team to support and speed up their workflows. As a TA, this will be common, as not only should you speed up your work, but you should also endeavour to speed up the people around you and their workflow.

Python, like software, has versions, so it's important to identify the version you are utilising in your package. As of this writing, the VFX platform determines the industry no longer supports Python 2 in 2020; current Unreal and Autodesk applications are all utilising Python 3.

6.1 Writing Standards

Everyone has their own way of writing code, in the same way, you have your own way of handwriting, communication, or process. While there are no right or wrong ways of writing code, there is inefficient and poorly written code; now how is that defined? Poorly written code is often described by how it does not adhere to defined writing standards and conventions. These standards aim to ensure code is written in a clean and tidy format to improve the work's readability for others. You may wonder why you must consider writing code for other people when you are the one writing it; this is because in a production environment, your work may be taken over by other people, or you yourself may revisit this code in a year's time and have forgotten what you have written and why you wrote it the way you did. For this reason, code must be as legible as possible to save time trying to reverse engineer what has been written rather than writing it neatly in the first place.

In Python, there are many style guides for writing code, such as **PEP8** (https://peps.python.org/pep-0008/). These are all guidelines to adhere to when writing code. In some studios, they will have their own writing style guides and they will supersede any format you may be familiar with. Ultimately, the aim with writing styles is consistency and readability.

6.2 Writing Efficiencies

When writing any form of code, there will be a golden path. This is the most optimal and perfect solution to a problem, but finding this path can be incredibly difficult. The problem in a production environment is that code needs to provide value quickly, but you do not want to rush it at the expense of compromising readability and the extendability of the system. This boundary is a very fine line to walk; you do not want to incur too much technical debt, but don't spend forever building something. If the work solves

DOI: 10.1201/9781003263258-6

a problem, it may not be the ultimate perfect solution, if your solution works and is clean, then it is no longer a problem—know when to move on. You and your work will only get better through experience, and experience comes from finishing tasks, not getting stuck circling around an answer.

The extreme side of this can become a detriment to not only you, your work and the team if you take coding standards, modularity and micro efficiencies to such an extreme that you do not stop until every critiquer or armchair developer out there is happy with the work you have made. The problem is that the code you spent months building for a simple system will never ship. You will fly past deadline after deadline, too busy getting caught up in this whirlpool of writing standards and efficiencies, resulting in the work never providing any return on investment. This goes back to the point regarding code needing to provide value—the best code is the code that gets written and used.

I would advise when starting any piece of code task, especially if it is in an unknown area, first focus on solving the problem to make the code work. Only once you have found that you are venturing into the correct pathway, then you can worry about abstracting the code and cleaning it up. Imagine spending all your time creating this immaculately abstracted function only to find out you've gone down the wrong pathway and the solution won't work, meaning your work is useless. Provide value first, then do a cleanup.

6.3 Python Basics

Let's dive into some of the basics of Python, for those familiar with other programming languages or even Blueprints, a lot of this will be familiar to you.

6.3.1 Variables

Writing Python, or any coding language, there are many similarities to algebra - one such similarity is the use of variables. In algebra, we often have X, and that X equals a value, in programming, this is no different—these are called variables. Variables can be used to store data! Whether that's a number, an object, or even a list, all data types can be stored as variables. Not only can we store "stuff," but it can also store states or modes. For the different data types, there are different terminologies associated with each:

- False/True States (0 or 1) are a **Boolean** data type.
- Decimal numbers (0.01, 0.5, 1.8) are a **Float** data type.
- Whole numbers (1, 2, 3) are an **Integer** data type.
- Text/Words (Hello My Name Is Matthew!) is a **String** data type.

Creating a variable is as simple as picking a name for your variable and defining it after an equals symbol. For example: X = "Hello". In this case, any time we use X in the future, we will receive "hello". While Python has many similarities to algebra, do not name your variables in an algebraic X, Y and Z style—name your variables adequately so that you can describe at a glance what is contained within. For example:

greeting = "hello world!"

6.3.2 Variable Collections

Variables don't just come in a single value; we are able to store groups of variables together in one of four collection data types: lists, sets, dictionaries and tuples. Collections are not only limited to multiple entries of a single variable type; you can store as many data types in them as you want. For example, you could store a string and a Boolean in the same collection.

Each different collection type has a different set of behaviours, making their use cases differ depending on the requirements of the collection. Table 6.1 showcases an overview of some of the different features:

TABLE 6.1

Python Collection Names and Their Behaviour

Collection Name	Example	Ordered	Modifiable	Duplicates
List	[A, B, C]	*Yes*	*Yes*	*Yes*
Set	{A, B, C}	*No*	*No*	*No*
Dictionary	{A:X, B:Y, C:Z}	*Yes*	*Yes*	*No*
Tuple	(A, B, C)	*Yes*	*No*	*Yes*

6.3.2.1 Creating A Collection

Creating a collection is just as straightforward as making a normal variable: a label followed by an equals symbol, then a particular type of bracket with the content inside separated with commas. We must ensure the syntax we use is appropriate for the type of collection you want to make; for lists, this means using [], Sets {}, dictionaries {} with paired items inside and a tuple uses {}. Here are some examples:

```
list = ['A', 'B', 'C']
Set = {'A', 'B', 'C'}
Dictionary = {'A':1, 'B':2, 'C':3}
Tuple = ('A', 'B', 'C')
```

6.3.2.2 Ordered Collections

An ordered collection means there is a particular order in which the variables inside the collection are defined; the position in a list is called the Index. Indices start at 0, so the first entry in an ordered collection is index 0, the second is 1, the third is 2 and so on. Unordered collections do not have particular indexes for the contained data.

To access a particular index inside an array, we can use square brackets with an index value contained inside to return the value of that index like so:

```
list = ['A', 'B', 'C', 'D', 'E']
print (list[1])
>B
```

If we find ourselves in a situation where we are required to find out a particular index value of an object contained in an array, we can use the Index method on an ordered collection to return the value. Here's an example:

```
list = ['A', 'B', 'C', 'D', 'E']
index = list.index('B')
print(index)
>1
```

The inverse of the operation can also be done; in a situation where we know the index but not the content, we can enter the list variable followed by the index in square brackets. This will return the variable at that index, like so:

```
list = ['A', 'B', 'C', 'D', 'E']
letter = list[1]
print(letter)
>B
```

6.3.2.3 *Modifiable Collections*

Modifiable collections are collections that, after their creation, can have their contents changed, whether that's removing, altering or adding new entries. Modifiable collections allow for all of these to occur. In the case of a list or dictionary, we can remove or insert entries from the collection, but tuples and sets do not allow for modification after generation.

There are several methods to remove entries from an array; the two most common are **remove** and **pop**. The remove method removes the first entry of the inputted value from the array, whereas the pop method removes a specific index from an array. Here's an example of both of them.

```
list = ['A', 'B', 'C', 'D', 'E']
list.remove('B')
>A, C, D, E
list = ['A', 'B', 'C', 'D', 'E']
list.pop(1)
>A, C, D, E
```

We can add entries to our collection with the **insert** or **append** methods. The append method will add a new entry to the end of the array, which will maintain the indexes of all previous entries. Insert, on the other hand, requires an index and will slot the entry into the middle of the array, pushing all the entries apart.

```
list = ['A', 'B', 'C', 'D', 'E']
List.append('Hello')
>A, B, C, D, E, Hello
list = ['A', 'B', 'C', 'D', 'E']
List.insert(1, 'Hello')
>A, Hello, B, C, D, E
```

6.3.2.4 *Duplicates in Collections*

Some collections allow for duplicate entries, meaning multiple elements have the same value in the array; lists and tuples allow for duplicates, but sets and dictionaries do not.

Be careful when dealing with collections that allow for duplicate entries, as when utilising an index method, there is the potential for it to return incorrect results compared to what you are looking for. For example, if you have a list with two duplicate entries at index 1 and 3, and you do not know where they are located in the array—using the index() method to find the second entry will return index 1, not your intended index 3. This can have the potential to cause some issues and catch people out—so watch out!

```
list = ['potato', 'tomato', 'strawberry', 'tomato']
index = list.index(''tomato'')
print(index)
>1
```

6.3.2.5 *Dictionary Collections*

The dictionary is the odd one out of the collections, where each of the other collections contains a single stream of items, and a dictionary is a list of pairs. This allows for unique behaviour to pair variables in the dictionary; if you feed one variable into the dictionary, it can output the other, like this:

```
Dictionary = {'A':'Potato', 'B':'Tomato', 'C':'Beansprouts'}
print (Dictionary['B'])
>Tomato
```

This is similar to how we have previously used an index, but instead, we use the dictionary with one of the paired entries, and it will return the other. This works both ways:

```
Dictionary = {'A':'Potato', 'B':'Tomato', 'C':'Beansprouts'}
print (Dictionary['Tomato'])
>B
```

6.3.3 Functions

A function is a section of reusable code that, when called, will perform a specific task. Instead of writing the same chunk of code over and over, we can define functions that encapsulate behaviour and then call that function when we require said behaviour. Functions are not only a static set of reusable code; we are able to extend their capabilities with inputs that can influence and change the behaviour of the function's internals. We can even make functions return information from the location that calls the function. Let's learn a little more about these capabilities.

6.3.4 Building a Function

Starting off, we need to build our function. We can do this via a procedure called a define, which sets up the function with a unique name of your choice and includes any inputs that may be required to operate the function. First, let's cover a basic function and expand it over time. To define a function, we must use the **def** keyword followed by the name of the function, parentheses and then a colon— like this:

```
def my_function():
    print("hello world!")
```

We have made a function called **my _ function** that, when called, will print the string "**hello world**. " Now that this is defined, we can call this function at any time by calling the function name with a parenthesis like this:

```
my_function()
>hello world!
```

With our function, we can keep calling my_function() as many times as we want to recycle the behaviour without writing the same commands over and over!

6.3.4.1 Inputs

Now that we have a basic function, let's expand some of its capabilities by providing inputs. With inputs, we can provide any form of data into the function when it is called, whether that's a Boolean or a string. The data can be passed through into the function to modify the internals of the function. To add inputs, we must modify our function definition. Let create a function that will benefit from the use of input variables. Inputs come in two flavours: positional arguments and flags.

6.3.4.2 Positional Arguments

Let's create a function that will add two numbers together to demonstrate a positional argument. To add a positional input, we must add new variable entries into parentheses, with each new input separated by a comma. The positional order of these variables is very important, not only for the definition but also when it is called; they need to match exactly for the function to work. The variables added here do not have to be predefined variables; these are new variables specific to the function that will be used on the internals of the function. Consider this like our earlier algebra analogy: with X and Y, these variable names are interchangeable, so use them inside the function.

```
def add_numbers(number_one, number_two):
    sum = number_one + number_two
    print(sum)
```

We have built a function called add_numbers that takes two inputs, and the internals of the function take these two numbers, add them together and store them in a new variable called sum. The variable sum is then printed. To use the variable, we can call it like this:

```
add_numbers(1, 5)
>6
```

6.3.4.3 Flags

An alternative but not mutually exclusive input for functions are **flags**; these operate the same as a positional when used inside a function, but when it comes to defining and calling the function, they are different: flags are entirely optional, out of order and best of all, they have a descriptor visible to the reader. To define a flag in a function, add a variable inside the parentheses just like previously, but this time add an equals symbol followed by a default value. This default value is what the variable will be if the flag is optionally absent when it is called. When using a flag and positional together, you must always enter the positions first, followed by the flags. An example of a flag in a function is like this:

```
def login(greeting="Hello", user="Matt"):
    print(greeting + user)
```

Since flags are completely optional, we can use as many or as few as we want, empowering us to do this.

```
login(user="Maxime")
>Hello Maxime
login(greeting="Hola ")
>Hola Matt
```

Since a flag is optional, it will default to its defined value in the function if it is missed when called.

6.3.4.4 Output—Return

When defining a function, we can also choose to add an output—this means that when the function is called, it can return information, whether that's a single value or multiple values from the inner workings of the function. Making a function return a value is very straightforward; all we need to do is use the **return** keyword followed by any variable we would like to return. Let's modify our earlier add numbers function to work with an output.

```
def add_numbers(number_one, number_two):
    sum = number_one + number_two
    return sum
```

To receive the value of the function when called, add a variable before the function; this variable will then become the value of the returned function like this:

```
answer = add_numbers(5, 10)
print(answer)
>15
```

We are not limited to a single return value either, we can send back multiple entries like this:

```
def function():
    X = 1
    Y = 2
    return X, Y
A, B = function()
```

Returns are optional; even if a function has a return value but you do not wish to grab it, you can call the function like normal without the risk of an error.

6.3.5 Conditional Statements

When building our scripts and functions, we will need to apply logic to them. We can't rely on our scripts merely being single command after single command, it is inevitable that we will need some checks to change behaviour based on the environment. To do this, we can use a conditional statement called an **if statement**. An if statement is a straightforward principle: if certain criteria are met, do X, if certain criteria are not met, do Y; or alternatively, even stop altogether. The formatting for an if statement is also simple; simply write the **if** keyword, followed by the criteria, and end with a colon.

```
if variable >= 5:
    # Logic here!
```

One key factor to consider in Python is the indentation. When moving to a new block of code, we must indent the line to indicate to the Python interpreter which block the code is associated with. When writing code on new lines, these are all part of the same block as they all share the same indent level of none, but since we are now creating a new block of code to perform based on criteria, we must indent all lines for that code. The indentation of code blocks will nest, so if we place another conditional inside this indented code block, we would have to indent a second time and again with each conditional. We can perform an indentation by pressing **Tab**.

Additionally, we can add an optional **else** keyword on the first line after the new code block, to trigger logic if the criteria are not met. Let's dive into some examples to make sense of it.

```
if variable >= 5:
print("This will print if the criteria is true")
else:
    print("This will print if the criteria is false")
```

6.3.6 For Loops

A for loop is a logic operation that can iterate through a sequence of objects and provide the current iterated object into a new code block, effectively looping the same piece of code over and over until all items in the list have been put through the block. This allows us to perform actions based on the contents of a list and can be quite useful for bulk operations. We can iterate through variable collections such as lists or even strings.

To create a for loop, we must first use the **for** keyword, followed by an **iterator variable**, the **in** keyword, and then an object to iterate through, such as a list. Finally, for the loop logic is then indented on the following line. The iterator variable is the reference you will use in the proceeding code block to describe the current iteration object; similar to how a positional argument in a function works, it's a placeholder to use in the next code block. The iterator variable can have any label, often it is used, but you can use a more descriptive variable name if you desire. Here's a generic example, followed by a TA-focused one.

```
# Example 01
list = [0, 1, 2, 3, 4]
for i in list:
    print(i)

# Example 02
joints = ['upperarm_r', 'forearm_r', 'hand_r']
for joint in joints:
    print(joint)
```

Often a plural descriptor can be used to clearly denote the list, and a singular label to describe the iterator—such as "joints" and "joint."

6.3.7 While Loop

A while loop is a logic operation that allows a block of code to keep repeating while specific criteria are met. This is where its name derives—while X is true, do Y. This logic loop will perpetually loop and not allow the script to continue until the criteria have changed, allowing the looping to end and the script to continue. The while loop relies on the criteria to release the script from the loop; otherwise, you can create situations where the criteria never change, causing the script to get stuck in an indefinite cycle—unless that's your intention!

To build a while loop, we start with the **while** keyword, followed by the criteria we want the while loop to keep working for, then a colon and finally our logic indented on a new line. Here's an example:

```
counter = 1
while counter < 4:
    print(counter)
    counter += 1
print('while loop ended')
```

The example has a while loop that will keep looping until the counter is 4 or over; the result of this script would print 1, 2 and 3, and finally "while loop ended" —as it, the loop would cause the counter to increase to 4, then end the loop and continue the script.

6.3.8 Comments

When writing code, you can enter a # to enable comments on a single line; this means everything after the # is ignored by the Python interpreter. You can use this opportunity to write comments for future you to explain why you are doing what you are doing. You may come back to this piece of code in 6 months, 1 year, 2 years or someone entirely different may take a look—you need to understand what is going on at a quick glance, and a simple comment is great for these.

```
# Comments can be made like this!
cmds.sphere() # or like this!
```

We are also able to write block comments with triple quoted speech marks to enter and exit comment mode, like this:

```
"""
This is a
Multiple Line comment
"""
```

6.3.9 Modules

To maintain the lightweight nature of Python, it only has a limited capability out of the box; while it can do many things, it cannot do a whole lot more. Rather than bloat the language with every feature set that every user will have to suffer with, the language opts for a module approach in which you can import a module that contains a specific set of functionality when you need it, so you only import what you need for your scripts rather than having every piece of functionality omnipresent.

Importing is as simple as using the **import** keyword followed by the name of the module; this has to be done in the script directly and before you call any functionality from the module. Here's an example of importing the math module and using the square root function to find the square root of 29:

```
import math
print(math.sqrt(29))
>5.385164807134504
```

6.4 Python Tips and Tricks

6.4.1 Help()

If you ever get stuck and cannot figure out how to use a function or module, you can access the help documentation directly from within Python using the help() function. By providing the help() with an object in parentheses, a breakdown of the help documentation relevant to the object will be printed into the history logs with an accompanied description to help you along as shown in Figure 6.1. Use Case - help (cmds.ls())

6.4.2 Print(Dir())

The dir() function is a similar help tool in that it will return a list of all attributes of the provided object. Unlike the help() function, this does not automatically log the information, so we must encapsulate the dir() function in a print():

```
print (dir (cmds.ls()) )

[… 'append', 'clear', 'copy', 'count', 'extend', 'index', 'insert', 'pop',
'remove', 'reverse', 'sort']
```

Dir() is context-sensitive to the object provided; notice how if you pass an array variable into the dir the returned values include operations such as pop, insert and append—all array-specific attributes, whereas if you provide a string, the array-specific attributes will be absent. This can be very useful to find out all the attributes available for different object types.

```
help(cmds.ls())
Help on list object:

class list(object)
 |  list(iterable=(), /)
 |
 |  Built-in mutable sequence.
 |
 |  If no argument is given, the constructor creates a new empty list.
 |  The argument must be an iterable if specified.
 |
 |  Methods defined here:
 |
 |  __add__(self, value, /)
 |      Return self+value.
 |
 |  __contains__(self, key, /)
 |      Return key in self.
 |
 |  __delitem__(self, key, /)
 |      Delete self[key].
 |
 |  __eq__(self, value, /)
 |      Return self==value.
 |
 |  __ge__(self, value, /)
 |      Return self>=value.
 |
 |  __getattribute__(self, name, /)
 |      Return getattr(self, name).
```

FIGURE 6.1 The console log for the Python help().

6.4.3 String Construction

When dealing with strings, you may find yourself needing to construct a new string from multiple strings, such as by combining strings A and B together or even injecting a variable into a string to build something entirely new. There are a handful of ways to achieve this; here are a few examples.

6.4.3.1 Method A—Variable + Variable

One of the simplest examples of this is to treat the strings like a maths equation, simply adding one string to another like so.

```
string = "hello" + "world!"
>string = "hello world!"
```

This can also work by adding other variables into the mix, but we must make sure to convert the variable into a string by surrounding the variable with str(variable).

```
username = "MattLake"
string = "hello" + str(username) + ", welcome to the show!"
>string = "hello MattLake, welcome to the show!"
```

While this can work for simple cases, with larger, more complex strings, this can grow in format to be very unreadable.

6.4.3.2 Method B—String Format - {}.Format

One alternative is the use of the. format method on a string; this allows us to inject another object at a defined point in the string. There are two steps to this: we must first add a {} where we require to add something into our string, and then we must add a. format() method at the end of the string with the object we want to inject in. Here's the same example case:

```
username = "MattLake"
string = "hello {}, welcome to the show!".format(username)
>string = "hello MattLake, welcome to the show!"
```

The format method also allows for multiple entries by entering an incremental number into the curly brackets/braces, then inside the format method you can add multiple entries to match the number of curly brackets you have; like so:

```
username = "MattLake"
string = "{0} {1}, welcome to the show!".format("hello", username)
>string = "hello MattLake, welcome to the show!"
```

Just like method A, while it can work for simple tasks, with multiple entries, this can start to get unreadable quite fast, causing the user to keep scanning from the beginning of the line to the end of the line to truly understand what is going on. To increase the readability of this method, we can use placeholder text instead of a number to get replaced, like this:

```
username = "MattLake"
string= "{greeting} {account}, welcome to the show!".format(greeting =
"hello", account=username)
>string = "hello MattLake, welcome to the show!"
```

6.4.3.3 Method C—F-Strings - {Variable}

Our final method is F-Strings (formatted string literals). With this method, we can inject variables directly into the string without any additional formatting, and it will read cleanly. To use this method, we must ensure our string is an F-String by beginning the string with an F/f outside the quotes. By doing this, we can simply format strings like this:

```
username = MattLake
string = f"Hello {username}, welcome to the show!"
>string = "hello MattLake, welcome to the show!"
```

Personally, I do think this is the best method, as the string reads clearly and does not require additional formatting—it all just works.

6.4.4 String Deconstruction

When working with strings, breaking them down into components is just as important as constructing them. Python includes some useful methods, including the split, partition and reverse partition methods, to break your strings down exactly how you desire.

The split method can be used to break a string into components in a list. We can define how the string is split via a separator value in the method, such as splitting a string up at every full stop, or if we leave the separator value blank, a default value of space will be used, which will split a string into a list with every word being a new entry in the list. Here's an example:

```
string = "namespace:lowerarm_r"
x = string.split(':')
print(x)
> ['namespace', 'lowerarm_r']
```

The partition method (**.partition**) will search for a particular set of matching characters and will split the string into three components in a tuple: the first entry will be every character before the found input characters, the second entry will be the found input characters, and the third entry will be every character after the found input characters. The partition method works forwards, so it will find the first set of matching characters; if there are multiple instances of the input characters, they will be ignored; only the first count will be used.

```
string = "character:controls:lowerarm_r"
x = string.partition(':')
print(x)
> ('character', ':', 'controls:lowerarm_r')'
```

The reverse partition method (**.rpartition**) has the same behaviour but performs in the opposite direction and instead finds the last matching character instead of the first, so it searches from the end to the start rather than the start to the end.

```
string = "character:controls:lowerarm_r"
x = string.rpartition(':')
print(x)
> ('character:controls', ':', 'lowerarm_r')
```

6.4.5 Slicing

Slicing is a technique that can be performed on any sequence object, with this technique we can take a slice out of a list, just like taking a slice out of a cake. If we have a list with ten entries, we can take entries 3–6 through this very easy method.

To slice a list, we use the same technique as receiving a particular index, but this time enter two numbers separated by a colon. The first number is the start index, and the second is the end index, like **[start:end]**. If we miss a start or end value but maintain the colon, the slice will interpret the missing value as the start or end of the list, depending on if it is the left or right number missing. Here is an example in action:

```
numbers = [1, 2, 3, 4, 5, 6, 7, 8, 9, 10]
print(numbers[3:6])
>[4, 5, 6]
```

This technique is not limited to collections; it can also be performed on strings.

```
string = 'lowerarm_r'
print(string[3:6])
>era
```

Another technique with slicing is to use a negative number—when used in the start index position, the value of the negative number will be removed from the string, or if used in the end position, it will remove that number of characters from the end. The latter technique is useful for removing predefined suffix lengths from names.

```
string = 'lowerarm_r'
print(string[-2:])
>_r
print(string[:-2])
>lowerarm
```

6.4.6 Remove Duplicates from Array

A quick trick to remove duplicate objects from a list is to convert it to a different variable type that does not accept duplicate entries and then convert it back. We can do this by converting the list to a set and then back to a list.

```
array = ['A', 'A', 'B', 'B', 'C']
array = list(set(array))
print(array)
array = ['A', 'B', 'C']
```

6.4.7 File Path

While not specifically a trick for Python, you may find yourself dealing with paths for files; these can be a multiple-step process to acquire manually; however, Windows offers a hidden shortcut for copying the path of a file! **Shift + Right Click** on a file will now reveal a secret option in the dropdown (Figure 6.2) labelled "**Copy as path**." This will copy the exact location of the file onto your clipboard, ready for pasting into your scripts! "C:\Users\Matthew\Desktop\Hello.txt"

6.4.8 Wild Cards

If we use the **fnmatch** module, we can search variables for wildcards. A wildcard allows us to search for specific criteria with a component switched out; for example, if we had a list of joints in a human, and we wanted to filter both the hand joints, instead of searching for both "hand_r" and "hand_l" we could search for a wildcard variant. Utilising a **?** wildcard will search for any single character in that position, while an asterisk ***** will match any character of any length. So in this case, we would search for "hand_?" and it would return both hands! Here's an example.

```
import fnmatch
joints = ["lowerarm_r", "lowerarm_l", "hand_r", "hand_l"]
filtered = fnmatch.filter(joints, "hand_?")
# filtered = ["hands_r", "hands_l"]
```

FIGURE 6.2 Windows OS copy as path option on the right-click menu.

Alternatively, using the asterisk version, which can denote any character or length of characters, can be used in cases like so; instead of searching an array for the specific suffix, it's searching for "spine" followed by any series of characters—so spine 01, 02 and 03 and spine ends are all flagged.

```python
import fnmatch
joints = ["spine_01", "spine_02", "spine_03", "spine_end", "neck"]
filtered = fnmatch.filter(joints, "spine*")
# filtered = ["spine_01", "spine_02", "spine_03", "spine_end"]
```

7

Python for Maya

As covered previously, Maya is very script-friendly, built upon the MEL language, it allows for an incredible degree of customisation to build features and toolkits the way you want them. Since Maya supports both MEL and Python, it can be a daunting decision for those just getting their feet wet with scripting and are stuck on which language to choose. I would recommend learning Python over Maya's Native MEL. The primary reason is that Python is a transferable skill beyond just Maya; many other packages, including Unreal, also support it, whereas MEL is only for Maya. Additionally, the entire suite of MEL commands is accessible through Python, meaning you get the best of both worlds if you use Python.

7.1 Maya Command Line

Located in the bottom left corner of the Maya interface is the Command Line (Figure 7.1); from here we can enter simple one-line commands to execute on our scene. To execute a command, first type a command into the text box and press Enter to activate the command. Make sure to select the appropriate language for the command, as noted by the text on the left. Clicking this button will switch between MEL and Python modes.

7.2 Script Editor

There is also a dedicated Script Editor available in Windows > General Editors > Script Editor, or alternatively, you can press the script editor icon (⊞) in the bottom right-hand corner of the interface. From the window shown in Figure 7.2, you can create and save multiple complex scripts with a variety of useful tools and error logging to diagnose your scripts.

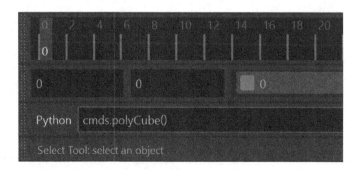

FIGURE 7.1   The Maya command line located in the bottom left corner of the interface.

DOI: 10.1201/9781003263258-7

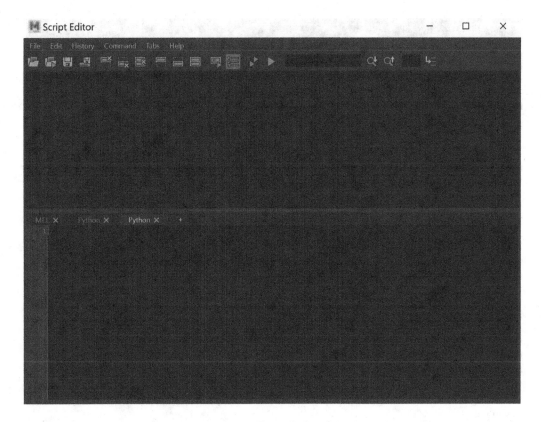

FIGURE 7.2 The dedicated scripting interface for Maya is called the Script Editor.

The interface has three distinct components: the toolbar, the history and the input panel (in vertical order). The toolbar features a variety of functionality to modify the behaviour of the script editor, such as saving your scripts, executing your scripts, or even clearing the history. *One button on the toolbar will clear your input panel - so watch out and do not lose your work!* The history panel is a log of all the actions, scripts, prints, and events that have happened in the scene. This area is very important for error logging and debugging! The input panel is your workspace; this is where you can create your multi-line scripts. The panel has tabs that allow you to store multiple scripts of both MEL and Python types.

Let's try a basic script to understand some of the fundamentals. First, open a new Python tab in the script editor, and let's start with your first print command. This command will log text into the history panel of your entered text. As a right of passage for all programmers, your first words should be "Hello World!". Type the function name, followed by the text in brackets, like so: **print("Hello World!")**

To execute the command, press the ▶ execute icon on the toolbar, or alternatively, press Numpad Enter. This will print your text into the history panel as shown in Figure 7.3! Well done!

```
print("Hello World!")
Hello World!
```

FIGURE 7.3 A successful first print log in Maya.

```
select -r pSphere1 ;
select -cl  ;
select -r pSphere1 ;
move -r -os -wd -1.221953 0 1.591834 ;
polyMirrorFace  -cutMesh 1 -axis 0 -axisDirection 1 -mergeMode 1 -mergeThresholdType 0 -mergeThreshold 0.001
// Result: polyMirror1 //
```

FIGURE 7.4   An example of the logs you will experience with Echo All Commands enabled.

One issue with the execution of the script is that it will be deleted from the Script Editor. To counteract this, you can first highlight the script (**Ctrl+A**), then execute it to prevent it from being deleted. With the flow being **Ctrl+A,** then **Enter** to execute and preserve your work.

7.2.1 Script Editor—Saving Scripts to Shelf

Scripts made in the Script Editor can be saved to your shelf as a button to act as a shortcut. To do this, open the relevant script tab, then click the **Save Script To Shelf** 🖫 button within the Script Editor's toolbar. This will then create a new shortcut button on your custom shelf.

7.2.2 Script Editor—Echo All Commands

A useful feature for getting a footing in scripting in Maya is the **Echo All Commands** feature. This can be enabled by **Script Editor Menu > History > Echo All Commands**. Once activated, every action, button or command that you perform while working in Maya, its activated MEL commands will be outputted into the history component of the Script Editor. An example of this output can be seen in Figure 7.4. You can then use the printed commands in your own scripts to automate your work as you go.

This feature can be a great introduction to scripting and can be used until you become familiar with the syntax and writing freehand. Keep in mind that the commands here are MEL, and they will need some basic conversion to Python if you are to use the provided commands in Python scripts!

7.3 Execute External Python Files

When developing scripts, you may opt to write in an external text editor, whether that's **Visual Studio Code** or **Notepad++,** you will need to know how to execute Python files outside of the scope of the interpreter in Maya or Unreal. Before we begin, make sure you have saved a **.py** Python file in your desired location. For demo purposes, our file will be called "**tech_anim.py**". Loading your scripts is similar to importing a module, we must do import followed by the name of your script—"**import tech_anim**". You'll notice executing this command will result in an error as your script does not exist—Python does not know where it is.

When importing modules, Python will only access directories that it knows about; these are listed under the sys.path directories, which include Python's installation location, where many modules are located. We can add our directories to the sys.path list to allow us to easily import a file from that directory.

```
import sys
folder = "C:\Users\Matthew\Desktop\Scripts\"
if folder not in sys.path:
    sys.path.append(folder)
import tech_anim
```

First, we import the sys module, followed by defining a string variable in our script folder (we use a variable as it is used twice). We then query the sys.path array to see if our folder already exists in the directories, if it does not exist in the directories list, we then append the folder to the sys list. This check is to make sure we do not keep adding the directory over and over again. Finally, with our script folder in the sys path directories, we can successfully import our script as Python knows about it.

7.4 cmds Module

Python is lightweight by nature and comes with minimal functionality out of the box, you must load modules into the scope of Python to extend functionality. The **cmds module** is one of many modules to access Maya through Python; there are many other modules such as **pymel** or **openmaya** but for the most part, the cmds module should cover the majority of tasks required in Maya. The cmds module has a variety of commands, from commands to create objects such as spheres, locators or joints to attribute creation and modification functions and even UI commands (which we will dive into in Section 7.5). In the following section, we will dive into several of the cmds commands and employ all our previously learned Python techniques to empower our workflows.

To load a module into scope, we must add additional lines at the beginning of the script, prior to any of the module's functions. To import, we must first determine the location of the module, which is Maya: "*from maya*" then "*import*" followed by the module name, which is *cmds*. The following line will import the cmds module—*from maya import cmds*

Now, to access any command from the module, we must first prefix the command's name with the module it's from. For example, the *sphere()* command must be prefixed by its module followed by a full stop. Like so – cmds.sphere(). This two-line script, when executed, will now interface with Maya to spawn a sphere!

The Maya help documentation (https://help.autodesk.com/) is very extensive for the scripting department and can be used to find any command and associated flags you require for the cmds modules.

7.4.1 MEL to cmds

Converting MEL to its Python cmds counterpart is very easy. Comparatively, how the languages are written is not too dissimilar, so converting one to the other is quite straightforward.

A MEL command would look like:

Sphere − name "george";

It's Python equivalent would be;

cmds.sphere (name = "george")

The first part of both commands is the function to call, Sphere. Where a MEL command can call a function directly, Python requires the module name first (cmds), followed by the function (sphere). This is one of the key differences: as Python is extendable by importing additional modules, the cmds module is the Maya commands—Python needs to know to call cmds's sphere function.

The second part of the command is the flags. Flags are optional parameters that can influence different behaviour from the function; in the example case, the name flag determines the name of the object that is created. There are many other optional flags on the sphere function, such as radius, pivot, axis, etc. While they both accept flags, the formatting of the command is slightly different. MEL expects a—followed by the flag name and the value for that flag. Python, on the other hand, reads a little more mathematically, with the flag=value for each flag, and all flags sur-rounded by brackets.

```
MEL = function -flag value
Python = module.function(flag=value)
```

While the majority of MEL commands exist in the cmds module, some do not. Always refer to the help documentation (https://help.autodesk.com/) to verify if the same command exists in the MEL and cmds modules. However, do not fret if you find an edge case that does not exist in cmds, as you can call native MEL commands directly in Python via the MEL module.

```
From maya import mel
mel.eval('INSERT MEL COMMAND HERE')
```

7.4.2 cmds.Ls()

The cmds.ls() command is a powerful utility that allows you to gather information about the scene; ls means list, meaning we can use it to acquire lists of nodes from the scene. The function has a ton of flags that allow you to gather almost any type of list data from your Maya scene, whether you want the selected nodes, all nodes of a specific type, such as a joint, or even all visible nodes—this command can do it all. Using the cmds.ls() command can be a great way to start your scripts, especially if you need to do a batch operation.

```
from maya import cmds
all_nodes = cmds.ls()
selected_nodes = cmds.ls(selection=True)
all_joints = cmds.ls(type='joint')
```

7.4.3 cmds.getAttr() cmds.setAttr() cmds.listAttr()

With a list of our scene nodes, how do we interact with them and gather or set information? There are several attribute-related commands, getAttr, setAttr and listAttr. getAttr will acquire the current value of a specified attribute on a specified node, setAttr will modify the value of a specified attribute on a specified node; and the listAttr function will return a list of all attributes available on a specified node. The listAttr is a good place to start when learning what types of attributes are available on a node.

```
selected = cmds.ls(selection=True, head=True)
attributes = cmds.listAttr (selected)
for attribute in attributes:
    print(attribute)
```

In the example, we acquire the first selected object via the cmds.ls() command, with the selection flag and head flag set to True. The head flag filters so that only the first selected object is returned, alternatively, we could use the tail flag for the last selected object. We then use the returned node on the listAttr command—since the listAttr returns a list, we can then iterate through each attribute with a for loop and print each one to be read in the logs. The output would appear similar to Figure 7.5.

Now that we know all the attributes of a node; let's start receiving some data. Let's use the cmds. getAttr() command to achieve this. The getAttr command has particular formatting; inside the paren-theses, the command expects the name of the node, a period, followed by the name of the attribute, for example:

```
value = cmds.getAttr('cube.translateX')
```

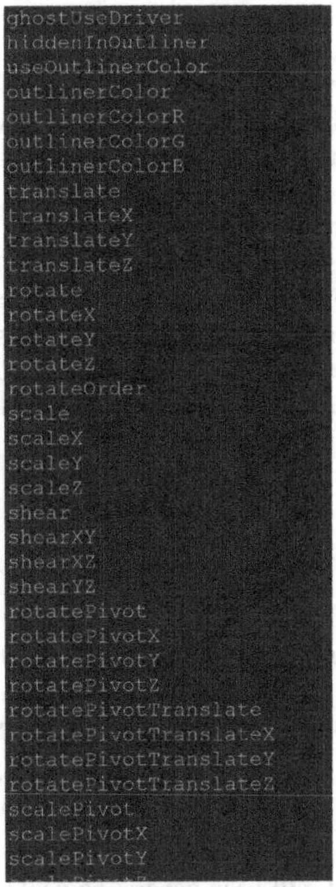

FIGURE 7.5 The print result of various attributes for the selected object.

But what if we have our node in variable format and not as a plain string, such as when iterating through a list? Well, we can use our previously learned f-strings like this:

```
selection = cmds.ls(selection=True)
for node in selection:
    value = cmds.getAttr(f'{node}.translateX')
    print(value)
```

And finally, let's use the cmds.setAttr() function to change attributes on a node! This function has the same formatting expectations as the getAttr, but has a second positional argument, the first is the node name + period + attribute name, the second is the value we want to set.

```
selection = cmds.ls(selection=True)
for node in selection:
    cmds.setAttr(f'{node}.translateX', 10)
```

This command will iterate through each selected node and set their translateX attribute to a value of 10. These simple commands of get, set and the list can be used to read and write to any node in Maya.

7.5 Building Maya User Interface

The cmds module empowers us with the capabilities to create our own user interface for Maya; whether that's a floating window or a docked tab, we can populate these interfaces with buttons, radio buttons, sliders, image buttons, text entry boxes and more! Each of these UI elements can have logic and functionality connected to them too.

The basic premise of the user interfaces in Maya is that there is a structure of nested containers that defines the layout of the interface. Think of it like a table of rows and columns, with each cell also having the ability to contain another table. UI elements such as buttons then reside within each cell of the layout.

At the top of the interface structure, we have the **window**; this is the container where the entire UI will reside. This window can be a floating window similar to the Script Editor, or it can be docked in the interface like the channel box. From inside the window, we can create **layouts**, which define the structure of the container, with different layouts having different structures such as a frame, row, column, tabs or even a scroll layout. There are many different types of layouts that each bring something different to the table. Finally, we have the **UI controls**, which are visual elements such as buttons, text or text fields that the user will interact with. The wonderful part of this structure is that it is all adaptive, so if you change the size of a layout, the other layouts will react and move along to keep everything neatly aligned.

7.5.1 Window Generation

Creating and generating our window requires two functions: first, the **cmds.window()** function, which creates the window ready for us to add controls to it; then, to show the interface, we must use the **cmds.showWindow()** function and provide it with our window's identifier.

```
window = cmds.window()
cmds.showWindow (window)
```

If we keep executing this script, it will keep generating new windows after new windows, which we don't want! So let's add some additional functionality to stop this. First, let's revise this code to provide our own unique identifier for the window instead of receiving and using the automatically returned value. We can predefine an identifier like this:

```
window_ID = 'window_tutorial'
cmds.window (window_ID)
cmds.showWindow (window_ID)
```

This script has identical behaviour as before, but now that we have a unique identifier, we can add additional functionality based on the unique ID. Next, let's utilise the **cmds.window()** function with a **query=True** flag to query if our unique ID exists already or not; this will return a True/False value. If it does exist, we can destroy the existing UI with the **cmds.deleteUI()** function and then generate the latest version of our UI.

```
window_ID = 'window_tutorial'
if cmds.window (window_ID, exists=True) :
    cmds.deleteUI (window_ID)
cmds.window (window_ID)
cmds.showWindow (window_ID)
```

7.5.2 Window Customisation

Now that we have our window, there are a variety of flags available on the cmds.window() command for us. Start with the **title** flag; this requires a string and customises the window's title bar label. The **width** and **height** flags are independent values that require an integer value; these will change the dimensions of the window. Alternatively, you can use the **widthHeight** flag, which requires a two-length tuple. The **sizeable** flag requires a Boolean value and determines if the user can change the size of the window.

We are also able to allow for our interface to be docked into the Maya interface with the **cmds. dockControl**() function. Provide the window's unique identifier to the **content** flag inside of cmds. dockControl() to allow docking in any direction. There is an additional **allowedArea** flag that requires a list of areas that you can dock to. This can be customised if you only want the user to dock to the left, right, top, bottom or a mixture of any of these.

```
cmds.dockControl (content=window_ID, allowedArea=['left'])
```

7.5.3 Parental Structure

When it comes to the content of the window, every piece of content needs to live on the lines between the commands for **cmds.window**() and the **cmds.showWindow**() command. This is so the content is created and parented to the window and exists before the window is shown. When we add new layouts and controls, they are automatically children of the last container, so our first layout is automatically a parent of the window. If we then create a rowColumnLayout followed by a button, the button will be parented in the first cell, the second button will be in the second cell and so on.

```
cmds.window(window_ID)
cmds.rowColumnLayout()
cmds.button()
cmds.button()
cmds.showWindow(window_ID)
```

If we desire to have a non-linear structure in your code, we can choose the specific parent of each UI element via the parent flag. In the same way that we built a unique identifier for the window, we can create a unique identifier for the layouts.

```
cmds.window(window_ID)
cmds.rowColumnLayout('rowColumnLayout_ID')
cmds.rowColumnLayout()
cmds.button(parent='rowColumnLayout_ID')
cmds.button(parent='rowColumnLayout_ID')
cmds.showWindow(window_ID)
```

The two buttons will be parented to the first rowColumnLayout, not the second.

7.5.4 The Layouts

The layouts are the blueprints for how the UI should look, some layouts have a table-like structure, such as the **cmds.rowColumnLayout**(), **cmds.rowLayout**() or **cmds.columnLayout**(). Other layouts are blank canvases like **cmds.frameLayout**(), and other layouts have special functionality such as a **cmds.scrollLayout**() which can scroll, and the **cmds.tabLayout**() creates tabbed interfaces, and the **cmds.menuBarLayout**() adds a menu bar.

Let's get acquainted with the table-like layouts, as they will fulfil the majority of UI tasks.

7.5.4.1 cmds.rowColumnLayout()

The **cmds.rowColumnLayout**() operates in either row or column mode; you specify one type, and then the other is an indefinite amount. If I required two rows, the column count would scale depending on the amount of content. Flag-wise, both types of row and column work based on a row or column count value, **numberOfRows** for rows, and **numberOfColumns** for columns - both of which receive integer values. Then there is an optional flag to determine the dimensions of the row/column: **rowHeight** and **columnWidth**. These values take a list of two-length tuples; the tuples contain the index of the row/column and then a dimension in pixels. For example, **rowHeight=[(1, 25), (2, 50), (3, 25)].** This would have the first row as 25 pixels, the second row as 50, and the third row as 25.

7.5.5 The Controls

The final piece of the puzzle is the controls the user will interface with. There are dozens of controls, some with multiple variants that provide additional functionality. Some of the commonly used controls are:

- **cmds.button()** - This control is a basic button.
- **cmds.checkBox()** - This control is an on/off tick box.
- **cmds.textField()** - This control is a field where the user can enter text.
- **cmds.floatSlider()** - This control creates a slider between numbers.
- **cmds.radioCollection()** - This control allows for multiple-choice selection.
- **cmds.radioButton(label='Option 01')** - must be used to add new entries.

7.5.5.1 Trigger Functions

With our controls filling our layouts, we can begin to add functionality triggers to the interface. Many of the UI elements have a flag called **command**, which is triggered when the UI is interacted with, not all feature this command, however, some, such as the cmds.radioButtonGrp() have a **changeCommand** flag that has similar behaviour—be sure to validate which function has which flag with the documentation.

The command flag takes a function name that you desire to trigger when the interface is pressed, alternatively, you can put a command directly in there.

```
cmds.button(label='print', command=print("hello!"))
cmds.button(label='function', command=my_function())
```

7.5.5.2 Lambda Functions

While that method will work for basic function calls, there is a big issue with commands calling functions that have any data passed through. When the UI is generated, it maintains whatever the values were at that point for its entire lifetime. So if you are passing dynamic values into the functions, they will always be the value they were when the UI was created, not when the UI is interacted with.

This can cause some problems, let's demonstrate.

```
def print_nodes(nodes):
    for node in nodes:
        print(node)
cmds.button(label='print', command=print_nodes(cmds.ls(selected=True) ) )
```

In this demonstration, we have a basic function that loops through a provided list and prints each entry in the list. There is a button that runs the function and provides the current selection to the function.

The problem with this setup is that the function will always print what the selection was when the button was generated, not when it was pressed. To get around this issue, we can introduce our new friend, **Lambdas**. We can utilise Lambdas in our function calls so that the data we send will be dynamically provided when called, rather than utilising the generation state. To use a lambda, we can suffix our command value with lambda x, like this:

```
command=lambda x:print_nodes (cmds.ls(selected=True))
```

7.5.5.3 Lambda X

You may be wondering what the x in the lambda x: syntax is for. This x is an argument for the lambda, similar to a function setup *(lambda arguments: expression)*. Often, UI functions can pass through additional telemetry, and we can use this X argument to hold the information. If the X is not used on the opposite side of the colon, then it is ignored, but often with Maya's interface commands, there are lots of extra goodies that can get passed through functions that we can benefit from.

```
def print_value(value):
print(value)
cmds.intSlider (changeCommand=lambda x:print_value(x))
```

With UI elements such as the intSlider, the function passes through the current value of the slider, removing the need to query the UI directly for the value.

7.5.5.4 Query Interface

When building a complex UI, we will inevitably need to query the state of the UI, whether that's the state of a checkbox, a text field's entry, or a radio button state. We will need to know the exact value to use in our scripts, but how do we do this?

Within every UI command, there is a flag called **query**. When set to True this changes the use case of all other flags provided, the same ones you use to set values are now changed to a True or False require-ment, and if set to True, they will return the value instead of setting it. For example, if we use query=True with label=True on a cmds.button(), it will return the string value of the label. Here are some examples:

```
checkbox_value = cmds.checkBox('checkBox_ID', query=True, value=True)
button_label = cmds.button('button_ID', query=True, label=True)
textField_text = cmds.textField('textField_ID', query=True, text=True)
intSlider_value = cmds.intSlider('intSlider_ID', query=True, value=True)
```

7.5.6 User Experience (UX)

"A user interface is like a joke. If you have to explain it, it's not that good,"

- Martin Leblanc

As Martin implies, if you need extensive documentation and handholding to explain to someone how to operate your user interface, it's just not that good. This could mean it is unintuitive, overloaded or unreadable. When creating a tool that's not for you, you should be considerate about building its interface for people who may not be as technically minded as you. Here are a few tips to enhance your UX with your own interfaces!

7.5.6.1 Collapsible Frames

The frame layout UI can be set to be collapsible and expandable, which will toggle the visibility of all the controls inside that layout. This, in turn, can be an excellent approach to adding focus to your interface, allowing the user to dynamically collapse and expand only the relevant section they are utilising rather than overloading the screen with all tools at all times, keeping the UI nice and clean.

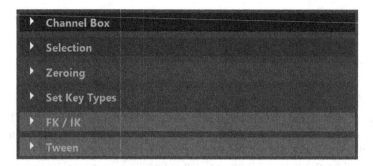

FIGURE 7.6   Collapseable frame layouts for Maya.

Adding the **collapsable** flag to our cmds.frameLayout() function will create a tab at the top of the frame layout, shown in Figure 7.6. We can then use the **label** flag to add a descriptor title to the frame layout.

```
cmds.frameLayout(label='frame title', collapsable=True, collapse=True)
```

Placing our UI elements into collapsible frame layout's is a great way to organise our interface!

7.5.6.2 Colours

While this may seem superficial, having colour-coordinated tools can go a long way towards training the brain to associate a specific colour with specific behaviour. Every UI element has the keyword **backgroundColor** that we can use to add colours to our frames, buttons, sliders, etc. I would recommend collectively colouring sets of similar tools with the same colour to train the user to correlate that colour with that type of tool. For example, all your IK and FK tools would be a singular colour, and every tool for keying would be another colour. This bundling of colours adds coherency and aids in training the brain, rather than the colours being random. This is demonstrated with buttons in Figure 7.7.

The backgroundColor flag requires a three-length tuple, with each value being a number in 0–1 space representing RGB. If you are more familiar with working with RGB in 0–255 space, you can take your 255 relative number, and divide it by 255 to get a 0–1 value. When picking colours for your interface, try not to choose garish 255 colours; try to pick a slightly muted colour, such as a pastel colour. Make sure it's not too dark or too light—it should be just right!

```
cmds.button (backgroundColor=(0.5, 0.5, 0.5))
```

7.5.6.3 Images and Iconography

Including icons and images in our user interface has the same benefits for our brain as associating a symbol with functionality. Even though the floppy disk has gone the way of the dinosaurs, the symbol is still our de facto icon for saving data; even our tape recorders are the icon for voicemail. Our brains are wired to create these correlations between the symbol and intended behaviour. We can employ this in our own interfaces to easily identify a specific icon in what would otherwise be a wall of text, the use of button icons is demonstrated in Figure 7.8.

FIGURE 7.7   Coloured buttons for Maya.

FIGURE 7.8 Images included in buttons for Maya.

An alternative to the cmds.button() function, we can use the **cmds.iconTextButton()** - this variant comes with all the standard button functionality but with the ability to include an image within the button. There are two important flags to set for the iconTextButton: **style** and **image1**. The style flag determines the format of the button and whether or not it should have an image and/or text. The following value must be set as a string - **iconOnly**, **textOnly**, **iconAndTextHorizontal**, **iconAndTextVertical** or **IconAndTextCentered**. The second flag is **image1,** which requires a path to the image file.

```
cmds.iconTextButton(style='iconAndTextHorizontal', image1='sphere.xpm',
label='sphere')
```

7.5.6.4 Acquiring Maya Icons

If you want to use pre-installed Maya icons in your tools, you can use the **Factory Icon Browser** tool to access every available Maya icon's name, and file type.

To access the **Factory Icon Browser**

1. **Right-Click** on any shelf script and select **Edit.** This will open the Shelf Editor (Figure 7.9).

FIGURE 7.9 The right-click menu on a shelf script.

2. In the **Shelf Editor** window, press the **Maya M** icon at the end of the **Icon Name** row (Figure 7.10).

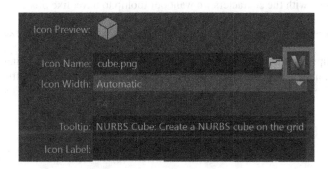

FIGURE 7.10 The Shelf Editor window exert.

3. The Factory Icon Browser Interface will open (Figure 7.11).

FIGURE 7.11 The Factory Icon Browser for exploring Maya icons.

4. Find your desired icon, then copy its name and extension into your script!

7.5.6.5 UI Tooltips

Often you may find yourself wanting to include additional information about a UI element but not wanting to clutter the interface with more text or rely on an external resource for the user to understand. This is where tooltips come in; each UI element within Maya has an **annotation** flag that can be added at creation. The annotation flag accepts a string value, which will appear to the user if they hover their mouse over the element. This is shown in Figure 7.12. We can use annotations as an opportunity to explain certain further details about the tools or even give a more thorough description of the button they are pressing.

By using the annotation keyword within the parenthesis of our UI element, such as a button, we can provide a string value with the characters we want our tooltip to have, like this:

```
cmds.button(label='press me', annotation='this is a tooltip example!')
```

By adding tooltips to our interface, we can keep our UI labels simplified, and only if the user requires additional information then our tooltip annotations can do the heavier lifting.

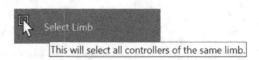

FIGURE 7.12 Tooltip example.

7.6 MEL Script Replacement

One of the neat aspects of Maya's deep MEL integration is that since most actions performed in Maya call a MEL script, we can find and modify the scripts directly to tailor our experience. Perhaps a popup dialogue is not to your liking, or perhaps you want to change or add functionality without having to deeply modify the software. We can jump into the MEL scripts to modify.

The MEL scripts live in the install directory of Maya, typically at the following location:

C:\Program Files\Autodesk\MayaXXXX\scripts

(switch *XXXX for the Maya version year*).

You can choose to modify the scripts in this folder directly, or a better option would be to have a duplicate of the script and import the duplicate; when the script is used, Maya will use the latest imported version, so the programme's default scripts will not be called and your edited version will be instead. I would recommend this pathway to distribute Maya modifications to other users too, this would prevent the user from being required to modify their software files.

The MEL command to import a file is source "C:/StringToFilePath"; This command can be called through Python via the mel.eval() command in the **mel module** if you would prefer to maintain Python usage.

```
from maya import mel
mel.eval('source "C:/StringToFilePath";')
```

8

Maya—Building a Skeleton

Once you have your character art ready and have fully audited it to ensure that it is up to scratch, you must begin the perilous task of bringing that character to life. That task begins in your DCC.

8.1 Rig Considerations

8.1.1 What Is Your Project?

Since the computational cost of your characters needs to be taken into account at all times, identifying the end goal of your project determines how we need to build our rigs. If the project requires a lot of characters to be on screen at once or for mobile platforms, then we must be very reserved with our polygon counts, joint counts and less intensive runtime calculations. If required, consider disregarding the finger joints, as this can be a fast way to remove 30 joints from the total joint count. If you are expected to have fewer characters on screen at any given time, you can be much more generous with your characters expenses. If you're using Unreal for offline rendering, don't be concerned about too many constraints—the world is your oyster when it comes to prerendering.

8.1.2 Identify Your Target Hardware

Knowing your hardware target will determine many of your limitations. When targeting mobile platforms, there are hard limitations due to strict resource allocations. For example, in Unreal, skeleton meshes are limited to having a 65k vertex count mesh, a 75 joint count and a limit of four influences per vertex in skinning. Whereas you are not bound by such limited constraints on next-generation hardware.

8.1.3 Software Choice

As we have picked Maya for our DCC and Unreal for our editor, we already know there are coordinate space differences between the two, with Maya being a right-handed Y-up and Unreal being a left-handed Z-up system. These differences are what we need to take into account when building our rig. Otherwise, we can introduce offsets between systems. An occurrence of this offset occurs even within Unreal's example rig, The Mannequin, which has a 90-degree rotation offset, resulting in any orientation calculation done within Unreal being 90 degrees offset from zero. We will cover how to account for this shortly.

8.1.4 Identify Your Style

This stems from the art and animation direction, but what are the needs and styles of the characters? Are they hyper-realistic characters requiring you to mimic real life in how your rig deforms,

DOI: 10.1201/9781003263258-8

with appropriate muscle and mass conservation, or are they stylised, larger-than-life characters with stretchy limbs?

8.1.5 What Does the Character Need?

Are they required to hold a prop, such as a weapon? Will they always be holding that weapon? If so, we need to rig the character and prop together. If there will be swappable props, we need to plan for that by rigging the character and prop separately.

8.1.6 Endeavour to Make Flexible, Catch-All Systems

Think of anything you may need in the future and avoid as much headache as possible, but do not worry—you won't always get it right the first time. A lot of this preparation comes from experience and doing multitudes of different characters, processes and projects.

8.2 Our Rig Project

For the purposes of this walkthrough, we will be rigging and animating a bipedal humanoid with the standard four limbs: two arms and two legs. While this will not be an exhaustive process for each type of character you can rig, a human is about as middle of the ground as you can get and is a very common character type to rig, with processes that will be learned that apply laterally across all of the rigging.

8.3 Joints/Bones

Joints/bones are the foundations of animated characters or objects; each joint is hierarchically linked to one another to determine a chain of articulation points. Joints and bones are the terms that are commonly used interchangeably, but there is one crucial difference between the two: a joint refers to a singular position with direction in 3D space, whereas a bone has length due to a start and an end position. Some packages use joints with bones as a by-product when additional children joints, while some packages have a bone length determined upon generation. The differences are demonstrated in Figure 8.1.

The joints of your skeleton are the location in which animation data is stored to be transferred from your DCC to the engine—due to this, it is imperative that all joints are immaculate and set up correctly before any animation is completed on them. If the angles on any joints are not appropriately set, you can have unnecessary data brought into the engine that can bloat your file sizes. For example, an elbow or knee joint should only bend in a singular axis; if your joint is incorrectly set up and it requires bending through three-axis to bend the character's elbow, then the angle is setup wrong and you are exporting three times as many curves.

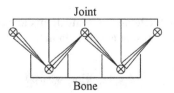

FIGURE 8.1 Diagram of what constitutes a joint versus a bone in 3D.

FIGURE 8.2   The fourth button in the display window will add a selection to a layer.

Endeavour to build the entire skeleton clean and strong the first time for your characters—everything is built upon the joints. Changing your skeleton mid-production is a risky endeavour and can cause a variety of issues that will take time to fix, including the retargeting of all pre-existing animation data to the new skeleton rig and proportions.

8.3.1 Scene Preparation

To begin rigging, we must bring our character art into the scene to work with. We can begin this process by either opening the file containing the character. To open - **Maya Menu > File > Open > Select Character File > Open**.

Once imported, let's prepare and organise our scene a little before rigging.

1. Create a group that contains all geometry.
   a. **Shift + Select** all geometry, then press **Ctrl+G** to create a group containing the selection.
   b. Rename the group a descriptor such as "geometry" or "geo."
2. Create a display Set that contains the geometry (Figure 8.2).
   a. **Select the geometry group**, then in the display tab of the channel box/layer window > select the last icon.
   b. Rename the display layer with a descriptive name.
3. Set the geometry display layer into reference mode, so it can no longer be selected.
   a. In the display window, press the third box on the geometry layer twice till it states "R" (Figure 8.3).

8.3.2 Joint Creation

Let's begin in Maya by enabling the **Rigging** menu set (**F3**). This will expose a variety of rigging-based tools. We will begin by building the very foundation of our characters, the skeleton. To build our skeleton, the tools we require are in the **Skeleton** sub-menu.

The first joint we are required to make for our skeleton is the **root** joint. This is the highest joint in the hierarchy, and all subsequent joints are children of it. We must keep our root joint at the top of the hierarchy and have nothing else be its parent. The root joint's function is to act as a reference point for the skeleton and will be very important when we move the character into the engine. The root should be located at world 0,0,0.

1. To create a joint, enable the **Skeleton > Create Joints** tool and mouse's left click into the viewport. This will create a new joint labelled "**joint1**."

FIGURE 8.3   The display layer settings.

2. To rename our joint, double-click the joint's name in either the **outliner** or the **channel box** and enter a new name. For this first joint, name it **"root."**
3. **Zero the translation** and **rotation channels** of the joint in the **Channel Box,** to ensure it's at world 0,0,0. Ensure the scale is set to 1 in XYZ—this means 100% scale.

8.3.3 Coordinate System Compensation

To account for the 3D coordinate system differences between Maya and Unreal, we are required to place an offset somewhere in the pipeline. This offset **must** exist somewhere in the pipeline to account for the coordinate space difference. If we do not, and we transfer a completely zeroed root into Unreal, the root joint would have a +90 degree offset in Rotate X and never be perfectly zero. We could keep the offset in Unreal, but then this offset will need to be accounted for throughout any skeleton orientation-based calculations at runtime. I recommend placing the offset into the Maya root at the beginning of the pipeline, as it is the least intrusive, so runtime calculations do not get unnecessarily complicated.

To compensate, we must put a **-90** degree rotation into **Rotate X** (or **Joint Orient X**). Later, when we move to Unreal, our root joint will be neatly zeroed.

8.3.4 Joint Visualisation

Joints can be difficult to visualise in the scene. You are able to increase the visual size of the joint by increasing its **Radius** attribute in the **Channel Box** to change the size on a per-joint basis. The Radius is a cosmetic attribute and does not scale the joint. Alternatively, you can increase the size of all joints globally by changing **Display > Animation > Joint Size**; the result of this change can be seen in Figure 8.4.

Do **NOT** increase the scale of the joint to make the joint visually look bigger.

The orientation of a joint can be difficult to determine at first glance because, unlike bones, which feature a clear start, direction and end, joints are simply points in space. Without viewing a joint's local axis **(Tool Settings > Axis Orientation: Object),** it can be hard to figure out its orientation. To aid in orientation visualisation, we can add children's joints with a translation offset in a single axis to make a bone visually appear—now we can clearly view the direction the joint is facing if we rotate the joint. We can merely add extra joints to our hierarchy to help with orientation visualisation (Figure 8.5). We do not have to keep these end joints long-term as they are merely for visualisation; label the joints accordingly so we know to remove them later, perhaps with a suffix such as "_end."

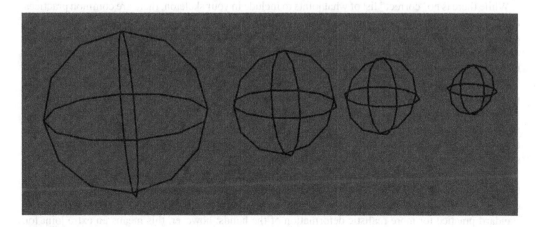

FIGURE 8.4 Using the radius attribute or joint size value will change the visual scale of the joint.

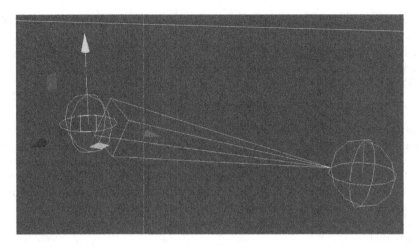

FIGURE 8.5   An example of using a child joint to visualise the orientation of a parent joint.

8.3.5 Skeleton Building

With our root joint in place, we must create the skeleton for the character. The joints we now make are the joints that will influence the mesh through skinning, so it's imperative that we build a strong foundation, as incorrectly placed joints can cause poor deformations.

Our aim here is to create a joint for each major component of our body and consider each joint to be responsible for each major moveable mass of the body. We should aim to mimic a real-world counterpart, but we do not want to build joints 1:1 with a real skeleton's bones or include every single bone; not only would this be incredibly computationally expensive, but you may also be shocked to find out that joints with skinning will not provide deformation results like it's the real-world counterparts.

Consider the animator when adding joints and how much control you want to give them, but then also consider the unnecessary control they do not require - you do not require to provide 24–33 bones into a spine to match a real human—between 3 and 5 will provide ample deformation and control. If you are on a tight joint count budget, you may opt to provide only one or two spine joints. There are a variety of optional joints you could endeavour to include, such as fingers, metacarpal joints or even toes—if your character has shoes, don't bother with toe bones!

While there is no "correct" list of what joints to include in your skeleton, there are common practices and assumptions that are made for a human. The 3DS Max's Biped, HumanIK, Unreal's Mannequin and Manny and Quinn, all share nearly identical structures, so research what standards are available, and if you plan to use any asset packs, I recommend using Unreal's standard as a starting point. The hierarchy shown in Figure 8.6 is a fairly typical starting point for a human.

The first major component after the root is the centre of gravity of the character—the pelvis. The pelvis then branches the hierarchy into the spine, left leg and right leg. Each leg has a thigh joint, a knee joint, an ankle joint, a ball joint and a toe tip/foot end joint. The spine follows up for an indeterminate number of joints, and where it reaches the final spine joint, we branch into the left and right arms and the neck. From the neck, we simply have a head joint, while each arm has a clavicle joint, a shoulder joint, an elbow joint and then a wrist joint.

A common difference for a standard human is how the hands are dealt with. For simpler characters, we can opt for a wrist joint which has child joints for each individual finger, with the wrist joint controlling the mass of the palm. However, the use of metacarpal joints for the fingers is becoming standard practice for more realistic deformation of the hands; however, this means an extra joint for each finger. Alternatively, we could opt for a third solution that is halfway between the two, where we

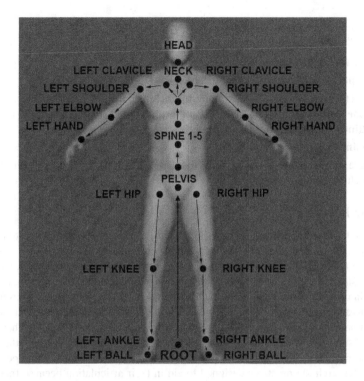

FIGURE 8.6 A hierarchy example for a human skeleton.

have an extra cup joint that the pinky and ring fingers are a child of—this cup joint could be rotated to mimic the benefits of a full metacarpal method. These variants and their weight distribution is demonstrated in Figure 8.7.

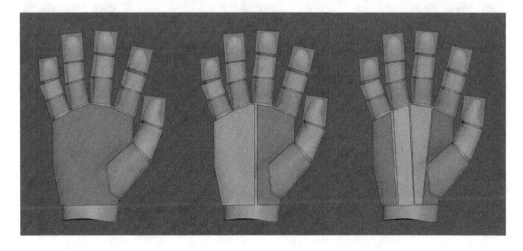

FIGURE 8.7 Three approaches to joint distribution and weights on the palm of a hand.

To add further joints to your skeleton, we can either duplicate an existing bone or utilise the insert joint tool to add new joints.

- **Duplicate the existing joint**.
  - To duplicate, select a joint, then select **Edit > Duplicate (Ctrl+D)**.
  - Parent the new joint into the hierarchy, by clicking the child joint, then press **Ctrl + Left Mouse Button** to select the parent joint, then pressing **Edit > Parent (P)** or within the **Outliner**, **Middle Mouse Drag** the child joint onto the parent joint.
- **Insert Joint Tool.**
  - Enable the **Skeleton > Insert Joint** tool, then drag from your parent joint to create a new child joint.

8.3.6 Placing Joints

Always refer to reference, as reference is always king! Skeletal anatomy should be a go-to for aiding with joint placement. Examine and study how bodies and mass are built and how they move. Look at rule sets for the body, like the fact that the forearm is five-sixths of the length of the upper arm, so when folding arms, the hands shouldn't fall short of aligning with the upper arm position. Use these learnings not only to apply joints in more appropriate positions but also to understand the direction of mass movement and orient your joints appropriately. Utilise your own body for reference; observe your movements in a mirror to see how your body moves and how each interconnected piece interacts with one another. Do not make the mistake of assuming how the body works when you have the world's best teacher attached to you.

Beyond anatomy studies, look to fields such as merchandising (action figures and poseable toys) or even robotics. Research the practices designed to aid in their articulation because that's all rigging is—building an action figure in 3D! There are many different types of joints featured in action figures, from ball joints, hinge joints and butterfly joints to double-jointed knees all of which provide different movements. These joints and behaviours can be applied to our rigging.

When placing your joints, ensure their positions are true to the character's skin by using their base mesh instead of their clothing for alignment. If you are placing joints within a character that has thick clothing, or armour, the best method for joint placement would be to rig their base mesh (*a naked skin-only version*). Placing your character's joints inside the base mesh allows you to more accurately see where the correct pivot points for each joint should be, rather than having to decipher where they

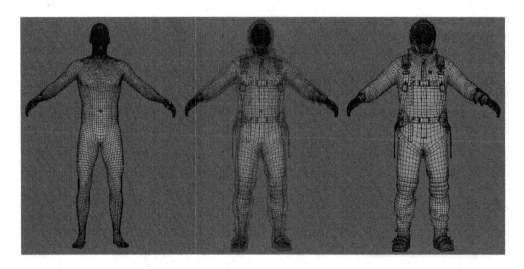

FIGURE 8.8 An example base mesh character and its outfit from Fort Solis.

would be within a mass of clothing. Figure 8.8 demonstrates this well, with a base body character that can be used for joint position reference instead of a space suit.

If you are creating a game that requires your character to have multiple outfits, this method is a must. This is so you can easily swap out the clothing layer, but the true skeleton remains consistent with the character under the clothing. If you created a skeleton based on the best deformations for that clothing set, the deformation may not look great for other outfits.

8.3.7 Joint Alignment

If you are struggling to find the centre point within a volume, a technique you could employ is to use a sphere and fill the volume where you are trying to place the joint as demonstrated in Figure 8.9; we can then snap our new joint to this sphere's position to get an excellent centre of volume.

1. Create a sphere by navigating to **Create > Polygon Primitives > Sphere**.
2. Utilise the **Move Tool (W)** to correctly position the sphere in the middle of the mass.
3. First, select your sphere, then select your target joint and apply a point constraint with maintain offset set to false (**Constrain > Point**). This will move your joint into position.
4. Cleanup! Delete your parent constraint and your sphere from the Outliner.

Alternatively, we could align multiple locators at vertices and then constrain an additional locator between the aligned locators to find an averaged location (Figure 8.10) This method is especially useful for hard-surface rigging to find perfect centre locations for areas such as pistons and hinges.

1. Create two locators (**Create > Locator**).
2. Use the **Snap to Points** 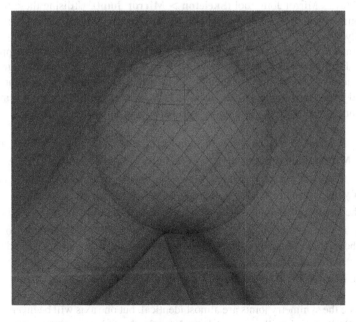 (**Hold V**) tool to align the locators with vertices on each side of the mesh.
3. Select the first two locators, then the target joint last.
4. Apply a point constraint (**Constrain > Point**).
5. Cleanup—Delete the parent constraint and two locators.

FIGURE 8.9   Utilisation of a sphere to find the centre of a volume.

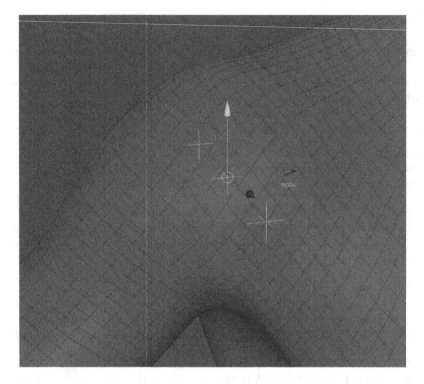

FIGURE 8.10   Use two locators snapped to vertices then acquire the half-way point for the centre.

8.3.8 Joint Mirroring/Symmetry

Any component that requires a mirrored counterpart, such as an arm or leg, can be automatically mirrored through Maya's Mirror Joint tool (**Skeleton > Mirror Joint**). Utilising these tools will allow you to focus your attention on only creating half of your character, saving valuable time from having to do it manually.

   To make the most of the mirroring tools, ensure your joints are orderly with an appropriate naming convention. Just like your file names, conventions should exist throughout all your work. Adding suffixes to your joints is an easy way to label the side of your joint, such as _R for right-sided joints or _L for left-sided joints; an example of this is shown in Figure 8.11. When applying symmetry to your joints, the mirror tool can be set to automatically rename your joints.

1. Select the first joint in the chain you wish to mirror, such as clavicle_r or thigh_r.
2. Open the **Mirror Joint Options** dialogue (**Skeleton > Mirror Joint > ▢**). See Figure 8.12.
3. Pick the appropriate mirror axis. This determines the 2D plane your joints will be mirrored across. If your character is facing positive Z, then select YZ.
4. Ensure the **Behavior** option is selected under **Mirror Function**.
5. Optional: If you have prefixed or suffixed joints, you can provide the label to search and replace the name for the opposite side. In this case, we are searching for _r and replacing it with _l.
6. Select the **Mirror**, and your joints will be mirrored!

   You may notice the symmetry joints are almost identical, but one axis will be inverted—if the joint is aimed down **Positive X**, it will now aim down **Negative X**. This symmetry ensures that when the

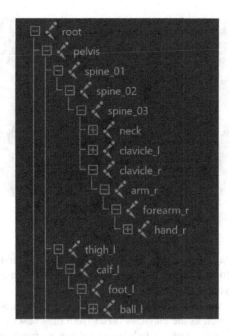

FIGURE 8.11 Suffix examples on a skeleton.

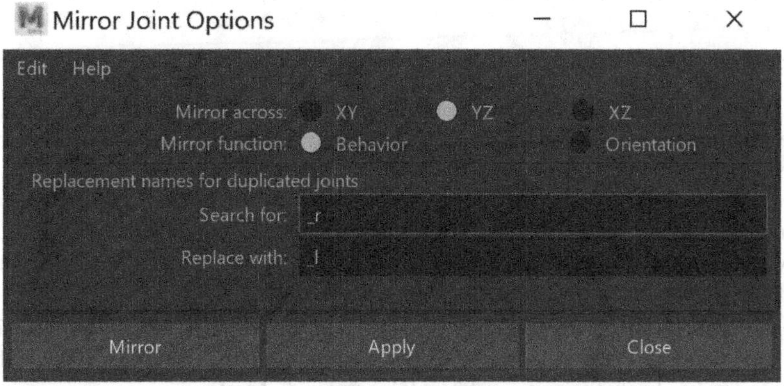

FIGURE 8.12 The dialogue interface for mirroring joints in Maya.

same axis is rotated between a joint and its mirrored counterpart, they will rotate in the same direction. So a rotation in a positive Y on the left and right arms would raise both. If both joints had the same aiming direction and a positive Y rotation was applied, one arm would raise and the other would lower.

8.3.9 Chain Joint Direction

When creating child joints in a chain, there is the potential for them to not have the correct direction. As demonstrated in Figure 8.13, the top chain of joints may appear fine on the surface, but if we view the translations of the second joint, it has translation in two channels. This is because the parent joint is not pointing at its child joint—causing the child joint to be offset from the direction the parent joint is facing.

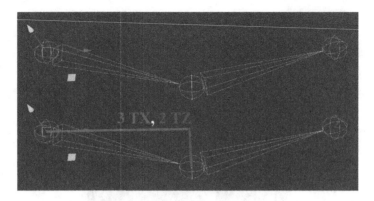

FIGURE 8.13   Joint direction issues with parent joints not aiming at their child.

An object's rotation axis can be displayed on a per-object basis by first **selecting the object**, and then go to **Display > Transform Display > Local Rotation Axis**. A small gizmo will appear at the location of the object, displaying its XYZ rotation.

Preventing multiple axes of translation isn't a one-shoe-fits-all solution, as certain joints will require multiple axes of translation, such as the clavicles offset from the chest or the thighs from the pelvis. It is not ideal to have unnecessary data, so let's try to remove as much of this as possible from the rig—we do not need unnecessary transforms!

There are two approaches to cleaning this data.

8.3.9.1 Manual "Aim" Process

The manual process for cleaning this data would be to utilise an aim constraint to point a joint at its intended destination, with an up vector object to determine its up axis. Once a joint is aimed in the correct direction, its child will only have a single axis of translation.

1. Before applying the constraint, you are required to dismantle your hierarchy because you cannot aim a parent joint at its child as it will cause an infinite cycle error. To unparent, **select the child joint**, press **Ctrl+P** or **Edit > Unparent**.

2. Let's create the aim constraint. **Select** the child joint **first**, then select the parent joint **second.** This selection order will tell the aim constraint which is the target and which is the object to aim at. Apply the aim constraint (**Constrain > Aim**).

3. By default, an aim constraint will utilise X+ as the aim direction, and the world's Y+ as the up vector direction. You can customise these settings via the Aim options dialogue (**Constrain > Aim > ▢**) before creation, or alternatively, after the constraint has been created, the settings can be modified in the **Attribute Editor**. **Select the aim constraint** node in the **Outliner**, open the **Attribute Editor** and navigate to the **Aim Vector, Up Vector** and **World Up Vector** options.

4. **OPTIONAL** If you desire further control over the up vector direction, and require an angle that does not correlate to the world's positive or negative X, Y or Z—then you can utilise an Up Vector object. To do this—Create a Locator (**Create > Locator),** then assign it to the aim constraint by **selecting** the **aim constraint** node in the **Outliner**, open the **Attribute Editor** and navigate to the **World Up Type** setting and change it to **Object Up,** then assign the locator into the **World Up Object** slot by **typing in the locator's name** or **middle mouse dragging** from the locator in the **Outliner** to the slot. Moving the locator will now change the up direction of the object.

5. Once you are happy with the orientation, **delete the constraint and locator**.

6. **Rebuild** the hierarchy by placing the child joint back under the parent joint.

7. It's clean! The child joint will now only have a single axis of translation!

8.3.9.2 Orient Joint Tool

Alternatively, Maya offers an Orient Joint tool (**Skeleton > Orient Joint**) that, when applied to a joint, will orient itself in the direction of its first child, but maintain the world positions of all descendent joints. To change the order of children, simply click **Middle Mouse Drag** the object in the **Outliner** to rearrange them in the order you desire.

By default, the Orient Joint tool will set the joint's X+ as your aim direction and Y+ as your up vector—using the world's Y-axis. While this may suffice for joints on a single plane, you may want to control the angle further. You can do this by navigating to **Skeleton > Orient Joint > □**. This dialogue will allow you to customise which axis you want for the aim and the up. Do note that the up vector angles snap to positive or negative X, Y and Z, and you do not get the minutiae of control over that direction as you would using an aim constraint with an up vector object.

When using Orient Joint, you may notice some discrepancies that may appear as errors on the surface. For example, as shown in the Figure 8.14, the selected child joint appears to have a rotation compared to its parent. The parent joint itself is facing in the direction of the child, but the local axes displayed on the gizmo are not facing the same orientation. So why does each rotation for the child joint in the channel box all equal 0? What is going on? Is this a bug? No—this is because the **Orient Joint** tool uses a system called **Joint Orientation**.

8.3.10 Joint Orientation

The Joint Orient attribute is akin to a second layer of rotations on top of the regular rotate XYZ attributes. Users who are not aware of this system can create messy skeletons with stacked rotations in both systems, as the true rotation of a joint is the combination of both of these values. A lack of awareness of joint orients can cause issues with your IK chains or even bring unnecessary animation data into the game, such as rotation through multiple axes to achieve a target rotation rather than just

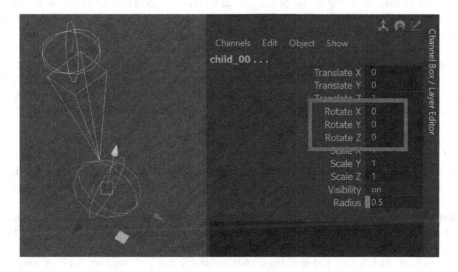

FIGURE 8.14 The joint has rotation, but the rotation channels are zero.

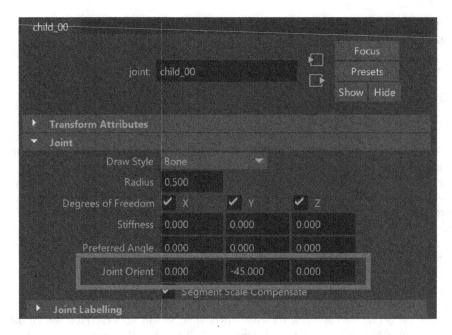

FIGURE 8.15 The joint orient attributes can be found in the Attribute Editor.

one. A joint's Joint Orient value can be viewed by going to **Attribute Editor > Joint > Joint Orient,** highlighted in Figure 8.15.

Certain processes within Maya put the rotation values of a joint directly on the Joint Orient rather than the normal rotation values—even the act of re-parenting joints will store the rotation there. These hidden values can cause havoc if you are not aware of them. One benefit of this system is that the channel box's rotations can be neatly zeroed while maintaining the skeleton's desired rotational pose. You can transfer rotations from your rotation XYZ to your joint orient XYZ by freezing the joint rotations (**Modify > Freeze Transformations**). The obvious downside to utilising this system is that the true rotation isn't visible by glancing at your channel box. You are required to hunt for it, but if you desire, you can make the joint orients visible in the channel box by **Channel Box > Edit > Channel Control > Select Joint Orient X, Y,** and **Z**, then click the right **≪ Move** button (Figure 8.16).

Moving Joint Orient rotations back to Rotate XYZ values is a slightly more involved process. You can manually move each individual channel back to the relative rotate channel and then delete its Joint Orient counterpart. Alternatively, you can orientationally constrain the joint with a maintained offset, which will lock the joint from any orientation changes, and then if you zero the Joint Orients attributes, the data will move into their corresponding rotate XYZ channels. Make sure to delete the constraint afterwards!

If you would prefer to utilise the regular XYZ rotation attributes but would like to bank your desired rotations with an easy method of restoring those values at any time—Maya offers an attribute called a **Preferred Angle**, which can be stored via **Skeleton > Set Preferred Angle**, this will store the current rotation values which can be restored by **Skeleton > Assume Preferred Angle**.

A similar system to Joint Orients can be seen on non-joint nodes when freezing their translation, but instead of a Joint Orient value, the "true" frozen translation is instead stored within the **Local Rotate Pivot** attribute within the attribute editor highlighted in Figure 8.17.

When rigging, pick where you will store your rotations, and pick rotation XYZ or joint orient XYZ—not both. You do not want to have stacked rotations.

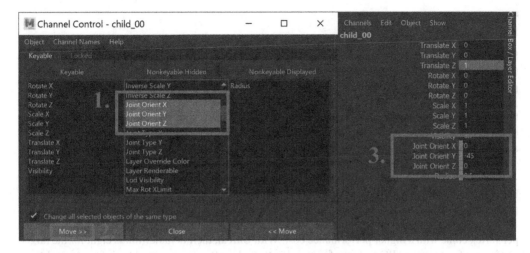

FIGURE 8.16 Use the Channel Control interface to move the Joint Orients to the Channel Box.

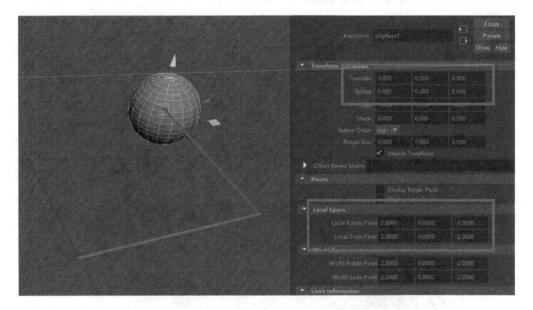

FIGURE 8.17 This cube has translation, but the translation channels are zero. The offsets are in the local rotate pivot instead.

8.3.11 Auto-Riggers

While I recommend building your own systems so you can understand the toolset and what the systems are doing, there are alternative methods to generating your skeleton rigs if you prefer a quick start. While there is a variety available from third-party vendors as plugins or scripts, Maya does come included with a bipedal auto-rigger called Quick Rig. Quick Rig is accessible via **Skeleton > Quick Rig.**

Quick Rig can give some great results in mere seconds but is prone to a variety of skeletal issues, including the ones we have spent the last few pages describing how to avoid. For the best results, build it yourself! Then you will know every facet of the rig is clean and proper; you will be building your character's whole animation system on top of this skeleton—so do not rush it, get it right and take your time.

8.4 Skinning

Skinning is a technology that allows you to associate a 3D model with joints inside a skeleton hierarchy so that when that skeleton articulates, the appropriate parts of the 3D model move and behave correctly. As a process, skinning works by assigning weight to each vertex to determine the percentage of influence each joint has on it. If a vertex is 100% weighted to a joint, it will inherit the transforms of that joint one to one; however, a vertex can be partially weighted between multiple joints, allowing for the final transformation of the vertex to be determined by multiple influences. To apply this weighting, a user can visually paint a weight heatmap onto a 3D mesh, as shown in Figure 8.18. Each colour of the heatmap corresponds to a specific weight value, with the darkest black being 0% and the hottest red being 100%.

When skinning, is it important to recognise the per-vertex influence count. This is the total number of joints influencing an individual vertex. This value is important to evaluate, as while it is not a problem in DCCs, some game engines have limitations on the number of influences they can support. It's a given that the more bones you use to help deform, the better the results are, but more influences per vertex come with a higher performance cost. With Unreal, their default limit is eight for the target platforms of console and PC and four for mobile - they also offer an uncapped limit for non-real-time projects. If you skin an object with a vertex limit of eight, but the engine of choice is limited to four—the character will deform differently between the two packages.

8.4.1 Applying Skin

Once we are happy with our joint placements for our characters, we are ready to move on to the next stage—skinning. Applying skin to the geometry via:

1. Select both the root joint and the geometry of the character.
2. Assign a skin cluster to the joints via the Bind Skin Dialogue (**Skin > Bind Skin > ☐**).
   a. **Bind to: Joint hierarchy**—This will add all joints in the hierarchy to the skinning. Be cautious if you are using end joints, as they will also be included and we will have to remove them later.

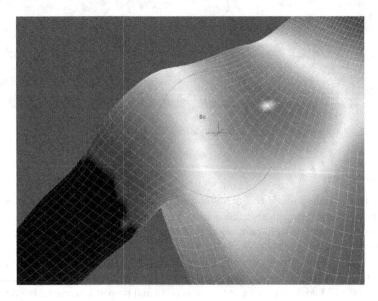

FIGURE 8.18 Coloured visualisation for skin weighting.

b. **Bind method: Heatmap**—The bind method is the automatic weighting method applied to give base weights. This is ultimately just a starting point, as we will manually improve the weights.

c. **Skinning Method: Classic Linear**—This option defines the method of skinning, since we are developing for real-time, we need to use Classic Linear as dual quaternions are not supported.

d. **Normalize Weights: Interactive**—This option defines how the weights are normalised (kept and updated into 0–1). Interactive will keep this updated consistently with any changes.

e. **Allow multiple bind poses: disabled -**

f. **Max Influences: 8**—Set this to the maximum supported by your engine, if you are developing for mobile set this to 4.

g. **Maintain max influences: enabled**—This option ensures the skin cluster does not exceed the maximum influences you have set.

h. **Press Bind Skin**

Once applied, this will define your skin cluster's bind pose. You can easily reset to the bind pose by selecting either the geometry or any joint in the skeleton, then use the Go To Bind Pose tool (**Skin > Go To Bind Pose**).

8.4.2 Range of Motions

Since you can only see your skin deformation happen when their joints move away for their bind pose, let's create a range of motions for the skeleton to test it! A range of motions is an animation that tests the extremities of each joint in each of its respective axes, moving between its minimum and maximum rotations and translations. Create a range of motions by iterating through each joint, rotating each operational axis between its minimum and maximum and storing a keyframe for each.

Once an animation is created, we can scrub through the timeline (**Hold K + Drag Left Mouse in the viewport**) while we are painting our skin weights to get a live preview of how our new weights are affecting our geometry. Alternatively, while skinning, press the middle mouse button to toggle the rotation manipulator from the Paint Skin Weights Tool. While in this mode, press and drag the middle mouse button to rotate the selected joint.

8.4.3 Skin Weights

With the range of motion applied, we can begin the process of assigning skin weights to our vertices. This will determine how much influence each joint has on each vertex to make it deform. To do this, either paint our weights or we can manually assign weights on a per-vertex basis.

8.4.3.1 Paint Weights

The paint skin weight tool can be accessed by first selecting our geometry, then either **Skin > Paint Skin Weights** or **holding the right mouse in the viewport and dragging to the Paint Skin Weights Tool.** Painting weights allows you to do just that—you can paint weights onto your mesh with a virtual paintbrush.

By default, your per-influence weights will be displayed in a linear black-to-white colour gradient, with white equalling 1 weight and black equalling 0. At times, this can be difficult to visualise as the difference between 0.95 and 1 is very minimal as it is light grey compared to white. To improve your visibility, under the **Gradient** category, there is a **Use Colour Ramp** checkbox, which will display a heatmap that will more accurately display your current weights. White is only for a weight that is equal to 1, then 0.99–0 ramps through red, orange, green, blue and finally black.

While painting, here are a few useful shortcuts that will speed up your workflow. You can easily shrink or increase the brush size by **holding B and dragging the left mouse button**. Additionally, **holding N and dragging the left mouse button** allows you to increase or decrease your applied weight value. These options can be manually configured under the **Stroke** category of the **Paint Skin Weights** interface. **Holding U and dragging the left mouse** will open a marker menu to quickly change the current paint operation (Add, Replace, Scale and Smooth).

Painting operations allow you to customise in what way your paint weights are added or removed from the pre-existing weight values. **Replace** will stomp over the pre-existing weights with your desired values, **Add** will add to the pre-existing values (up to 1). The **scale** will scale the existing values, so if your input value is set to 0.9 (90%) and your existing weight value is 0.5, the resulting weight value will be 0.45. **Smooth** also does as it says, it blends and smooths the weight values of the vertices it is painted on. The **flood** button (Alt+F shortcut) is a useful shortcut that allows you to apply a weight value across the entire model or selection without the need to paint.

Also included within the paint weights interface is a shortcut to the **Hammer Skin Weights** tool (**Hammer icon** under the influences list or **Skin > Hammer Skin Weights**). If you ever notice any spikes in vertices or want to smooth a vertex's weight to the result of its surrounding weights, then use this tool. It requires one or more vertices to be selected to be applied.

When painting, keep scrubbing your timeline (**Hold K + Drag Left Mouse in the viewport**) to review your new weights with the range of motion you made!

8.4.3.2 Manual Weight Assignment

Weights can also be assigned manually through the component editor's tables. Don't use this for normal workflow, but for some edge cases, it is invaluable to know.

1. First, select one or more vertices on your model (**Vertex mode by F9, or Hold Right Mouse in the viewport and drag to the Vertex option**).
2. Open the Component Editor (**Windows > General Editors > Component Editor**).
3. Open the Smooth Skins tab.
4. Each vertex will be a new row, and each influence has a column—change these values to whatever you desire.

8.4.4 Weighting Techniques

There is no magic method to weighting your meshes, and you will get better the more you paint and learn from experience. Don't be afraid to make big paint adjustments; just try something out. We are in a digital world where we can undo—go big! Don't waste time doing small increments—a Goldilocks approach works extremely effectively. Always overshoot the amount you think you want to paint, then under paint and then you will find the perfect value somewhere in the middle—it will be. Just right! While there is no silver bullet to making the perfect weight values, here are a few techniques and tricks that can speed up your workflow.

8.4.4.1 Influence Locking

When you are working with dozens of influences, using paint weight tools such as Smooth can cause undesirable results as weights can be distributed onto any influence. To get around issues like this, we can isolate the influences we want to work with by locking out the ones we do not. Directly within the Paint Weights interface, the first column on the left of each influence allows you to set the locked state of that influence. Additionally, right-clicking in the list of influences reveals options such as the ability

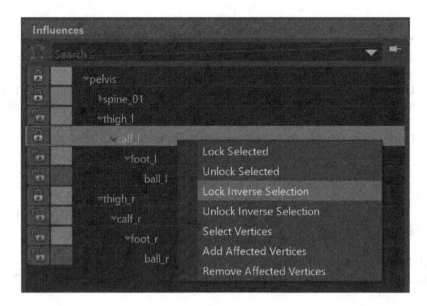

FIGURE 8.19 Lock and unlock weights with the pad lock icon, or bulk lock/unlock via the right-click menu.

to lock the inverse selection, which will lock all influences but those selected (Figure 8.19). This is a fast way to lock out all influences except the ones you are concentrating on.

8.4.4.2 Selection Isolation

The paint weight tool can be combined with the selection tool to isolate an area to paint on your models. With the selection tools (**Select a Model, Hold Right-Click, Drag to Vertex/Edge/Polygon**), you can select any element, be that a vertex, edge or polygon, then re-open the paint weights tool and your paint actions will only be applied within the selected area. Remember to deselect your vertices, edges or polygons when you decide to continue painting the rest of your weights!

8.4.4.3 Mirror Skin Weights

Akin to our skeleton's symmetry, Maya lets us mirror our skin weights from one side of a character to another. This is extremely helpful, especially for symmetrical characters, as it saves valuable development time. To mirror your skin weights, first, select your geometry and then use the mirror skin weights tool (**Skin > Mirror Skin Weights > ▢**). Just like when mirroring your skeleton, you will need to define a mirror plane, but this time with a direction (whether you are mirroring + to - or - to + space), so if your character is facing Positive Z and I want to mirror right to left, I need to set **YZ** with **positive to negative disabled**.

While its default settings may get you respectable results, the tool can sometimes get confused when trying to copy weights from one side to another, especially when skeletons become more complex, such as in situations where multiple joints are located in the same place. To counteract this, we can set up **Joint Labels** to help the mirror tool distinguish between each joint and its mirror counterpart.

1. Select your joint.
2. Navigate to the **Attribute Editor** (**Ctrl+A** cycles between Channel Box & Attribute Editor).
3. Open the **Joint** category, and then the **Joint Labelling** sub-category.

4. Fill in the appropriate settings for your joint.
   a. **Side**—Determines the side or centre status of your joint.
   b. **Type**—This is a quick access label for distinguishing body parts, if you desire to determine your own labelling, then choose **Other**.
   c. **Other Type**—With Other selected in the Type option, this text box will enable. Enter a unique name without any side labelling. For example, a "hand_r" joint would be labelled "hand."
   d. **Draw Label**—If checked, this will render the text of the joint's label on the joint in the viewport.

Be sure to utilise the additional resources to find a script that will automatically label and assign the side of your joints!

Once all joints have been appropriately labelled, we can now set the Mirror Skin Weights tool to use the labels.

1. Select the geometry.
2. Open the mirror skin weights options dialogue (**Skin > Mirror Skin Weights > ☐**); see Figure 8.20.
3. Re-apply the mirror direction settings.
4. **Set Influence Association 1** to **Label** to use the new joint labels.
5. **Set Influence Association 2** to **One to One**. Alternatively, the Closest Joint option uses a guess by the position but can cause issues with joints in close proximity or identical places, so only use if necessary.
6. Enable Normalisation of your skin weights - this will ensure all skin weight values are normalised 0–1.
7. Mirror your skin weights!

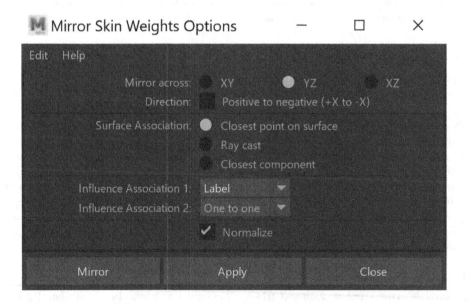

FIGURE 8.20 The mirror skin weights options.

8.4.4.4 Copy Skin Weights—Mesh to Mesh

You can copy skin weights from one model to another, which is particularly useful for updating mesh to transfer the weights from the old mesh to the new version, or if you are utilising a base mesh pipeline with a character, you apply skin weights to the naked base mesh and then copy the weights from it to each clothing piece to give you a good starting point. To copy weights, we can utilise the Copy Skin Weights tool found under the Skin menu.

1. We must first select the mesh containing the source of our skin weights.
2. Then select the destination mesh where we want to transfer our skin weights.
3. Open the Copy Skin Weights options dialogue (**Skin > Copy Skin Weights > ◻**).
4. Apply the following settings:
   a. **Surface Association**—Typically, you can set this to **Closest Point on Surface**, but if you are transferring between two models with identical UVs, containing zero UV overlaps, we can set it to **UV Space**.
   b. **Influence Association 1 - Labels, 2 - One to One, 3 - Closest Joint**.
      i. Only utilise the Labels option if you have properly set up your joint labels as we defined in the previous section.
   c. **Normalize – True.**
5. Click Apply and the weights will transfer between meshes.

8.4.4.5 Copy Skin Weights—Selection to Selection

Copying skin weights also works not only from mesh to mesh, but combined with the selection tools, you can copy weights from mesh components to another mesh or even to specific mesh components— meaning you can transfer weights from a selection of vertices on your source mesh to another group of selected vertices on your destination mesh while leaving all vertices outside the selection untouched.

1. Select your destination mesh for where the weight will end up.
2. Open the **Maya Marker Menu (Hold the Right Mouse Button)** and drag to the **Vertex** selection mode. This technique works with other selection modes such as edge or face.
3. Select your vertices where the weights will be transferred too.
4. Re-open the **Maya Marker Menu** and select **Object** selection mode. This will ensure your vertex selection is not deselected!
5. Select your source mesh, where the weights originate from.
6. Re-open the **Maya Marker Menu**, and select **Vertex** selection mode.
7. Select the vertices you wish to copy weights from.
8. Return to **Object** selection mode again through the **Maya Marker Menu**.
9. We now treat the situation like a standard copy weights procedure—by selecting the source mesh first, then the destination mesh second.
10. Use the copy skin weights tool (**Skin > Copy Skin Weights**).

8.4.4.6 Copy Skin Weights—Simplified Mesh To High Poly

Let's say you are dealing with a mesh with a complex topology where all the standard painting tools are failing to give you a smooth gradient weighting in an ample amount of time, or if you are dealing with a mesh that may have air pocket gaps in between the mesh but you want to maintain your skinning smoothly across, such as with a spring mesh. To solve this problem, you can utilise a simplified

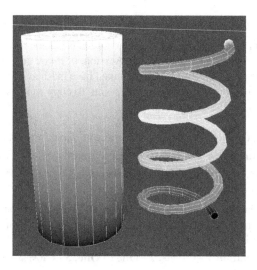

FIGURE 8.21   You can copy skin weights from a simple mesh to a more complex one.

mesh that removes all of this complex mesh data and acts as a simple "blocking" of the area you are working on. This could be merely a cube, cylinder or even an extremely low level of detail mesh of the model you are skinning. This method makes the task of skinning a spring, shown in Figure 8.21, a trivial task.

Apply skinning to your simplified mesh, paint your weights on this mesh as you would expect to see your final result, and then treat it like you would any other mesh you would transfer data from by selecting the destination mesh, then the source mesh and use the copy weights tool. The copy weights tool does not require both meshes to be exactly the same—use this to your advantage!

8.4.4.7 Copy Skin Weights—Vertex to Vertex

If required, you can also copy the weight values of an individual vertex and paste those exact values onto other vertices. This can be a little time-consuming to do en masse, but it is invaluable for instances such as ensuring a lip or edge maintains the same thickness or even sealing different meshes together by ensuring their vertices have identical weight values.

1. **Enter Vertex Mode (F9)** and **select the vertex** you want to copy the skin weights from.
2. Use the **Copy Vertex Weights** tool (**Skin > Copy Vertex Weights** or **Ctrl + Alt + C**).
3. Select the vertex or vertices for which you want to paste the skin weights onto.
4. Use the **Paste Vertex Weights** tool (**Skin > Paste Vertex Weights** or **Ctrl + Alt + V**).

In the previously described instance of using the simplified mesh technique to copy weights to a spring mesh, the whole spring would have a perfect gradient across the entire mesh; however, each edge loop of the coils would grow and shrink in size as it articulated—which is not ideal! Along with the use of the simplified mesh, we could then use the vertex copy weight tool to copy a single vertex weight from an edge loop of the spring and then paste those values to its neighbouring sibling vertices on the same edge loop with the vertex paste weight tool to ensure we had equal weight for all vertices on that edge loop, repeating for each loop throughout the spring. This solution is shown in Figure 8.22.

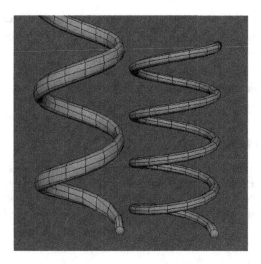

FIGURE 8.22   Copying vertex weights to a loop can improve the deformation.

8.4.5 Moving Joints After Binding Skin

Once you begin skinning and testing your deformations with the range of motions, you may inevitably recognise that you may have misplaced your joints, or that they are not in the most optimum position. Do not be deterred if this happens—rigging is an iterative process, but let's make the most of not losing work and preserve any skinning work we have done at this point. We cannot simply move our joints into our new location, as it'll move the mesh because it now has skinning applied. We could delete our skin cluster and then move the joint to its new location and reskin—but we would lose all our skinning work. Now how can we move our joints while preserving the skin work we've already done? Here are a few methods to achieve this.

8.4.5.1 Move Skinned Joints Tool

While your geometry is selected, there is a Move Skinned Joints tool (**Skin > Moved Skinned Joints**) that allows you to translate your joints and maintain their skinning data. Once enabled, select the joints you want to move and the originally selected geometry will turn transparent to identify that the tool is active, and you can begin moving any joints freely. The big downside of this tool is that it only supports translation movement; if you switch to rotation or scale, then the tool will reset. However, there is a method to access full joint transformation control through the skin cluster function via scripting.

Included within the additional resources is a script to toggle the full Move Skinned Joints transformation functionality.

8.4.5.2 Export/Import Skinning Data

We are able to export and import our skinning data to an external file, this process can be useful for situations requiring skin data to be transferred between different Maya files.

The XML method:

1. Select the geometry you wish to save the skin weights for.
2. Open the Export Weights Dialogue (**Deform > Export Weights**).
3. Click the **folder icon** and pick a desired export path and name.

4. Click **Export** and a. XML file containing your weight data will be exported.

   You are free to unbind your geometry and reposition your joints into their new locations. Once you have reapplied skinning to the geometry, you can import your weights.

5. Open the Import Weights Dialogue (**Deform > Import Weights**).
6. Click the **folder icon** to find the appropriate XML weight file.
7. Click **Import** and your skin weights will be reapplied!

8.4.5.3 Unbind Keep History

Alternatively, there is another method in which you can unbind the geometry from the skin cluster but ensure the skin cluster does not get deleted—meaning the skin weights work will be preserved in the skin cluster. Once you rebind the geometry to the skeleton, the weights will reassign and begin deforming your mesh again. This method also updates the bind pose and is the most hassle-free process.

1. Select your geometry.
2. Open the Unbind Skin Options Dialogue (**Skin > Unbind Skin > ❒**).
3. Select **Keep History** from the **History** dropdown menu.
4. Select **Detach**.
5. Move your joints into your desired location.

Rebind geometry to the skeleton by selecting the root joint and geometry (**Skin > Bind Skin**).

8.5 Corrective Joints/Helpers/Solvers

You may notice as you preview your range of motions that some areas do not look as good as you want, no matter what you do. Areas such as the wrists can look like a twisted coke can when the hand is twisted (Figure 8.23), or even the elbows and knees, that completely lose their volume when the limb is folded. Sometimes this can seem like a losing battle, but do not fret! There are methods to solve this. We just need some extra help from additional joints to improve the skinning deformation of a mesh. *Only consider adding additional joints if your joint budget can accommodate it!*

Let's start by diagnosing the issue we have with the wrist deformation before we begin to tackle it. When we twist the wrist, we can see all the deformation happening in between the segments highlighted in intense black—whereas when you twist your wrist in real life, the twist is spread across the entire forearm.

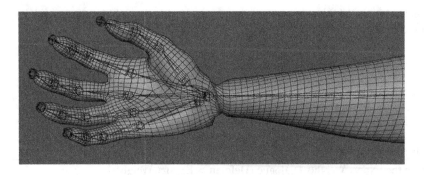

FIGURE 8.23 Problem deformation area on the wrist when joints are at their extremities.

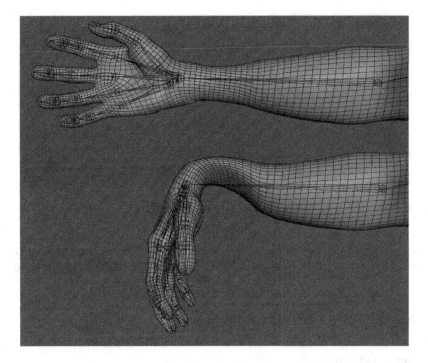

FIGURE 8.24 Spreading the skin down the wrist will not fix this problem, just make it worse.

Could we not just add additional weight up the forearm onto the wrist? While it would fix the wrist twist issue, it would cause another problem visible when rotating the wrist is pointed down, warping the arm shown in Figure 8.24.

To solve this wrist deformation, we require to disperse the twist rotation of the wrist along the forearm while maintaining the forearm's orientation so it does not move in other directions with the hand.

1. **Add a leaf joint to the forearm,** which is in an identical location to the wrist—this will be our wrist twist corrective joint.
2. Create an end joint under the twist corrective so we can see its orientation. It should look something like this (Figure 8.25).

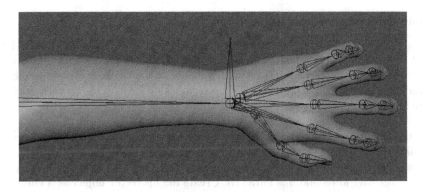

FIGURE 8.25 Adding a leaf joint to a twist corrective helps see its orientation.

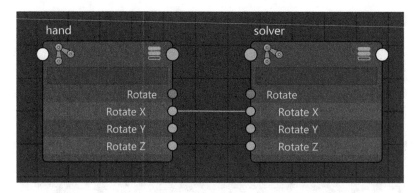

FIGURE 8.26   Connecting the rotation X attributes together in the node editor.

Now, we are required to set up the twist corrective to only have the twist of the hand joint's rotations. Like most problems in 3D, there are a variety of ways to solve this with varying degrees of success.

8.5.1 Solution 1—Direct Connection (Beginner)

A simple method is to use a Direct Connection between the twist orientation of the hand and drive the twist orientation of the wrist.

1. **Select** both **the hand and the wrist corrective joints**.
2. Open the **node editor** (**Windows > Node Editor**).
3. Press the **Add selected nodes to Graph** button [image].
4. **Expand** the "**rotation**" dropdown on both nodes and **connect the Hand's twist. rotation** (X in this instance) **to the twist rotation of the wrist joint** (Figure 8.26).

Now when we rotate the hand, the wrist will also rotate. While a direct connection is the simplest approach, it is also the weakest. This is because the values are a 1:1 connection, and if any gimbal singularity begins to occur, the gimbal will occur on both joints, causing undesirable results. This issue is easy to reproduce if you pitch the wrist up to the point where the Euler values flip. While this is the simplest method, it may suffice for your needs. If it does not—we can try alternative methods.

8.5.2 Solution 2—Aim Constraint (Intermediate)

An alternative approach, an aim constraint with an up vector to isolate the rotation of the hand, can be applied. Aim constraints experience gimbal singularities if the two aim vectors (target direction/up direction) become aligned. While it is a flawed technique, we have control over where the fault line will trigger based on moving the up vector. The up vector along the most infrequently used axis will benefit the final result.

1. For this setup, we require an **Up Vector Object**. *This object will be used in the aim constraint settings later.* This object can be a locator, transform or even another joint. If you intend to transfer your rig setup between different packages, such as Unreal, use a joint so you do not have to rebuild it is universal. **Create the up vector object as a child of the hand.**

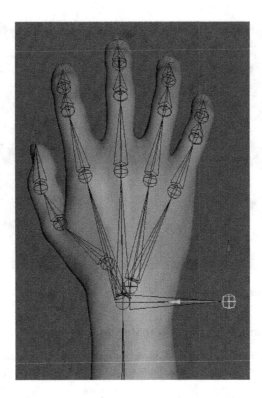

FIGURE 8.27   A new up vector object added.

2. **Add an offset to the up vector object**, making it directly parallel to the hand on the left or right side (as shown in the image), this will place our up vector alignment along the axis that will be less frequently used than the other two axis (Figure 8.27).

3. With our joints in place, we must now isolate the rotation. **Apply an aim constraint** between the wrist and the forearm joint. **Select the target joint**; the forearm, then **select the destination**; the wrist. (**Constraint > Aim > ☐**). In the dialogue options,

   a. Set the **World Up Type** to **Object Up.**

   b. Enter the **up vector object name** in the **World Up Object.**

   c. Set the **Aim Vector** and **Up Vector** relative to the directions of your joints. The aim vector denotes the direction in which the joint should point to its target, and the up vector denotes the direction of the up vector object. Set only a single value in each vector to 1 or -1. If the X direction of your joint is pointing to the forearm, then you must do 1,0,0. If it's pointing away, it would be -1,0,0 for example (Figure 8.28).

   d. Then hit **Apply.**

4. Rotate the hand joint, and you will see the aim constraint has isolated the twist rotation solely on the wrist. Since the wrist aims at the forearm, it does not move as that is a single plane, but as the Up Object moves around caused by the hand rotation—it causes the wrist to spin; our desired result!

Ultimately, this solution, just like the first solution, has a gimbal problem—but in this case, we can control where that gimbal problem occurs by placing the up vector object in particular places. With Euler angles, you will always have to suffer the gimbal problem, and sometimes the best you can do is just avoid it wherever possible… However, there are more advanced methods to escape the gimbal.

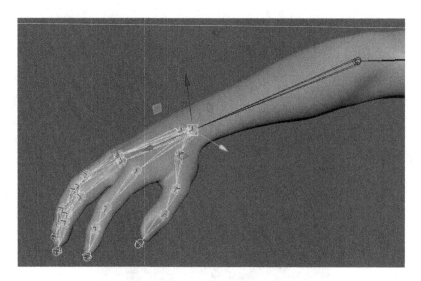

FIGURE 8.28   Visualising the orientation of the joint for the aim constraint axis.

8.5.3 Solution 3—Aim Constraint Alternate (Intermediate)

Once you have an understanding of using an up vector object, we can take advantage of the aim constraint to perform a similar operation, but without the need for a dedicated up vector object.

1. Unlike the other methods, we require our **wrist joint to not be aligned with the hand** and to be in between the forearm and hand positions. **Let's move our wrist 80% of the distance between the forearm and wrist**.
   a. A trick to do this is in the channelBox you can apply maths equations to the current value such as *= for multiply, += to add, -= to subtract or/= to divide. In this case, if we have a channel value of 25, we require 80% - enter *=0.8 to acquire 20, which is 80% of 25.
2. **Apply an aim constraint** between the wrist and the hand joint. **Select the target joint**, the hand, then **select the destination**; the wrist. (**Constraint > Aim > ◻**). In the dialogue options:
   a. set the **World Up Type** to **Object Rotation Up**.
   b. enter the **hand's name** in the **World Up Object.**
   c. **Set the Aim Vector** relative to the directions of your joints.
   d. **Set the Up Vector & World Up Vector to a matched vector different** from the aim vector.
   e. Then hit **Apply.**
3. With the Object Rotation Up as the World Up Type changes the behaviour of the aim constraint to take the up from the up vector object's up. This means we can have the Aim Target and the Up Vector Object be the same without issue. Rotate the hand and observe the rotation taking place on the wrist.

8.5.4 Solution 4—Matrices (Advanced)

To fully solve the gimbal issue, a more complex approach would be required—we can use matrix nodes to separate the twist from the swing. Matrix nodes are additional nodes that can be enabled through the plugin manager (**Windows > Settings/Preferences > Plug-in Manager**) labelled

matrixNodes.mll; enable the **Loaded** and **Auto Load** checkboxes. Once these nodes are enabled, we can begin putting together our system.

1. First, let's create our wrist joint as a child of the forearm. Making the joint a sibling to the hand will ensure we do not inherit any unwanted transforms we could get if the wrist was a child of the hand.

2. Next, open the Node Editor (**Windows > Node Editor**).

3. Add the hand and wrist joints into the node editor (will add selection).

4. Create an **AimMatrix** node (**press the tab then type the name of the node you desire**).

    a. We will use an aim matrix node to isolate the swing and twist orientations of the hand joint.

5. Connect the **Hand's Matrix** attribute to the **Primary Target Matrix** of the **AimMatrix** node.

6. We must now customise the **AimMatrix** node to ensure its aim vector correctly corresponds with our **hand** joint's aim direction.

    a. Select the AimMatrix Node, then open the Attribute Editor to find the **Primary Input Axis** and **Primary Target Vector** values.

    b. In this instance, our hand's aim axis is X—so set the X to 1.

    c. The **Output Matrix** value of the **AimMatrix** will now provide the swing value of the hand joint with no twist. We could use this for other solving processes, but we still require the twist, not the swing.

7. To get the twist, we must remove our new swing matrix from the original hand matrix to get the twist matrix.

    a. We can achieve this by inverting our new swing matrix through an **InverseMatrix** node.

    b. Next, create a **multMatrix** node. Then connect both the original hand matrix and our new inverted matrix into the **multMatrix** node.

    c. The output **Matrix Sum** will be our desired twist matrix!

8. To use this twist matrix, connect the **Matrix Sum** from the **multiMatrix** node into our **wrist's Offset Parent Matrix**—and tada! When you rotate the hand joint, the wrist joint will now only have a twist applied to it without any swing! Unlike the previous two methods, this will not flip! The node graph should look a little like Figure 8.29.

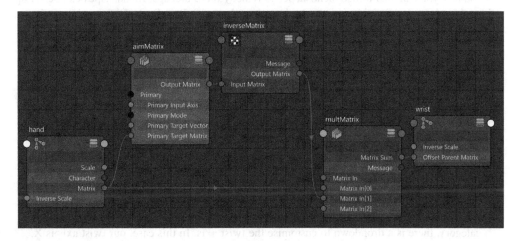

FIGURE 8.29 Matrix nodes utilised in the node graph to isolate the twist.

As demonstrated, there are many alternatives to achieving this same end goal, and there are many more. Once you are happy with your desired approach, be sure to add the new corrective joint to your mesh's skin cluster (**With the mesh and joint selected, Skin > Edit Influences > Add Influence**) and continue skinning! Continue adding additional correctives all over your character to prevent visual issues such as mass loss, bending metal, clipping or undesirable deformations—within reason and your budget of course!

Included with the additional resources is a variety of corrective joint examples with different approaches and types of challenges—dissect them, learn from them and apply their approaches to your own work!

8.6 Blendshapes/Morph Targets

A blendshape, otherwise known as a morph target, is an alternate version of a 3D model that is identical in every way except the position of vertices; through a blend value, the original version of the model can blend their vertex positions to the alternate positions. It is, in effect, an alternative method of deforming a mesh instead of skinning. Blendshapes can be stacked, and multiple can be blended at once to get the desired deformation.

In rigging, blendshapes are most commonly used for corrective deformation purposes and facial poses for animation. The former of the two is for use when a skinning solution isn't fully working as one would expect; a corrective blendshape can be used to fix the deformation instead of additional joints. As for facial animation, blendshapes can be used for facial expressions, these can then be blended by an animator to get the desired face shape. Beyond rigging, blendshapes are utilised for alternative purposes, such as the stylised rendering of 3D characters, to ensure they maintain a consistent 2D visual look to the final render when moving between different camera angles. This technique involves automatically blending between blend shapes based on the camera angle of the subject.

Blendshapes are more expensive computationally when compared to skinning, so if a skinning solution can be devised, that may be a better course of action. However, blendshapes offer an entirely artist-driven workflow, but that also comes with the overhead of requiring art support to produce the shapes.

8.6.1 Corrective Blendshapes

Corrective joints are not the only method you can utilise to fix any unwanted or bad deformations in your models—you can also utilise blendshapes to remedy these hiccups. Blendshapes can be set up to trigger based on specific joint poses and orientations through a Pose Space Deformation (PSD).

So let's fix our previous example of wrist deformation, but this time—with a blendshape!

1. Let's begin by opening the **Pose Editor** tool (**Windows > Animation Editors > Pose Editor**). This is where we can create, customise and configure blendshapes to trigger based on specific stimuli.

2. While our hand joint is selected, press the **Create Pose Interpolator** button in the **Pose Editor** window. This creates a node that will keep track of and drive the relationships between the hand joint's pose and the blendshapes we will now create. This will create three default entries in the right-hand side of the interface—neutral, neutralSwing and neutralTwist.

3. Next, we need to ensure our **Swing** and **Twist** are properly configured for our joint. Swing refers to two axes dealing with up, down, forward and back motion, while Twist refers to a single axis of rotation which is the rotation around the joint. To change this, enable the Advanced Options (**Pose Editor Window > View > Advanced**). In the **driver settings** category, there is a dropdown to customise the twist axis. In this case, our twist axis is X. Changing this attribute defines both swing and twist.

4. Next, pose your skeleton in a way that breaks the deformation—in our forearm twist instance, we need to twist the hand in X.

5. Select **Add Pose** in the **Pose Editor**. This will create a new blendshape that will be blended depending on the proximity of the hand's pose from the bind pose. A dialogue option will open, allowing you to customise the name of the newly created blendshape. Select **Create Pose Shape**.

6. Next, let's rename the name of the pose itself for clarity. This is different from the blendshape mesh we just created.

7. Since we only want this pose to be driven by the twist of our hand, let's select **Twist Only** in the **Type** column for our new pose.

8. Next to the newly created pose is an **EDIT** button. If the button is highlighted in red, this means you are in edit mode. If it is not—press it to enter edit mode.

9. Now, we can enter a component edit mode (face, edge and vertex) and begin to edit our mesh to modify our blendshape into a shape that appears like our desired deformation. Feel free to use any and all sculpting tools to help achieve this.

   a. Soft selection is very useful in this situation too (toggle soft selection by pressing **B**). You can grow/shrink the selection area by holding B and dragging the left or right mouse.

10. Disable edit mode in the pose editor when you are happy.

11. Now, if you rotate the hand joint back to the bind position—the blendshape will not be blended in. The more you rotate the hand joint closer to our newly created pose, the more the blendshape will fade in.

Do not feel constricted to using one technique or the other—you can freely mix and match corrective joints with blendshapes however you please! While all deformation problems can be fixed with each solution, for some problems, it's just faster to use one solution than the other.

8.7 Organisation

As with all your work, keeping on top of your organisation and tidiness should be paramount—your skeletons are no exception. The organisation in all facets of your work should be treated like how you would like to receive a file from someone else. You never know when your assets will be used by other people or even yourself in the future, long after you've forgotten how you've done this work. Make sure everything is neat and easy to understand and digest. Here are a handful of recommendations to make your scenes more organised.

8.7.1 Outliner

- **Clear naming conventions:** K your naming conventions consistent across all name groups. Employ consistent use of prefixes or suffixes. Don't name one object "L_Hand" and the other "Hand_R". Consistency is key!

- **Groups:** When opening the scene outliner, you should expect to see each section of the scene neatly organised with clearly defined groups and your skeleton root in the root of the scene. **Do not put your skeleton in a group!** Do not have dozens of items scattered in the root of your outliner either; this is messy! Make a group for your geometry, your working files, your locators, etc.

  - Groups can be created by pressing **Ctrl+G** or **Ctrl+G** with objects selected will automatically make the selected objects a child of the new group.

- **Sets:** Sets are collections of objects and/or components that can be grouped without the need for hierarchical changes. Once created, a set and its contents are visible in the outliner as a list. Sets can be useful for organisation purposes, or they can even be used as a shortcut to quickly select multiple items in the scene (right-click on the set, select items).

To create a set,

1. First, select the objects or components you wish to collate into a set.
2. Create a set (**Create > Sets > Set**).
3. A new set will be generated in the outliner—now rename the set as you please.

To add new objects to a set after it has been created,

a. Method 1—In the outliner, right-click a node, select Sets, then Add Selection to Set.
b. Method 2—In the outliner, the middle mouse drags objects into the set to add them.

8.7.2 Display Layers

Another method of organisation is the Display Layers interface (Figure 8.30). Creating display layers allows you to create groups of unrelated items, similar to sets, but display layers come with additional functionality that can be controlled on a per-display layer basis. The three buttons on each display layer have specific functionality. The **V** option is for visibility control—this will simply toggle the visibility of all items included in the layer. The **P** option is for playback—if P is enabled, the items in the display layer will render when playback is occurring and will not render if disabled. The final box will cycle through a blank option, T or R. Blank means the layer is in a normal state, but T corresponds to the layer being in a template state—this will render the layer in a wireframe, and it cannot be selected. Finally, R means the layer is in reference mode; meaning it cannot be selected but renders normally.

8.7.3 Colours

Colours, while they may seem trivial to some, are very powerful tools when used correctly. Colours can be used to employ a design language to your scene—this methodology extends beyond just your scenes; it's a fundamental concept in UX. Employing a very specific colour palette per object type, everywhere you find that type of object, be that in the display layer, outliner or even in the viewport, will provide cohesion that will instinctively allow you to quickly find that type of object.

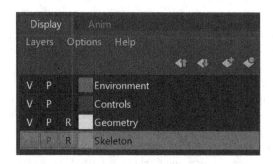

FIGURE 8.30 The display layers interface.

8.7.3.1 Display Layer Colour

Applying colour to a display layer is as simple as clicking the square () directly to the left of the display layer name. This will open a dialogue enabling you to customise the colour of that display layer.

8.7.3.2 Viewport Colour

With the **node selected**, open the **Attribute Editor** then navigate to the **Display** category (or **Object Display** category for shape nodes), and then open the **Drawing Overrides** category. Tick the **Enable Overrides** checkbox, then customise the **colour** attribute to control the viewport colour of your node.

8.7.3.3 Outliner Colour

With the **node selected,** open the **Attribute Editor** then navigate to the **Display** category (or **Object Display** category for shape nodes). Enable the **Use Outliner Colour** checkbox, and then customise the colour in the attribute below it. Outliner colour can be applied on a per-node basis.

Manually applying colour to many nodes in this manner can be tedious and time-consuming; be sure to use the tool included in the additional resources that allows you to quickly apply and customise colour assignments in your scene!

8.8 Skeleton Evaluation

Skeletons are always evolving, so do not expect to nail every facet of a rig the first time—as your project develops, new challenges will arise or your work will be used in a context you never intended it to be used in. Be comfortable with going back to the drawing board with some aspects, or even rebuilding entire sections of your skeleton.

Evaluating your skeleton is how you'll ensure you are putting your best work forward. Consider every joint area and how the deformation is working. Is it working well? Does the joint need fixing with corrective joints to preserve volume and mass? Or does it just need some skinning tweaks? Be sure to audit your skeleton for consistency, and test test test!

And remember, if you ever do have to fix or change your work—try to use a pipeline that is the least destructive to the work you've already done, you don't want to waste that work, so let us try to keep it!

8.9 Animation Transfer—Part 1

HumanIK (HIK) is an animation middleware that is built into Maya—it is a full-body IK solver that can be utilised to animate with their control rig system or, more importantly, used to retarget animation data from one humanIK character to another. This is especially useful for loading motion capture data onto your skeleton or control rig, or even for transferring data from a differently proportioned skeleton to a new skeleton.

To set up a character for HIK, requires the character must be "**characterised**". This is a process of defining each major body component for the HIK system (pelvis, spine, head, arms, fingers, etc.). To define your skeleton properly, it requires the skeleton to be in a T-Pose, so it can be used as a universal delta to transfer data between other characterised skeletons. Since each characterised skeleton will be T-Posed, it's easier to retarget data across. Do not worry if your character was not created in a non-T-pose position, we can simply rotate the limbs into the T-Pose to complete this process, then use the **Skin > Go To Bind Pose** tool to return. Once the skeleton is characterised, you can then utilise HIK's control rig to animate with or map characterised animation data onto your skeleton.

8.9.1 Characterising the Skeleton

1. First, let's verify the HumanIK plugin is enabled (**Windows > Settings/Preferences >
   Plug-in Manager**) For **MayaHIK.mll** enable the **Load** and **Auto Load** checkboxes.
2. Open the HIK interface (**Window > Animation Editors > HumanIK** or press 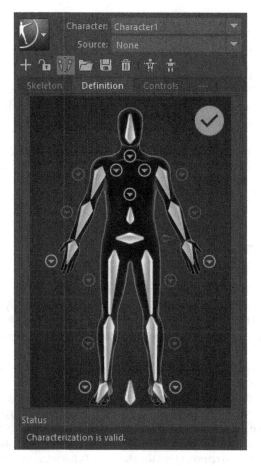 in the
   top right of the Maya interface); see Figure 8.31.
3. Press the **Create Character Definition** button to begin the characterisation process.
4. Name our character (**HumanIK window > HIK Icon > Rename Character**).
5. We must now assign each of our character's joints to the HumanIK interface, this is as
   simple as **selecting the joint**, then **right-clicking the corresponding body part** in the
   interface, and then selecting **Assign Selected Bone**.
   a. Repeat this step for all body parts.
6. If the status indicator in the top right goes red, there is a problem with your characterisation!
7. Once you have entered all animation joints and the characterisation is green noting no errors—
   press the **padlock icon** at the top of the HumanIK window to lock your characterisation.
8. Congratulations! You have now successfully characterised your skeleton. Be sure to save
   your scene to preserve the characterisation.

FIGURE 8.31   The HumanIK interface.

This is part 1 of the characterisation process, to take full advantage of HumanIK we can also connect our control rig to the system to load animation data onto the control rig too. We will cover this in the next chapter.

8.9.2 Transferring Animation through HIK

Once fully characterised, we are now able to drive one HIK character with another, as long as they are both fully characterised! If they are, then it is a straightforward procedure.

1. **Import** or **Reference** an animation file that contains a characterised character with animation.
2. At the top of the HIK window, in the **Character** dropdown, select the character you wish to receive the animation.
3. In the **Source** dropdown, select the character you wish to copy the animation from. Once applied, the character will immediately be driven by the source character.
4. The HumanIK system exposes a variety of retargeting settings allowing you to customise how the animation is mapped from one character to another. To access these settings **HumanIK window > HIK Icon > Edit Character Definition > Edit HIK Properties**. The attribute editor will open exposing these options—feel free to experiment with the attributes to see the differences they make to the retarget. While there are too many options to discuss, here are a handful of the more powerful options.
   a. **Match Source**—This determines whether the destination character should compensate for differences in proportions. If enabled, mapping a run animation from one character to another will maintain any distance metrics between the two, so stride lengths will be increased or shortened to ensure the same distance is travelled. If disabled, the proportions of the character are taken into account so the character will move at a relative speed for their limb length.
   b. **Mirror Animation**—This will flip the animation along a mirror plane.
   c. **Floor Contacts**—If enabled, this will modify the animation so that hands and/or feet do not go through the floor plane.
5. The next step is to bake the animation onto your character. **HumanIK window > HIK Icon > Bake > Bake To Skeleton**.
6. With the animation on your target character, we must now disconnect the character from the Source dropdown.
7. Finally, remove the additional character from the scene.

8.10 Exporting the Skeleton

Exporting your skeleton is the process of packaging up your work from Maya into an intermediate file format, such as FBX, so we can transfer all the necessary data into the engine. Unfortunately, this is not as straightforward as **File > Export All**—we need to prepare our scene by removing any work-in-progress content or unnecessary data.

8.10.1 Working File and Export File

Preparing your file for export can be a destructive process for your working files. Objects that you may want to keep in your scene for future development purposes will need to be stripped away for export. This is where a separation between your working file and an export file can be useful. To put it simply, you work within your work-in-progress file, and then when you are ready to export, you clean your scene to export and save another copy as your export file. This export file is a first-stage intermediate export file; you will never work on or change anything in the export file, but it gives a much clearer view into what exactly is and is not being exported from the scene. To continue any work, we will re-open the work-in-progress file. Naming convention-wise, using a _**WIP** or _**EXP** suffix on the file name to denote **Work In Progress** or **Export** respectively, can be very clear to define which file is which.

8.10.2 Cleaning the Scene

Cleaning your scene is as simple as deleting all unnecessary content you do not want to see in the final in-game product—this includes any rigging work such as simplified skin meshes or base meshes from your skinning processes, any unnecessary joints such as end joints or unskinned joints, and any locators or systems you are using. Essentially, remove all content except your skeletal hierarchy and your skinned geometry.

A useful technique for quickly cleaning your scene would be to place any and all content you want to delete in a set in your WIP file; you can then quickly access this set at any time and easily delete its contents, making the file ready for export.

8.10.3 FBX Export

With our EXP file prepared, let's begin the export.

1. To start, let's export via **File > Export All**.
2. A dialogue will open—export to a path consistent with your WIP and EXP files. Choose a file name accordingly, and select FBX as the file format.
    a. Keep all naming consistent across file types and status. For example
       i. **SK_Human_WIP.ma/SK_Human_EXP.ma/SK_Human.fbx**
3. Press **Export All**.
4. An FBX Export Dialogue interface will appear—this controls various parameters for which components to export and convert from your scene and which components to leave alone.
    a. A good starting point with the FBX settings is to select the **Preset - Autodesk Media & Entertainment** at the top. We can create our own presets too!
    b. Expand Geometry and Disable **Triangulate**.
       i. This isn't necessary for export as the engine will triangulate the file, but your work can be easily salvaged from a non-triangulated FBX.
    c. Expand and Enable **Animation**.
       i. Disable **Bake Animation**.
       ii. Enable **Deformed Models**, **Skins** and **Blendshapes**.
    d. Expand and Enable **Constraints** and **Skeletal Definitions**.
    e. While not necessary for your skeletons, enabling **Cameras** will be beneficial in the future.
    f. Save your preset—**Edit > Save Preset**.
    g. Press **Export**, this will create a new FBX file ready for engine implementation. We will continue this integration later.

9

Maya—Building a Control Rig

Before implementing our character into the engine, we must develop the animation control rig. A control rig is a set of animation-friendly controls and tools that drive a skeleton rig to behave in a particular way, allowing for faster pose manipulation and animation development. Control rigs can contain as few or as many features as desired; each feature helps animation in a specific way, so some functions may not be necessary depending on the project, but certain core features are essential.

Never confuse complexity with quality when evaluating a control rig's features set—as usability determines a rig's quality. More features and components mean a more computationally expensive control rig. If the rig can't play in real-time, then it is not usable. The rig shouldn't require playblasts to preview animation; this is an unacceptable workflow. If the features are not designed and implemented intuitively, the rig is not usable. To counteract the disadvantages of feature-rich control rigs, certain development approaches may choose modular versions of a control rig, each with a different number of features, allowing you to pick your preferred feature set for your particular animation task while maintaining performance. Alternatively, some approaches just stick with a fundamental features approach, which is enough to get the job done and minimise any issues, and create specific alternative rigs for bespoke issues rather than an all-encompassing solution.

Be careful while considering new technology for control rigs—while it can appear new and shiny, there is the potential for the technology to be unproven in a shippable pipeline. Before integrating a new method or technology into your control rig pipeline, test and verify it won't cause any problems. At a minimum, new technology can break backward compatibility with older software versions.

9.1 Rig Separation

Before starting construction of our control rig, we must remember to keep the control rig and skeleton rig separate within the scene. The control rig must serve as a separate layer that drives and manipulates the skeleton through constraints and connections. This separation ensures a clean workspace with clear dividers as well as a straightforward process for exporting animations since we intend to only export skeletal joints from our Maya scenes and not any control rig components. This rig separation lets us update the skeleton rig and geometry without affecting the control rig's systems. Simply delete and load the new skeleton rig, then reattach the control rig.

9.2 Building Controls—Fundamentals

Controllers are the most common components of a control rig and are the most user-facing as they are the only visible part of the control rig. In-world controllers drive other nodes through relationships such as constraints or direct connections; driven nodes can be anything from a constrained joint to direct connections into systems such as IK or foot roll. Controllers expose the manipulation of one to all nine of the Cartesian transformation values of translation, rotation and scale; X, Y and Z,

DOI: 10.1201/9781003263258-9

depending on what the controller requires. On the surface, a controller is simply a transform node with a visual shape node attached. The shape itself is purely for selection purposes. In an ideal world, controls should be placed on or near the body part they influence, but exceptions can be made if there is a cluster of controllers on top of one another.

First, let's create a group that will contain our control rig (**Edit > Group** or **Ctrl + G**)—let's adhere to our chosen naming conventions such as "control_rig" or "controlRig" depending on which case type you chose. All components of our control rig should reside within this group. Then add another group as a child of the control rig group and label this group "controllers." As you may have guessed, we will keep our controllers here.

9.2.1 Controller Transforms

When creating a controller, it is recommended that the controller should match the transformations of the joint it will be driving. This is so that pivots and axes will be matched, allowing the controller to have the appropriate bend planes and ultimately eliminating any offsets between the controller and the driven joint. However, a problem will occur when you make a controller match the joint's transformations—the controller will now have transformation offset values visible in the channel box to make it match the joint's position and orientation. Unfortunately, this will not suffice, as we want each of the transformations to be zero—this is to avoid several workflow problems for the animator, such as not being able to easily reset a controller back to its original position. Generally, having a non-zero controller transformation is bad practice and not a clean workflow.

You may be familiar with the Freeze Transformation tool—however, **do not use it** to try to solve this problem, as it does not fix it and causes issues. While the attributes may appear to be zeroed, the transformation offset is merely moved into the **Local Rotate Pivot** attribute visible in the **Attribute Editor > Pivots** (shown in Figure 9.1). The object's orientation, on the other hand, will become destroyed and match that of its parent or the world.

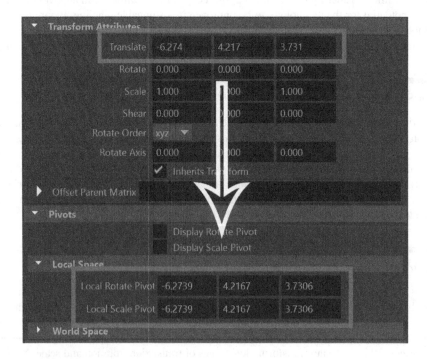

FIGURE 9.1 Freezing translation merely moves the offset to a hidden attribute.

So, how do we get around this problem while maintaining the position and orientation of our controller at the joint position while maintaining a neatly zeroed channel box? One solution is to utilise **offset parent groups**.

9.2.1.1 Offset Parent Groups

This is a simple solution that involves an additional group that the controller is parented to. This group then has the offsets applied to it instead of the controller as shown in Figure 9.2. The result is that since the controller is a child of the offset group, transformations are preserved and attributes are neatly zeroed. This means all controllers require two parts-an offset parent group and the controller node itself.

9.2.1.1.1 Creating an Offset Parent Group Control

1. Create a group (**Edit > Group** or **Ctrl + G**). This will act as our offset parent group. Make sure to move it into the control rig's controllers group!
2. Create another group and parent it to the offset group. This will be our controller.
3. Match the parent group's transforms with the joint the controller will influence.
   a. First, **select the offset group** (target), then **select the joint** (source), and then use the Match Transformations tool (**Modify > Match Transformations > Match All Transformations**).
4. Now the new group, controller and joint will all be aligned. The controller will have a clean channel box.
5. We can then drive a controller via constraint—pick the best-suited constraint for the joint. For example, if the limb requires just rotation, then apply an orientation constraint.

9.2.1.2 Offset Parent Matrices

While the use of parent offset groups has been a common process for many years, Autodesk released a feature in Maya 2020 called Offset Parent Matrices. This feature also provides the flexibility that parent offset groups provide without the need for additional groups. Their use is more intermediate and requires more setup than the simple process of offset parent groups. I recommend understanding the offset parent group workflow thoroughly before tackling this workflow.

The offset parent matrices pipeline involves offsetting controllers and driving joints through matrices rather than via offset groups and constraints. This greatly reduces the number of nodes and connections within the control rig, which is a huge performance optimisation.

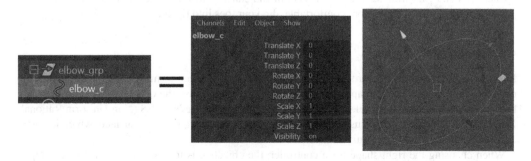

FIGURE 9.2 A controller node under a parent offset group allows for clean transforms.

9.2.1.2.1 Creating an Offset Parent Matrix Control

1. Create a group (**Edit > Group** or **Ctrl + G**). This will be our controller. Make sure to move it into the control rig's controllers group!
2. Match the controller's transforms with the joint the controller will influence.
   a. First, **select the controller** (target), then **select the joint** (source), and then use the Match Transformations tool (**Modify > Match Transformations > Match All Transformations**).
3. Next, let's set up the Offset Parent Matrix on the control to remove the transform offsets. **Select the controller**, and then open the **Attribute Editor**.
4. Expand the **Transform Attributes** & **Transform Offset Parent Matrix** categories.
5. **Move each transform value** from the **Transform Attribute** category into the same value in the **Transform Offset Parent Matrix**.
6. Be sure to **delete the Transform Attributes** values after, otherwise the controller will have a double transformation.
7. We now have a controller with preserved transforms and a clean channel box.

This workflow also allows for joints to be driven by a controller's offset parent matrix, which can make our rig even more economical; however, this only works within Maya. Since we are building our rigs for the game engine, in situations where we will need to bake animation keys to export, driving a joint with the offset parent matrix causes some fundamental problems caused by the same benefit we are utilising to zero our controllers. When animation is within the scene, the joint's attributes will all be zero since they are driven by the offset parent matrix—no matter what pose they are in. When baked, the animations maintain these zero values without breaking any data. So we can still be required to drive the joints via a constraint.

9.2.1.3 Groups or Matrices

So, groups or matrices? Which should I use? Realistically, any option will work because they both address the same problem, but you must consider their advantages and downsides. In the end, the offset parent matrix workflow has better performance since it has fewer connections and nodes, but you will also have to understand matrices to expand their functionality, and they are also not backwards compatible, so they won't function in Maya versions prior to 2020. While utilising the group offset workflow may be more computationally expensive, you save production time on the setup due to its simpler workflow. Both pipelines are valid workflows, so use whichever you feel most comfortable with.

For this book, we will be utilising the Offset Parent Groups workflow, as it has cross-software applications and isn't limited to Maya. I recommend starting with this workflow to understand the principles, then once you are more comfortable, dip your toes into the matrices workflow.

9.2.2 Controller Shapes

Beyond its functionality, a controller's shape is the element we need to make sure the animator can reach the most easily. These shapes are what will be selected to use the controller. A controller can have any shape added to it for selection, though most people choose NURBS (Non-Uniform Rational B-Spline) curves. You can also use different shape types, such as a NURBS surface, which lets you choose a volume rather than a curve shape.

When choosing the right shape for a controller, the objective is to make sure that it is as simple to select as possible when the control rig can be in any pose and the camera can be facing in any direction. To find the controller, the user shouldn't have to dig through geometry or toggle display layers on and off; it should be simple and obvious. By using colour theory to design your controllers, you can tell the user what kind of controller they are or even which side of the character they are on. A common practice in the computer graphics (CG) industry is to match the colours of a control rig to those used in aviation, where central objects are yellow, left-sided controls are red and right-sided controllers are green. However, since by default Maya colours an item green when it is selected, you will frequently encounter blue used in Maya rigs instead of green. Many of the curves that can be generated in Maya are made up of multiple shapes; for example, the square is actually four line shapes, not a single shape.

Also consider the controller's function. If you use a ball shape on a controller that deals with rotation, at a glance, it is much harder to determine the rotation of the object. It is because of this that their use should be limited to positional controllers. This is why it is useful to use shapes that you can determine orientation with, such as squares, so it is clearly visible if the rotation has been modified.

9.2.2.1 Creating Shapes

1. Navigate to the **Curves/Surfaces** tab at the top of Maya (Figure 9.3).
2. Pick a **NURBS Curve** or **Surface**—in this instance, let's start with a circle. This will generate a new object in the scene. While we do not want the newly created object in the long run, we only care about its shape node.
3. Access this shape node by enabling **Outliner > Display > Shapes**. The curve object will now have an additional dropdown on the node, exposing the shape node.
4. Unlike normal transform nodes, we cannot drag or reparent a shape node to another parent. We can use a Maya command to easily do this.
   a. First, **select the shape node** in the outliner.
   b. Then **select the controller node** in the outliner.
   c. In the bottom left-hand corner of the screen, there is a MEL command box. Enter the following command: "**parent -r -s**". This command is the parent command, with two flags; "-r" is the relative flag that preserves the local transforms of the shape itself, and the "-s" flag allows this command to run on a shape node.
   d. **Press Enter**—This will move the shape node to the controller object.
5. Tidy up—**delete the old curve transform** from the scene.
6. We can then **use the Control Vertex** tools to move, scale or adjust our new curve shape. **With the object selected, hold right-click to open the marker menu** and select **Control Vertex**.
7. Adjust the shape as you see fit, as moving vertex positions do not affect the controller's transform, just its visual shape!

Included within the additional resources is a tool that will allow you to skip this manual process and quickly apply shapes to selected objects!

FIGURE 9.3 The curves/surfaces shelf tools.

9.2.3 Controller Conventions

Ensure your tidy conventions and organisational practices extend to your control rig. We are required to make sure all controls are clearly legible so the user can understand exactly what they control. While there are many forms of conventions and practices that can be adhered to, the most important one is that you are consistent. Prefixing or suffixing nodes with different dénommers to identify what their use case is could be very useful, such as labelling controls as "_ctrl" or even shorter "_c," or groups as "_group" or "_grp." An easy-to-understand method would be to match the names of controls and groups to the joints they drive—so if the joint is "upperarm_r" the associated nodes could be "ctrl_upperarm_r" or "upperarm_r_ctrl."

9.2.4 Controller Hierarchy

When building controllers for the control rig, there are two approaches to consider for your hierarchy structure: flat or nested (Figure 9.4). Nested controllers are those that are built in a typical parental-like manner, with each controller being a child of another controller, so that when the parent controller is moved, the child inherits those movements, as do the child's children. An example of this would be an upper arm controller with a forearm controller as a child, then the hand is the forearm's child, and so on. This is a straightforward approach, similar to building a skeleton. Flat, on the other hand, refers to controllers that are all created as siblings to one another, which means that all controllers exist in a single group and there is no hierarchy relationship between connected controllers; instead, chains of controllers are linked through constraints to inherit the parent controller's transforms. In the same configuration as before, there would be a controller group that included the upper arm controller, forearm controller and hand controller, but the hand controller is constrained to the forearm controller and the forearm to the upper arm.

When using the control rig, you would not be able to tell which solution was used unless you looked under the hood. There are some fundamental differences between each approach, each with advantages and disadvantages. Using constraints to hold a control rig together is more computationally

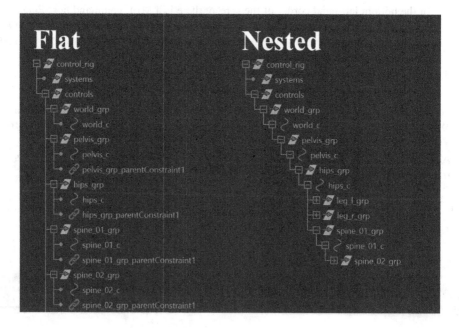

FIGURE 9.4   A nested hierarchy versus a flat one.

expensive than a simple nested hierarchy structure, but this cost may be insignificant unless there are hundreds of controllers in a scene held together in this manner. This additional cost is offset by the fact that a flat structure provides pipeline flexibility in instances that require the control rig's hierarchy to be changed, as any animation work completed on the control can be preserved. The nested solution can cause a handful of usability problems for the animator. The most visually facing issue is the viewport selection highlighting—Maya will highlight the selection with all of its children, making it harder to visualise what controller is actually selected. The isolation tools will not only isolate the selection, but it will also isolate all the children, making the tool not useful.

This is due to the way Maya stores data; all data for a node, including its animation data, is based on the node's long name. The long name is the full hierarchy path to the node within Maya-for example, a spine_01 controller in a controllers group would have the long name "**control_rig/controllers/ spine 01_c.**" A hierarchy version of the same controller's full path could be "**control_rig/controllers/ root_c/pelvis_c/spine_01_c.**" If the full path of this node is changed, the stored animation data for that node will be lost. Let's say we want to add another hip sway controller in between the pelvis and the spine; the full path would change in the hierarchy structure but would remain the same on the flat structure. Of course, this benefit is only available if there are hierarchy changes, but it allows for the flexibility to change the structure of the control rig while preserving any animation data.

We will be building with the flat controller workflow for our control rig, as the slight computation expense is a worthy sacrifice to make for the workflow and user advantages.

9.3 IK/FK Switching

IK/FK switching is a feature that allows a control rig to provide the best of both IK and IK in a limb. Rather than the control rig limb being exclusively locked into FK or IK, an animator can pick when they want to use FK and when to use pure IK, or even a blend between the two. As previously discussed, there are inherent benefits and drawbacks to the utilisation of both IK and FK systems. If you want to plant a limb, IK is superb for that but incredibly difficult to achieve with FK. With this feature, you get the best of both worlds! It's worth noting that not all rigs need an IK/FK switching solution; this is only if the rig requires the functionality of both systems—in some cases, just an IK solution could suffice, such as in the legs where FK is infrequently used.

While the concept may seem complicated, the setup is quite straightforward; the IK/FK system operates on the simple premise of having three duplicate chains of the limb. The first chain is driven by an IK solution, the second is driven by an FK solution and the third is then constrained to both of these chains. There is then animation control over how much control the IK and FK chains have over the third chain via an 0–1 float attribute. Having this as a float allows the user to control the blend between chains at decimal values, rather than a hard switch behaviour like you would get with a Boolean.

9.3.1 Setup IK/FK Switching

For this setup, we will be walking through an IK/FK setup on an arm limb, but this setup is the same for legs.

9.3.1.1 FK Setup

1. Begin by duplicating the three joints of the skeleton's arm limb that we will be setting up for IK/FK switching. These include: the upper arm, forearm and hand joints. (**To duplicate, select the joints and press Ctrl+D**).
2. Rename these joints to indicate they are an FK duplicate (for example, "**fk_hand_r**").

3. We do not want to include these joints in our skeleton—these joints are only for our control rig system. Let's create a new group under our control rig group, for which we will put all our systems and non-controller components of the control rig. Let's call it "**systems**." To further categorise the systems, let us create another group within systems for our IK switching—"**ik_fk_switching**," and a final group to specify which limb it is, to compartmentalise each limb's IK/FK switching. For this case, let's use "**ik_fk_arm_r**."

4. Move the duplicate joints into this group.

5. Create three controllers for each joint; **fk_upperarm_c, fk_forearm_c** and **fk_hand_c**.

   a. Ensure these are connected to one another, be that through hierarchy or constraints, so the upper arm controller influences the forearm, etc.

6. Orientationally constrain the controllers to their respective joints (**Constrain > Orient**).

7. **The FK portion is complete**—These controllers should behave like standard forward kinematic controls for now.

9.3.1.2 IK Setup

1. Duplicate the three limb joints for a second time, but this time rename with the "**ik_**" prefix instead of "**fk_**." Be sure to place these in the ik_fk_switching's limb group too!

2. We must set the preferred angle of our joints for the IK to work properly. The preferred angle is the "rest" or default for the joint. To do this, **select each IK joint**, then **Maya Menu > Skeleton > Set Preferred Angles**, or **hold right-click in the viewport to show the Marker Menu and select Set Preferred Angles**.

   a. The preferred angle value can be seen in the Attribute Editor > Joint.

3. Next, we must create our IK system.

   a. Enable the Create IK Handle Tool—**Skeleton > Create IK Handle**.

   b. **Select the ik_upperarm joint**, then **control + left mouse button to select the ik_hand joint.** This will then generate an effector and an IK handle.

   c. Parent the ikhandle under the ik_fk_switching group, and rename it corresponding to your limb.

4. Next, create a single controller. This controller will drive the IK handle and, in turn, the IK chain. Label the controller "**ik_hand_c**." Ensure the controller has translation and rotation exposed.

5. **Parent constrains the ikHandle node to the ik_hand_c controller.** First, **select the ik_hand_c** controller, then **control + left mouse button to select the ikHandle**. Add a parent constraint (**Constrain > Parent**). This will cause the IK handle to move when the controller is moved. This is better for the user.

6. While the controller will translate the ikHandle, the rotation of the controller will not move the hand joint. We must add an additional orientation constraint to do this. **First, select the ik_hand_r joint**, then **select the ik_hand_c controller** and then add an orientation constraint (Constrain > Orient).

7. Now we have a single controller driving the IK chain. However, we want to be able to control the twist of the IK chain with a controller—we can add a Pole Vector controller to add this functionality.

8. **Create a new locator** under the ik_fk_switching's limb group. This will be our pole vector.

9. Rename the locator to **pole_vector_arm_r**.

10. We must now constrain the locator to the ikHandle as a pole vector. We can do this by **first selecting the locator**, then **select the IKhandle**, then **Maya Menu > Constrain >**

Pole Vector. The locator will now twist the IK chain if translated, but we want a nice user-friendly controller, not a locator.

11. Create another controller for the pole vector locator.

12. Cleanup time! Our controllers should be the only user-facing components, so let's set the Visibility of the systems group to False, and lock the value by right-clicking in the channel box and selecting Lock Attribute.

13. We now have an operational IK chain driven by two controllers.

9.3.1.3 Switching Setup

Now we have two independently operating chains for both IK and FK, we will now create a third chain that blends between the two based on user input.

1. **Duplicate a third and final copy of the skeleton's limb**.

2. **Prefix each joint's** name with "**blend_**."

3. Next, **iterate through each joint in the chain** and **orient constraint** it to **both equivalent FK and IK joints**. This should result in each blend joint having an orient constraint with two inputs, the FK and IK versions of the joint.

4. **We will now create a controller that will act as an attribute holder.** The attribute on this control will change the state of the IK/FK limb.

   a. **Create a controller object.**

   b. Rename the controller to correspond to the whole limb.

   c. Add a float attribute to the controller, to do this -

      i. **Select controller**, then **Maya Menu > Modify > Add Attribute**

      ii. **Choose an attribute name** such as FKIK.

      iii. Select **Float** in **the Data Type.**

      iv. **Set minimum to 0, maximum to 1 and default to 0.**

      v. Select **Add.**

5. We must now connect the attribute to various controls and constraints. **Open the Node Editor (Maya Menu > Windows > Node Editor)**.

   a. Add the attribute controller and all three orientation constraints on the blend joints into the graph by **shift-selecting each node** and then **press the add selected nodes** button ▣ in the Node Editor window.

   b. Expand the node's attributes by pressing the **Show Primary Attributes on Selected Nodes button** ▦.

   c. **Connect the output of the FKIK attribute** to the **input of the IK joint's weight** in each constraint. This means the IK joint's weight will be one-to-one with the attribute value, if the value is 1, the weight is 1, and if the value is 0.2 the weight is 0.2.

   d. We require an inverse value for the FK, if our attribute is 1 we require 0, if it is 0.2 we require 0.8. We can do this with a **reverse node**. Create a reverse node (**press Tab and type** "reverse").

   e. **Connect the output of the FKIK attribute** to the **inputX** of the reverse node.

   f. **Connect the reverse node's outputX** to the **FK joint's weight in each constraint.** We now have reversed behaviour for both IK and FK limbs, the attribute now drives which control is active and during decimal values one limb fades out as the other fades in.

   g. At whole numbers, only a single limb is active, so from a user perspective, we do not need to visually see both IK and FK controllers at the same time. Connect the same attribute and reverse node outputs to each controller's visibility and they will toggle on/off.

h. Finally, with the system complete, we must **connect it to our game skeleton. Constrain each blend joint to its original game skeleton joint.**

i. Congratulations—You have successfully set up an IK/FK switching limb. Repeat this section for each limb of your character!

9.3.2 Reverse Foot

With our IK/FK chains setup for the leg's thigh, calf and foot, we will require a bespoke setup to be able to control the foot posing with accuracy. We will not have good enough control over a foot with FK alone; this is where a reverse foot setup comes into play. A basic reverse foot setup adds several controllers or attributes that allow for animation control over each component of the foot—these areas of control are points at the toe tip, ball and heel. The ball allows for the foot to roll properly; this also brings the IK ankle along for the ride to be in the correct place for the foot's positioning. The heel and toe tip allow for peel from the tip or heel of the foot, pivoting the entire foot. This process is demonstrated in Figure 9.5.

To prevent an infinite cycle, where one node is driving a node that is driving that node in return, there must be an operation order to the chain—so out of the three controls we will make, there must be a hierarchical order. This unfortunately means the last ones in the chain can't affect the first in the chain. For this reason, we must order the controls in a manner that provides the best use case and the most control at any given time. Since a reverse foot is particularly useful for doing a foot roll for a walk, having the influence be driven based on a foot roll would be best. This means the heel drives both the ball and the tip, but neither modifies the heel. We will then have the toe tip affect the ball.

9.3.2.1 Setup

1. Begin the foot roll setup by **creating a new group** in the leg IK group; this is where our foot roll system will reside. Label the folder "foot_roll_" with a suffix denoting the side.

2. Next, we must determine our pivot locations. We will have three locations: the heel, ball and toe tip. The heel should be placed under the heel point, on the corner of the geometry. The toe tip should mirror the heel but be at the front of the foot. The ball point will reuse the position of our ball joint.

   a. **Create a locator for the heel, ball and toe tip** (Figure 9.6).

   b. **Create a parent offset group for each locator** to zero the locator transforms.

   c. Place the offset groups in the foot roll group.

3. **Parent constraint the locators and parent groups:**

   a. **Parent constraint** the **foot tip group** to the **heel locator.**

   b. **Parent constraint** the **ball group** to the **foot tip locator**.

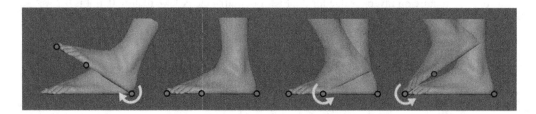

FIGURE 9.5 How the reverse foot rig controllers will manipulate the skeleton.

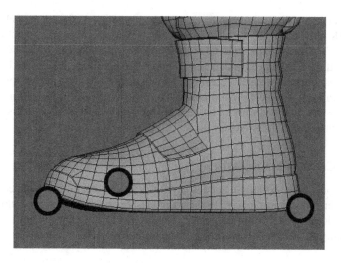

FIGURE 9.6 Placement locations for the foot.

4. From your original skeleton, **duplicate the foot ball and toe tip joints** and **parent to the leg's IK duplicate chain**.
5. Create two IK handles with the IK Handle tool.
6. **Skeleton > Create IK Handle - Select the ik_foot joint,** then **control + left mouse button to select the ik_ball joint.** This will then generate the ball IK handle.
7. **Skeleton > Create IK Handle - Select the ik_foot joint,** then **control + left mouse button to select the ik_ball joint.** This will then generate the toe IK handle.
8. **Parent both ik handles** to the **toe tip locator.**
9. **Parent** the **original leg IK** to the **foot ball locator.**
10. **Parent constraint the foot heel parent offset group** so the **IK foot controller** now drives it.

With the foot roll system setup, we now need to choose our method of control for the animators. We can either use a controller or an attribute holder with attributes to drive the axis of the foot roll system. Creating the controllers is just a matter of performing the techniques we have learnt previously for each controller, while the attribute holder requires float attributes that can be directly connected from each attribute to a specific attribute on each locator.

I prefer controllers as it feels a lot more tactile to manipulate the controller in-world, which is consistent with other controllers. Additionally, I prefer to keep away from hiding content away from the user and keep all controls easily accessible on the surface view.

9.4 Space Switching

Space switching allows a controller to dynamically swap inherited transforms between multiple controllers as if it were a child of that controller. In layman's terms, it's a switcher that toggles the weight of a parent constraint's targets that affect a particular controller—these targets are known as spaces. The controller can animate in that space while retaining its inherited transforms. It can do all this without being a descendant of the driving controller. If you are utilising a flat controller hierarchy and constraining controller groups together, this is an expansion of that system, but instead of just one controller parent driving the controller, we can control and switch between multiple.

Space swapping as a utility can come in very useful if you need to animate a character touching their face. The IK hand controller would be in world space throughout the animation, moving only when the world did. When a character touches their face, the animator can space-switch the hand into the head's space. If the head moves, the hand will move like it's attached since it's in its space. When the character stops touching their face, swapping back to the original space stops the inheritance. Without space swapping, simple animation tasks like this would need to be painstakingly animated by hand. All the contacts would need to be keyed, which may cause various drifts due to no proper planted connection between the two controllers.

9.4.1 How to Create a Space Switch

Before we create our space switch, we need to do a little bit of preparation. We need to decide which spaces we want our controller to inherit. In this example, we are going to apply multiple spaces (clavicle, hips and world) to the IK controller. Once you have decided, follow either of the two following sections, depending on which offset workflow you have utilised.

9.4.1.1 Offset Parent Group Workflow

1. **Select all the chosen spaces**, then **select your controller's parent group**.
2. **Apply a parent constraint**, with **maintain offset enabled**.
3. **Select the new parent constraint node**, and **open the channel box**.
   a. At this point, we can test our space's influence on the controller. We can do this by **setting all constraint weights to 0** and **setting the space we want to test to 1**. If we now transform the space, our controller will inherit those transformations.
4. While the spaces are functional with just a parent constraint, this is not a user-friendly workflow for the animator. Let's improve this by setting up an easy-to-access enum attribute on the controller to switch between the spaces. To do this, **select the controller and then Modify > Add Attribute**.
5. A new interface will pop up, allowing us to customise our attributes.
   a. Enter "**SpaceSwitch**" for the attribute name.
   b. Enable **Keyable**.
   c. Select **Enum** for the Data Type.
   d. In the enum names section, **add a new entry for each space**. In this case, I will add three entries: clavicle, hips and world.
6. Next, we will connect our enum to automatically switch the constraint's weight values. To do this, we must **open the Node Editor** (Windows > Node Editor) and **add our controller and parent constraint by selecting each** and then pressing the **Add selected nodes to Graph** button ▦ in the Node Editor window.
7. We must repeat this step for each space we have.
   a. Add a condition node (**press Tab and type "condition"**). In this instance, we can use the condition node to switch the weight of the constraint based on the selected enum value.
   b. **Connect** the **controller's spaceSwitch** enum attribute to the **condition's first term**.
   c. **Connect the condition's Out Color[0]** to the **parent constraint's first weight**.
   d. We must now set the condition node's second term. **Select the condition node** and open the **channel box.** We can set the second-term attribute here. The value we enter must correspond to the space's order in the enum we created; if it is the first entry, it should be number 0, the second entry is 1, the third is 2, the fourth is 3, etc. If the selected enum

equals the second term set, the condition node outputs 1, if it does not, it will output 0. This will switch the constraint's weight on and off.

    e. **Repeat this step for all spaces, using a unique condition each time.**

8. We now have an animator-friendly enum driving the space switch!

9.4.2 Animating with Space Switching

Now that we have set up our space switching to be very easy and intuitive for our animators, we still need to fully understand how to work with the system, as while it is useful, it is not without its quirks. A problem occurs when switching a controller between two spaces and the spaces themselves have moved from the transformation they were originally constrained in. Upon swapping, the controller will appear to "pop" to a new location. This is because when we established the spaces, we created an offset between each space and the controller. Think of this offset as a transform attached to the space's transform. If the space moves—this transform's location and orientation will move with it. Then, when we swap into that space, the controller will snap to that offset's transform. The controller's local transforms will then be applied on top of that offset's location.

How do we work with this pop? The solution is that we are required to perform a stepped key on the frame of the space switch that will return the controller to its exact position before the switch. So how do we go about getting the controller's previous position? We cannot just copy the local transforms, as they will be different between spaces. We are required to get the world transforms from the controller and then re-apply. A manual way of acquiring a world transformation would be to create a locator (**Create > Locator**), then match the locator to the controller's transformations (**Modify > Match Transformations > Match All Transformations**), perform a space switch and then match transforms again, but this time from the locator to the controller to reapply the original transforms. While this does work, it is long-winded and requires multiple steps for the animator to perform. We can make this better through scripting! Maya offers a command called xform, which allows us to access the world space positions of objects. We can use this to our benefit to improve it.

Acquire transforms:

```
translation = cmds.xform(selected, query=True, translation=True,
worldSpace=True)
rotation = cmds.xform(selected, query=True, rotation=True, worldSpace=True)
```

Apply transforms:

```
cmds.xform(selected, translation=translation, worldSpace=True)
cmds.xform(selected, rotation=rotation, worldSpace=True)
```

Included within the additional resources are script examples that include functions for acquiring and pasting world transformations.

9.5 User Experience

The key consideration when building a control rig is the target audience—the animator. The control rig's whole purpose as a toolkit is to empower animators to do what they do best—animate! Let's focus on creating an intuitive UX that someone with little to no technical experience would be able to utilise, or little familiarity with the rig-they should be able to pick it up and play, not read extensive documentation or jump through ten hoops to animate. The age-old rule of KISS applies here: Keep it simple, stupid! By removing as many hurdles from the animator's path as possible. The more convoluted a tool or process is to complete, the less likely it will be that the tool or process will even be used.

9.5.1 Cleaning the Channel Box

Ultimately, since we are setting up a control rig for animators, we want to remove as much fuss from hindering an animator as possible, so they can focus on doing what they do best: animating! With that in mind, animators will spend a lot of time using the channel box on controllers, so let's make sure it's clean for them.

9.5.1.1 Lock, Hide and Non-Keyable

Not all attributes need to be exposed in the channel box for each controller. Some controllers may only require rotation, such as FK controls, or some may only require translation, such as a pole vector control for IK-so how do we go about hiding and locking attributes that don't need to be visible or used?

Directly within the channel box, you can right-click on attributes and set attribute states by selecting one of the following:

1. **Locked (or Unlock) Selected**—This will lock the attribute to a specific value and it cannot be modified.
2. **Hide Selected**—This will remove the attribute from displaying in the channel box.
3. **Make Selected Non-Keyable**—This will allow the attribute to be modified but not animate, maintaining a single value will be maintained.

Additionally, there is a dedicated **channel control** interface for further control. Accessible via **Windows > General Editors > Channel Control** or **Channel Box > Edit > Channel Control**. From this interface (Figure 9.7), you can control the state of each attribute of the selected object.

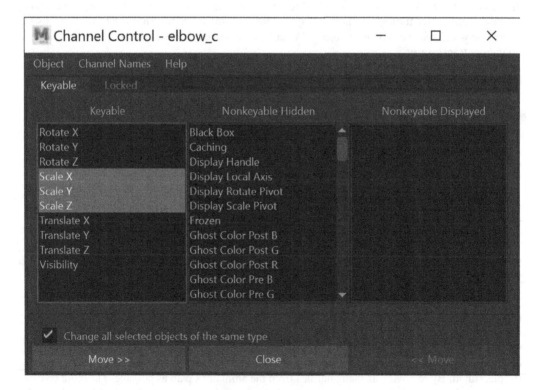

FIGURE 9.7   The channel control box can be used to lock and hide attributes.

Moving an attribute from one column to another defines the specific state. You can easily select all the attributes you want, then press either of the Move buttons to sort them into the appropriate column.

This interface can also be used to make attributes easier to access for the user by displaying hidden attributes within the channel box—a simple example of this would be to expose the Rotate Order attribute for any orientation-based controller. This will save the user several clicks when navigating to the attribute editor to find the attributes.

If you are using parent offset groups for your controllers, be sure to lock the attributes from being modified so the animator does not accidentally break the rig!

9.5.1.2 Hiding Controller History

The channel box displays all the history and information associated with each node. This includes all shapes, any math nodes or constraints, etc. An animator does not need to see this information, and it clutters the channel box.

Each node within Maya has an attribute called "isHistoricallyInteresting"; this flag controls whether the node is useful for construction history. By default, this is set to True, but if we set this to False, then the nodes are hidden from the channel box. This attribute can only be changed via code, as there are no UI elements for it. To change this attribute, you can use the Python command—**cmds.setAttr("nameOfNode.isHistoricallyInteresting", False)** *(Ensure you change the nameOfNode with the name of your node!)*. Included within the additional resources is a tool that will automatically clear all nodes from the selected object's channel box—be sure to give it a try!

Additionally, if the user has the Arnold renderer installed, this will add lots of attributes to every node in the scene. By default, these attributes are set to autokey, which can cause problems with bloated file sizes and slow the scene down due to the density of animation data. If you do not need to use Arnold, disable it in the plugin editor to clear up the channel box further (**Windows > Settings/ Preferences > Plug-in Manager > mtoa.dll unload**).

With these two steps alone, we are able to improve a controller's channel box to only display the relevant data, only attributes that need to be displayed and no additional nodes displayed in the history— Figure 9.8 is much better for the animator!

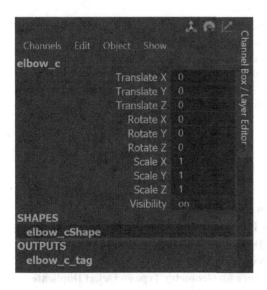

FIGURE 9.8 How a channel box can be cleaned up for the animator.

9.5.2 Controller Node Tag

From Maya 2017 onwards, Autodesk provided a feature that enables riggers to tag their controllers with a controller node—rather than just being a normal node that drives joints, this tag allows for special behaviour and properties to be associated with controllers that add a handful of benefits that will greatly improve the rig's usability. Tagging a controller is very simple. Simply select the controller, then navigate to **Rigging Menu > Control > Tag as Controller**. If successful, you will notice an additional node added to the history list in the channel box for the controller.

The first benefit is that tagged controllers have their own exclusive show/hide option within the show filter (**Display > Show/Hide > Show/Hide Controllers** or **Viewport > Show > Controllers**). This filter supersedes the object type, so if geometry, curves or even surfaces are tagged as a controller, this filter will hide them all without discriminating against a specific object type. This is useful for the user to quickly toggle the visibility of controllers specifically.

The second benefit is that tagged controllers allow for a custom pick walking hierarchy independent of the actual hierarchy. If you are not familiar with pick walking, this is a feature that allows you to utilise the arrow keys on the keyboard to navigate through hierarchies, with up navigating to an object's parent, left and right cycling between siblings and down selecting a child node. Since a control rig can potentially not be hierarchically correct like the skeleton is, pick walking through a control rig could place the animator on nodes they should not touch, such as parent offset groups. Controller tags allow us to set a custom hierarchy to pick walk-through. To determine a parent-child hierarchy, we must first select the child controller, then select the parent controller and then go to **Rigging Menu > Control > Parent Controller**. Now, if you select the child controller and press up on the arrow keys, the parent controller will be selected regardless of hierarchy. Repeat this for all your controllers.

The last, and perhaps the best, is the performance gains given by the control rig if controllers are tagged appropriately. In Maya, if your character does not have any animation on the control rig, Maya will choose not to parallel evaluate the software across multiple CPU threads or do any GPU acceleration. However, if the control is tagged as a controller, Maya now immediately makes Maya parallel evaluate and accelerate any deformation on the GPU when the user manipulates the rig. These performance gains will be felt drastically in your rig.

9.5.3 Shareable Attributes

While the use of an attribute-holder controller is common practice, it is possible to share attributes across multiple controllers via instanced shapes. An instanced shape allows for multiple transform nodes to share the same shape. We can use this to our advantage by adding attributes to the shape, and then the attribute is accessible wherever the shape is instanced. This means in instances such as an IK/FK system, the attribute can be available on every single controller, reducing the number of clicks the animator has to perform to find the relevant attribute and removing the need to have an attribute holder controller.

9.5.3.1 Instanced Shapes

Let's start with the basics of shape instancing before we fully utilise it.

1. Begin by **Enabling Shapes** in the **Display** dropdown in the **Outliner**.
2. Create a standard poly cube—**Maya Shelf > Poly Modelling > Poly Cube**.
3. To instance the shape, we must perform a **Duplicate Special** operation. **Select the poly cube, Maya Menu > Edit > Duplicate Special > Options**.
4. In the Duplicate Special Options, choose **Instance** for **Geometry Type** and select **Duplicate Special**.

5. Expand both **pCube1** and **pCube2** in the **Outliner**, and observe the **pCubeShape**. This object is instanced between the two transform nodes, if one is changed the other will also be changed. Names, attributes and modifications will apply on both sides.

6. **Select the pCubeShape** and add an attribute via **Maya Menu > Modify > Add Attribute**. For this demonstration case, add any variable type.

7. With the attribute on the shape, select one transform node, then the other. Observe the fact that the attribute is available on both nodes! If one attribute is changed, the other also changes. We can use this to our advantage to share attributes across many controllers so they are universally accessible rather than all in one place.

9.5.3.2 *Moving Shapes*

With our instanced shapes created, we may want to move the shape onto a pre-existing node. We cannot simply move the shape node between transforms, we are required to use the Parent command.

1. To use the Parent command, we are required to **select the Shape node first, and then the destination transform node**. The selection order is the source and then the destination.

2. In the **command line**, use the **Parent command** with the **relative flag** and **shape flag** set to **true**.
   a. MEL Long Name—**parent -relative –shape**.
   b. MEL Short Name—**parent -r -s**.
   c. Python Long Name—**cmds.parent(relative=True, shape=True)**.
   d. Python Short Name—**cmds.parent(r=True, s=True)**.

3. The shape will then move to the target node.

9.6 Animation Transfer—Part 2

Continuing from Animation Transfer part 1 in the previous chapter, we will now connect our new control rig to our HumanIK character so we can also transfer animation onto the control rig.

1. Open up the HumanIK interface (**Window > Animation Editors > HumanIK** or press the button ▓ in the top right of the Maya interface).

2. **Select the relevant character** in the **Character** dropdown.

3. Select the **Definition** tab.

4. Click the **Create Custom Rig Mapping** button ▓. This will create a new tab called "**Custom Rig**". The character's HIK name will also be appended by (custom rig).

5. Next, assign your FK controls for your character to the relevant UI elements. Similar to assigning your skeletal joints, simply **select a controller** in the scene, then **right-click the relevant body part** in the HumanIK interface, then click **Assign Selected Effector**. Repeat this process for all body parts displayed in the interface.
   a. When assigning each controller to the relevant body part, ensure you enable or disable **Map Translation** and **Map Rotation** within the **Mapping Controls** section. For controllers that control both translation and rotation, such as the pelvis controller, both are required to be enabled. If the controller only controls rotation, such as an arm, disable the translation setting.

6. Once all controllers are assigned and mapping controls are set up, the control rig definition is complete!

You are now able to load animation data onto the control rig through the same method described in the previous chapter!

It is important to note that, as shown in step 5, we are only setting up FK joints, so this will bake the animation onto the FK controllers only. We would have to copy the FK to IK to use this data on our IK. We will cover how to do this in the scripting chapter.

9.7 File Referencing

Referencing is the process of externally loading additional 3D scenes into your scene without importing the data directly. The additional data will be accessible in the scene without truly storing the data in the file. Since the scenes are externally referenced from other files, this keeps the main scene as lightweight as possible. This process can be utilised for animation purposes—the pipeline would include an animator to reference a control rig in their scene rather than directly working in the control rig scene. Since the control rig is an external reference file, the new scene will only save additions and modifications—meaning only animation is saved into the file. This will keep animation files super lightweight! This process can also be used for referencing sets (scenery or furniture) or even props (weapons or interactable objects). The beauty of the referencing pipeline is that all updates made to external references are automatically updated into the scene too—which is fantastic for control rig or skeleton updates, as these will automatically appear in the animation scenes.

To add a reference to your scene, choose **File > Create Reference (Ctrl + R),** then select your desired file to reference. This will immediately load the file as a reference. To further control your references, navigate to the Reference Editor (**File > Reference Editor**). This window will allow you to add, remove or even reload any reference without re-opening the scene. The reference editor also exposes functionality to view the edits made to a reference (**Right-click a reference > Reference > List Edits**). This will show every attribute modification that has been made in the scene and is useful for debugging any unwanted edits that have been made.

Make sure that whoever animates with your new control rig, whether animators or yourself, uses this pipeline!

9.8 Evaluation

The job isn't done when the control rig is built. The next step is to test, test and test! Rigorously test all features of your control rig to find any bugs or unintended behaviour before you deploy the rig to the rest of the team. Put the rig through all the processes it will be used for: create gameplay loops, animate a cinematic, load data between rigs and then test, test and test again.

Then, once you're satisfied with the rig, expand your testing pool by providing the control rig to others to put it through its paces and provide feedback. Will the control rig meet not only the project's needs but also the needs of the animators? Remember, this control rig is for the animator; it's not for you. This is what they will use every day, so accommodate their needs and iterate based on their feedback. Do not start production on any animations until the control rig has been tested and all users are confident it will meet project and team needs.

Once everyone is happy with the rig, it's time to move to production. While control rigs can stand on their own, their feature set and usability can be expanded with tools; we will discuss tool development in a later chapter.

Be sure to view the files included in the resources to see various demonstrations on how to tackle some of the previously covered topics!

9.9 Exporting Animation

Once there is an animation on your control rig and you want to export your animation into the engine for use within your game, there is an export process we must go through to cleanly get our animation exported. This process is not as simple as File > Export, unfortunately.

Exporting data in the cleanest way possible from Maya is a destructive process, this means we will partially destroy our scene to get our animation data. Due to this destructive nature, I recommend saving your scene before exporting, as well as the utilisation of _**WIP** and _**EXP** variants of your file to denote work in progress and export similar to the skeleton. In the exporting process, an EXP file can be useful for debugging any issues with your exported animation data.

9.9.1 Step 1—Bake Animation

The first step in this process is the baking of our animation. Baking is the process that involves simulating every single frame and storing a keyframe for each of those frames so objects save their correct values. This will also collapse any constraints, connections or driven keys into keyframes so they are only driven by animation.

This step is important because currently within the animation scene, the control rig and its controllers contain all the animation data, but instead, we need this information on the skeleton joints as they are the objects we will export.

1. Select the root joint in the Scene Outliner.
2. Let's bake! (**Edit > Keys > Bake Simulation > ❑**).
3. We will be presented with a Bake Simulation Options window, from this we can customise the options that best suit our needs.
   a. **Hierarchy**; since we have only selected our root joint and we must bake all joints, select **Below** to bake all joints below the selection.
   b. Enable driven channels to ensure all driven keys are baked down.
   c. Disable control points and shapes as they are unnecessary.
   d. Select our bake region; we can either manually enter a time range to bake that duration or bake based on the time slider.
4. Hit the bake button!

9.9.2 Step 2—File Cleanup

We must now clean out the scene of non-animation export assets; this includes our control rig and geometry, leaving only the joints behind. This destruction is very straightforward.

1. Simply select the geometry group, control rig group and any other nodes from within the **Scene Outliner** except the root joint.
2. Press the **Delete** key on your keyboard.

9.9.3 Step 3—FBX Export

With our joints baked and the scene cleaned, we can now export!

1. To start, let's export via **File > Export All**
2. A dialogue will open—Export to a path consistent with your animation file, so they can be found together. Name the file accordingly, and select FBX as the file format.

3. Press **Export All**, once defined.

4. An FBX Export Dialogue interface will appear—this controls various parameters for which components to export and convert from your scene.

   a. A good starting point with the FBX settings is to select the **Preset - Autodesk Media & Entertainment** at the top. We can create our own presets too!

   b. Expand and Enable **Animation**.

      i.   Disable **Bake Animation**, as we have already cleanly baked.

      ii. Enable **Deformed Models**, **Skins** and **Blendshapes**.

   c. Expand and Enable **Constraints** and **Skeletal Definitions**.

   d. While not necessary for animation data, enabling **Cameras** will be beneficial if you export camera animation.

   e. Be sure to save your preset for the future! (**Edit > Save Preset**).

   f. Press **Export**, this will create a new FBX animation file ready for the engine. We will continue this integration later.

9.10 Maya Game Exporter

Now that we understand how to get a clean bake through manual means, let's explore **Maya's Game Exporter** which can be used to export animations automatically with a nice interface. The Game Exporter is a built-in Maya plugin that is enabled by default and can be accessed via the **Maya Menu > File > Game Exporter.** If the option is not available, you must first enable the plugin **Maya Menu > Windows > Settings/Preferences > Plug-in Manager >** Search for **gameFbxExporter.mll.**

Navigate to the **Animation Clips** tab to view the toolkit for exporting animation data from your scenes. From this window, we are able to add and batch export multiple animation clips from a single scene, with each clip having a bespoke name, start frame and end frame. We must define a shared path for all the files to export. By default, the game exporter will export all assets into the scene and bake down the animation, however, we only require joints to export from our scenes. We can achieve this by changing the Export All option to Export Object Set. With this choice, we can export a specific object set. I recommend adding a set that contains only joints to your control rig file by selecting the joints. Maya Menu > Create > Sets > Set. We can save the Game Exporter settings via the top option's preset saver. Press the drop-down with Anim Default on it and choose New Anim Default to save your current export presets.

10

Introduction to Unreal Engine 5

Epic Games' Unreal Engine 5 is the game engine of choice—this application is where all our content will be collated and connected together with gameplay logic (Figure 10.1). Just like with Maya, let's introduce ourselves to Unreal to make sure we are all on the same page, as there are some quirks with Unreal's workflow that may be unfamiliar to a few. Let's jump in.

10.1 Interface

10.1.1 Viewport

The viewport is your window into the world of Unreal! Since Unreal is a game engine, it comes with some very intuitive methods of exploring your world in the viewport with game-like controls—while holding right-click, the WASD keys will navigate left, forward, right and back, respectively, with mouse movement allowing for view rotation similar to a first-person game. Additionally, Q and E will also lower or elevate your camera view, and the mouse wheel will zoom in and out.

In the top left of the viewport (Figure 10.2) is the viewport options icon, followed by a perspective switcher, a view mode switcher and a show filter. The viewport options include options to modify the viewport's current field of view, and there is even a screenshot tool. The perspective option can toggle between orthographic and perspective rendering. Additionally, there is a setting for enabling a cinematic viewport, which will letterbox the viewport and expose tools to add grids and action-safe

FIGURE 10.1 The Unreal Engine interface.

DOI: 10.1201/9781003263258-10

FIGURE 10.2   The viewport tools for changing perspective, view mode or filter.

areas. The view mode switcher can be used to change the rendering style, whether you want to see the game in wireframe or unlit—you can do it here! The show filter allows the user to toggle flags for rendering, so whole categories can be turned on or off at will.

Unreal's viewport has a concept called "Game Mode"; this can be toggled on and off with **G** or via the Viewport Options icon in the top left of the viewport. This mode toggles the viewing experience that the end user will see. Some objects in Unreal are visible when not in game mode, such as the player start, VFX particle emitter locations or even trigger volumes—once you move to game mode, these all stop rendering.

10.1.2 Details Panel

The details panel (Figure 10.3) is where you will find context-sensitive information about the object you have selected in your scene: each component, variable, transform and even function can be accessed via the details panel for an object. Think of this like the attribute editor or channel box from Maya.

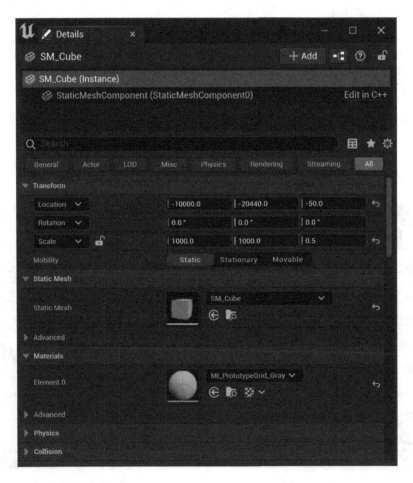

FIGURE 10.3   The details panel for Unreal.

10.1.3 Scene Outliner

The scene outliner window is the list and browser of all the contents present within the current open level; this does not include all content in the game, only the current level! Each mesh, VFX and blueprint will all show up in this list if they are present within the level. The scene outliner can be neatly organised into groups to help categorise the content.

When adding new content to the scene, it will always be added to the root directory, but if you are working with folders, this can be tedious to keep doing; fortunately, you are able to set a particular folder in the Scene Outliner to be your **"Current Folder."** You can do this by **Right-Clicking on the folder in the Scene Outliner**, and click **"Make Current Folder."** From this point onward, all new content added to the scene will populate in that folder! Very useful!

10.1.4 Content Browser

The content browser is the main point of access to explore and modify all content in the project; imagine the scene outliner, but project-wise instead of level-specific. The browser is your replacement for Windows File Explorer, but for your project's files.

10.2 Unreal Engine Workflow

Before we dive too deep into Unreal, there are a few workflow quirks with Unreal's workflow that you should understand.

10.2.1 UAsset Content

All data that is created or imported into the Unreal Engine is converted into a proprietary file type known as UAsset (Unreal Asset). This means that all content within the engine exists as this file type. While not all engines operate in this manner, it is prudent to be aware that your data has been converted into another format, and the file's new form cannot be simply edited in File Explorer in this new format since it is binary data. The Unreal editor does provide methods for exporting data from the UAsset format back to its native intermediate format, which is extremely useful (**Right Click The Asset > Export**).

Non-UAsset files will not be displayed in Unreal's content browser either—because of this, it is wise to keep editor content and source files in two different directories; this includes working files (.MA, .MB and .PSD) and intermediate files (.FBX, .OBJ and .TGA).

10.2.2 UAsset Redirectors

Moving content around in Unreal isn't as straightforward as one may think either. UAssets are connected together through chains of references, with each file storing where each connected file lives, creating a giant spider web of interconnected files; if one link breaks, it can all fall apart. When you move a file in the editor, the file is not truly moved. This is because upon moving, the content is moved to its new location as intended, but a new file is left in the original file's place. This new file is called a "redirector." Since each connected file remembers where the other file lives, these redirectors act as relays to tell the connected file where the moved content is, without having to change connected files.

By default, redirectors are hidden in Unreal's content browser, but they can be made visible via the Show Redirectors filter. (**Content Browser > Filter > Other Filters > Show Redirectors**). If you are not aware of redirectors and have the visibility filter disabled, the engine can behave as if it has phantom folders that cannot be deleted and appear empty.

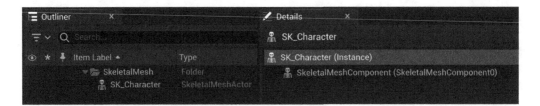

FIGURE 10.4 A skeletal mesh asset in the scene becomes a skeletal mesh actor with a skeletal mesh component.

You can "fix" a redirector simply by right-clicking the redirector asset and clicking "fix up" or "fix up redirectors" by right-clicking a folder—this will then modify all connected content to know about the new location and remove the redirector.

Moving content outside the editor in the Windows File Explorer is strictly forbidden. Do not do this. This will break all content references to the files moved.

10.2.3 Unreal Engine Terminology

While there is a wide variety of Unreal-specific terminology, there are four primary distinctions between **assets** that we must be aware of—**Asset, Actor, Component** and **Pawn.**

An **asset** is essentially a file; it is the object type you will find in your content browser. An asset can be used inside other assets, such as a material asset applied to a skeletal mesh, or even within the scene.

An **Actor** is a scene object that contains components. When an asset is used within the scene, it creates an actor that has a component of the asset you used. For example, if you add a skeletal mesh to the scene, you will find the asset type is, in fact, a *Skeletal Mesh Actor,* not a *Skeletal Mesh*, and the details panel will reveal a SkeletalMesh component attached (Figure 10.4). Blueprints (BP) can also be made as an Actor type, which is basically an empty container for components.

A **Component** is a sub-object of an Actor that contains specific functionality. Some components can be added that are assets, such as static meshes, skeletal mesh or even other BP. There are a variety of components that can be added, from lights to collision volumes or even AI logic.

Finally, a **Pawn** is a controllable actor—whether it's controlled by player input or AI. It's essentially an actor with extra behaviour attached for player or AI input.

10.3 Blueprints

BP sit at the heart of Unreal, they are a node-based scripting tool that allows artists to create gameplay functions and behaviour without touching a single line of code. Entire games can be made within BP, as long as they are created efficiently. Different asset types can be added to BP as components, such as models and lights—this allows you to create characters, weapons, vehicles or environmental pieces with logic. BP are impressively powerful, and there is very little you cannot achieve with them—all the standard tools and processes that you would expect from a code language are all accessible in BP. They can be used to create logic, with programming-like behaviour—functions, events on a timer, etc.

10.3.1 Event Graph

The event graph of a blueprint is the blank canvas on which you will begin to script your logic and functionality (Figure 10.5). By default, BP contain a single Event Graph, but multiple graphs or even collapsed graphs can be made to organise portions of the Event Graph, the latter acts similarly to a

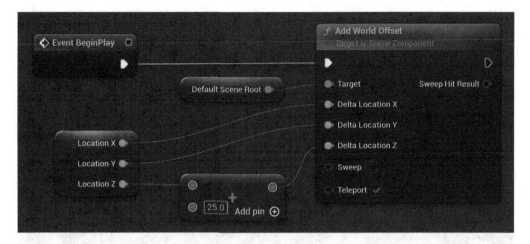

FIGURE 10.5 Event graph of a Blueprint, featuring nodes connected to the begin play event.

folder or group. To create a new event graph, simply click the **+** icon in the **My Blueprint** panel to get a new canvas. Existing nodes can be collapsed into a sub-graph by **selecting the nodes, right-clicking and selecting Collapse Nodes**.

Nodes can be easily added to the event graph by **right-clicking** in any blank space; this will bring up a context-sensitive window providing you with all the available nodes you can generate. Nodes are objects that can have a variety of behaviours, from a function call to a variable setting or reading or input detection.

Each node (Figure 10.6) consists of a variety of pins; the left-hand side pins are **Input Pins**, and the opposite sides are **Output pins**. The top pin on either side is the **Execution Pin**; these pins are connected to one another to create a flow of execution between nodes, determining when they get activated. All other pins are data pins; these can carry different types of information into or out of a node, whether that's a number or a reference.

Nodes do not execute simultaneously within Blueprint; unlike in Maya, where everything happens in parallel to one another, Unreal differs in the fact that there is an execution order—certain logic triggers before others. The execution flow is shown by the white execution wires that connect from

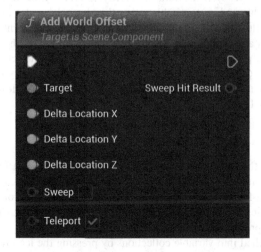

FIGURE 10.6 An example node featuring input and output pins.

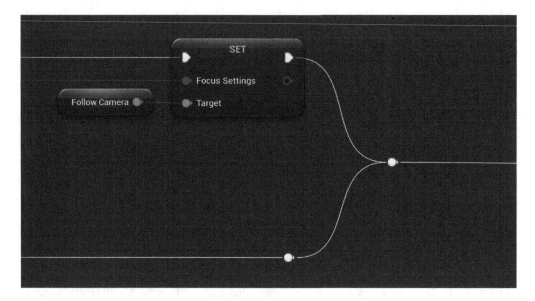

FIGURE 10.7   Re-route nodes for execution wires.

node to node, naturally flowing from left to right in the direction of the connected pin's arrow. This is wise to keep in mind if building logic where one piece of the system drives another, that system needs to be calculated before the driven component.

For organisation purposes, you can employ reroute nodes along your execution and data wires - **by double clicking on the wire**, a reroute node will be generated, allowing you to control the wire's path and reducing the spaghettification of the blueprint nodes (Figure 10.7).

A shortcut to remember is the **Q key with nodes selected**; this will vertically align all selected nodes so they neatly line up. Incredibly useful for organising your nodes!

10.3.2 Functions

Just like within code; the BP system offers the ability to create functions—these are mini-Event Graphs that can be reusable and customisable rather than bespoke nodes for identical systems over and over again. Once built, a function is accessible like a normal Blueprint node and can be called upon demand, with input and output pins at your disposal. From within the **My Blueprint** window, functions can be made by pressing the **+ icon** on the functions tab. Once created, choose a name for your function (*Remember CamelCase or snake_case!*) and begin building your logic. **Selecting your function**, then navigating to the **Details panel** will expose the ability to **add Input and Output pins** to your functions (Figure 10.8).

10.3.3 Variables

Variables are containers that hold data or references to other objects, just like in code, they can be a single piece of data or multiple piece in an array, set or map. The data can vary from float values containing numbers, transformation values or just a simple boolean (true or false). Variables can be used to maintain properties of a blueprint, such as keeping track of a system over gameplay, such as, health which could be represented as a number (Figure 10.9).

Variables can be switched into variable collections by pressing the icon next to the variable type; this will switch between single, list, set and dictionary (Figure 10.10).

FIGURE 10.8 The creation of input or output variables from a function.

FIGURE 10.9 Various variable types, with different colours denoting different variable types.

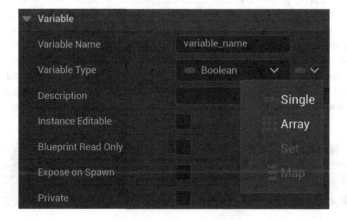

FIGURE 10.10 The interface button to switch a variable between a single, array, set or map.

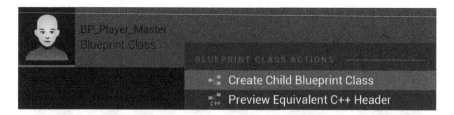

FIGURE 10.11 Right-click a blueprint to find the option to create a child Blueprint.

10.3.4 Events

Blueprint Events are similar to Functions but are called based on gameplay events rather than called by proceeding gameplay logic. These events could be anything from the game starting, input being registered, entering a trigger volume or any custom event determined by us. Two of the most common events, which are in every blueprint by default, are **Begin Play** and **Event Tick**. Begin Play is an event that is triggered when the game starts or when a new blueprint is loaded in a level—this is particularly useful for any setup logic that you may need to do. Event tick is another event that runs on every tick of the game, meaning it perpetually runs. This event has a high potential to be misused and can very easily be abused, causing poor performance in your games. This is because the event is constantly triggered dozens of times a second, if a lot of logic is tied to this, then it can lead to performance slowdown. These can all be added to the blueprint via the right-click context-sensitive menu. While there are many other types of events, you can create your very own Custom Event by accessing the right-click context sensitive menu and typing "Create Custom Event." This will create a custom event node that you can call just like a function.

10.3.5 Inheritance

The structure of BP allows for an inheritance parent -> child structure; this pyramid structure allows for a parent class to have core functionality that all children inherit, but then the children can have their own unique functionality to differ from the siblings. These child BP can even have their children's BP too. For example, imagine you have a game with multiple playable characters, you can create a master blueprint that has the core foundations that all characters will share; movement systems, inventory, animation systems, etc. Each character may have their own special ability, so instead of the master blueprint including this functionality, causing all characters to have it active at all times, instead the functionality is only added to a child blueprint of the master one.

To create a child blueprint, press the Create Child Blueprint Class from the right-click menu as shown in Figure 10.11. This child blueprint will have access to all the same functions, variables—it behaves as the same graph that you can build and expand on. Not only can you add new functionality, but you can also expand on previous implementations of functions or events.

We can override existing functions via the dropdown menu in the functions category of My Blueprint window, as shown in Figure 10.12. Functions will now have an additional Parent node (Figure 10.13); this node executes the functionality from the parent function. We can choose to disconnect this so the parent function does not execute, or we can make it execute and add additional functionality.

FIGURE 10.12 A hidden dropdown labelled Override will only appear when hovering over the Functions tab.

FIGURE 10.13 A function, and its parent function call.

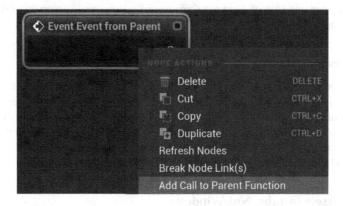

FIGURE 10.14 Add Call to Parent Function command accessible via the right-click menu.

This same setup applies to events, however, we need to manually create the Parent node by pressing the **Add Call to Parent Function** button from the right-click menu on an event (Figure 10.14).

10.3.6 Blueprint Casting

Blueprint casting is a method to communicate from one blueprint to another with exposed access to a blueprint's entire suite of functionality. If you attempt to access a reference to the actor, you will find limited exposed functionality, and you will not be able to call functions or set variables found on that blueprint (Figure 10.15).

For each type of Blueprint there is a unique cast node, and casts have to be performed targeting that specific Blueprint class—there is no universal cast. In our example, we are attempting to acquire the animation Blueprint asset from the Get Anim Instance node, our Blueprint is called ABP_Master, so we must use the Cast To ABP_Master node (Figure 10.16).

FIGURE 10.15 A failed attempt to find the relevant animation blueprint's values.

FIGURE 10.16 Casting to the ABP class allows for the blueprint's values and functions to be accessed.

Performing a cast to the correct class will convert the reference into the appropriate class for access; if the cast is successful and the input actor reference is of the type of the casted class, then all access is exposed.

10.4 Useful Editor Settings

Before we dive deeper into Unreal, here are some useful settings you can apply to your editor to get the most out of your workflow.

10.4.1 Load Level at Startup

When opening a project in Unreal, it will default to opening what the project has set as its "Editor Startup Map"—this is a single level set in the Maps & Modes section in the project settings. While this can be customised to your liking, with differing levels for the editor versus the game, there is an additional editor setting that will store the last level you were in and reopen that on startup. This option can be found in—**Editor Preferences > General > Loading & Saving > Load Level At Startup > Last Opened** (Figure 10.17).

10.4.2 Open Assets in Tabs, Not Windows

Another useful usability option is to enable Unreal to open new assets in docked tabs instead of the default option, which is to open in a new window, which can cause content to be lost in layers of multiple windows and can become frustrating. There is an option to have all content open in tabs instead. You can set this to be automatic within **Editor Preferences > General > Appearance > User Interface > Asset Editor Open Location > Main Window.**

10.4.3 Show Frame Rate and Memory

While developing, it may be useful to know the current frame rate and memory usage of your editor and scene. Within editor preferences, you can enable this; **Editor Preferences > General > Performance > Show Frame Rate and Memory**. Once enabled, the FPS, memory allocation, object count and stalls will be detailed in the top right of the Unreal interface (Figure 10.18). Keep in mind that the framerate and memory usage will not be 1:1 with the expected frame rate and memory usage of your cooked builds, as the editor itself has some overheads.

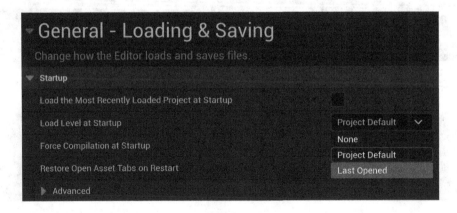

FIGURE 10.17   Load level at Startup option in the editor preferences.

FPS: 120.1 / 8.3 ms   Mem: 6,482.51 mb   Objs: 117,249   Stalls: 6

FIGURE 10.18   Editor frame rate and memory allocation at the top of the Unreal editor.

10.5 Customising Your Engine's Inis

Getting the most out of your editor does not stop at editor preferences; you can customise your editor on an ini level. Ini (.ini) is a configuration file type that is used in many programmes, Unreal uses these extensively to customise all aspects of the editor, from inputs to rendering settings to even editor defaults. I find it particularly useful to customise the ini files to set various default presets for all users of the editor. For example, when importing a skeletal mesh into Unreal, there are various options that can be set and often these defaults need to be changed. From within the ini files of Unreal, you can customise what these defaults are, so you can apply settings that will catch 90% of the situations so they do not have to be set over and over again, speeding up the workflow for all users of the editor.

We will cover a variety of useful commands you can utilise in your project ini!

10.5.1 BaseEditorPerProjectUserSettings

Within the **Engine/Config/BaseEditorPerProjectUserSettings.ini** resides a plethora of editor settings; here we find and alter the settings to our liking. Under the **/Script/UnrealEd.Fbx** category, include the settings for when importing skeletal meshes and art into the engine (Figure 10.19).

```
bImportMaterials=False
bImportTextures=False
bReorderMaterialToFbxOrder=True
NormalImportMethod=FBXNIM_ImportNormals
bUpdateSkeletonReferencePose=True
bUseT0AsRefPose=True
bImportMeshesInBoneHierarchy=False
bImportCustomAttribute=True
bDeleteExistingCustomAttributeCurves=True
bDeleteExistingMorphTargetCurves=True
bDoNotImportCurveWithZero=False
```

10.6 Unreal Usability Tips and Tricks

10.6.1 Coloured Folders

We can add a splash of colour to our content browser's folders via the Set Colour tool (**Right-click a folder > Set Colour**). This can help your brain associate a specific folder with a specific colour, making it easier to find. This coloured folder approach is demonstrated in Figure 10.20.

10.6.2 Reload Content

Have you ever found yourself too deep into modifying a file and realised you need to go back? Well, you're in luck, as Unreal has a function to reload your content to its last saved state, undoing any modifications you have made to it; **Right-Click The Asset In Content Browser > Asset Actions > Reload**.

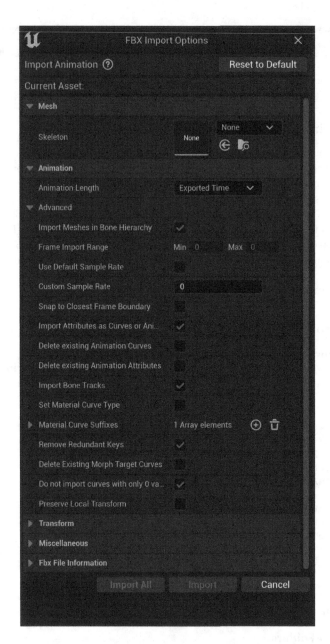

FIGURE 10.19   The FBX import dialogue default options can be changed via the ini settings.

FIGURE 10.20   An example of coloured folders in the editor.

10.6.3 Blueprint Wire Tips

Create Node From Wire—While dragging a wire in Unreal, hold **Ctrl** then **release the left mouse button** to be prompted with the option to create a node.

Detach & Drag Wire Pin—Ctrl + drag a connection to detach it.

Reroute Nodes—Double-click a wire to add a re router node; useful for organisation!

Highlight Wire—Hold Shift and click a wire to highlight it.

Connect Pins Without A Dragging—Shift-click two pins to have them connect!

Disconnect Wire—Hold Alt and click a pin to disconnect it.

Delete Node Keep Connection—Hold Shift & Delete any node to maintain the connections on either side.

10.6.4 Blueprint Variable Shortcuts

When dragging variables into your Blueprint graph, you will be prompted with a window to pick between the Get or Set nodes. Did you know that when dragging, if you press **CTRL** prior to the release of the left mouse button, the Get node will spawn or if you press **ALT** instead, it will spawn the Set node! (Figure 10.21).

10.6.5 Bulk Edit Assets

If you are fed up with going through multiple instances of the same file type to change a value over and over again? Be fed up no more with the Bulk Edit via Property Matrix tool; with this tool, you can modify the values of multiple assets at once—if they are of the same type (texture, animation, skeletal mesh, etc.).

To open the Bulk Edit via Property Matrix.

1. Select all assets you wish to modify in the Content Browser by **Shift + Left Mouse** clicking each asset.
2. **Right-click > Asset Actions > Advanced > Bulk Edit Via Property Matrix**.
3. The property matrix interface will open, navigate to the **Display panel** on the right side and expand each of the tabs to find your chosen variable to change.

10.6.6 Slomo

Entering the slomo command followed by a number can be used to change the simulation speed of the world. The preceding number is a multiplier for the simulation speed, where 1 is normal, 0.25 is quarter speed and 10 is ten times the speed. To enter the command, **press tilda ` while playing in editor**, then enter slomo followed by a number such as **slomo 0.2**, then press **enter**.

The utilisation of slomo into a decimal place can be a great technique to analyse animation graphs or visuals; since they can play back at a slower rate than intended, you will be able to see blending

FIGURE 10.21   The get/set variable will result in one of the two nodes being created.

issues or mistakes much easier. Alternatively, utilise slomo at a faster speed, to save time by speeding up the game's simulation, everything happens faster!

10.6.7 ShowDebug ANIMATION

Activating the ShowDebug ANIMATION command will display an array of telemetry on the screen with statistics covering which animation is playing, what animGraph nodes are active, what additives are running, which curves are active, their value and much much more. Activate by pressing via Tilda, then entering ShowDebug ANIMATION, then press enter!

11

Unreal—The Skeleton Setup

11.1 Import Skeleton FBX

Let's get our previously exported character skeleton FBX integrated into Unreal.

1. **Open the Content Browser** in your Unreal project.
2. **Navigate to or create a folder directory for your character's skeleton**. As always, keep organised and don't have your assets scattered around your project, keep assets and asset types consolidated.
3. **Press the IMPORT button** at the top of the Content Browser interface.
4. A dialogue window will pop up; **navigate to and select your skeleton's FBX file** in the file browser, and then press Open.
5. The FBX Import Options window will appear.
   a. **Enable** the **Mesh > Skeletal Mesh** option.
   b. **Enable** the **Mesh > Import Mesh** option.
   c. Set **Mesh > Import Content-Type** to **Geometry and Skinning**.
   d. **Mesh > Skeleton**
      i. **Leave this blank for a new skeleton to be created**.
      ii. If sharing a skeleton, pick the existing skeleton.
         A. Only choose this option if the skeleton hierarchies are shared; you cannot have misordered or differing hierarchies for skeleton sharing. A perfect example of this would be multiple human characters; they can all share a skeleton, but a spider could not share it. We will cover skeleton sharing in more detail.
   e. **Disable Animations > Import Animations**—We will be importing animations separately later, there will be no animations in our FBX.
   f. Expand the **Mesh > Advanced Tab**
      i. **Enable Update Skeleton Reference Pose**
         A. This option updates the Skeleton's reference pose (bind pose); although we are creating a brand new skeletal asset, enabling this option will ensure it applies every time the character is updated in case joints move.
      ii. **Enable Use T0 As Ref Pose**
         A. Enabling this option will use frame 0 as the reference pose; this is to be used in conjunction with the previous setting.
      iii. **Optional Import Morph Targets**
         A. If the character mesh utilises blendshapes or morph targets, then enable this setting; otherwise, keep it disabled.

DOI: 10.1201/9781003263258-11

iv. **Optional Import Mesh LODs**

    A. If the character mesh includes Level of Detail meshes, enable this option. If we do not, disable it and we will manually re-enable it later.

v. **Normal Import Method—Import Normals**

    A. By default this option is set to Compute Normals, this must be changed to Import Normals as we want to preserve the artist's work and model normals and not recompute them.

vi. **Optional Create Physics Asset**

    A. With this option enabled, a physics asset will be automatically generated for the character mesh. If it is disabled, you can manually create a physics asset.

g. Under the Materials, it is optional to disable Texture and Material imports; I would recommend disabling these options and setting up the materials yourself. To disable:

i. **Material Import Method - Do Not Create Material**

ii. **Disable Import Textures**

h. Once all the settings are set; select **Import**

i. *Reminder; you can set the default the FBX dialogue settings in the Engine/Config/ BaseEditorPerProjectUserSettings.ini with options like Use T0 As Ref Pose being bUseT0AsRefPose=True*

6. Upon import, it will create three different files.

a. **A skeleton asset (*SKEL_*)**

i. Metadata parent asset for the structure.

b. **A skeletal mesh asset (*SKM_*)**

i. Asset containing geometry, transforms and skinning information. This is the asset we will use for the character going forward.

c. **A physics asset (*PHYS_*)**

i. Physics-based asset used to create a simplified primitive version of the character that can be used for simulations, dynamics or collision.

7. Make sure to save each asset!

11.2 Character Assets

With our skeleton FBX imported, Unreal will generate three different asset types that will unify to create your character in real time. The three assets are a **Skeleton**, **Skeletal Mesh** and finally a **Physics Asset** (Figure 11.1). The character you build in your DCC is split into the two former asset types, and the Physics Asset is an additional optional asset.

11.2.1 Skeleton Asset

A skeleton is the foundation of the character; every other asset associated with the skeleton is linked to this asset, which means all animation sequences to animation BP are interconnected to this skeleton. A skeleton is essentially a metadata asset containing all the data for a character. This data includes the skeletal hierarchy structure, how animation data is applied to that hierarchy, as well as any animation curves, notifies or sockets associated with a character. Due to this, it is a very important but delicate file that must be looked after and dealt with care. If this asset breaks or a setting is incorrectly applied, this can cause knock-on effects to every single asset associated with the skeleton. So be careful with it and test any changes thoroughly!

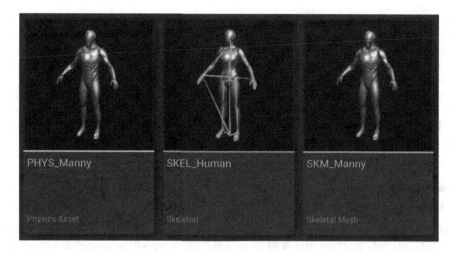

FIGURE 11.1   The three skeleton uassets: physics asset (left), skeleton (middle), and skeletal mesh (right).

Unlike a DCC skeleton, an Unreal skeleton asset does not contain joint transforms or any geometry or skinning data—this data is stored in the skeletal mesh asset. A skeleton can be shared between multiple skeletal meshes that share a matching hierarchy, including fewer or more joints, while a skeletal mesh only has a single skeleton assignment. Skeleton assets are signified by the colour light blue.

While in the Skeleton asset, the Unreal Menu > Window has a plethora of additional windows for accessing all the additional information for this skeleton. The Animation Notifies, Anim Curves, Anim Slot Manager and Animation Data Modifier windows each can be used to view a list of every item from their respective category in a nice list; these windows can also be used to clear out any old curves or notifies from every single associated animation.

11.2.2 Skeletal Mesh Asset

The skeletal mesh asset is where you will get the most direct translation between your FBX character and engine. The skeletal mesh as an asset contains your entire character's render geometry, joint transformations, skinning data, material assignments, level of detail assets and settings, as well as any mesh-specific settings such as physics asset assignment or even cloth settings. Multiple skeletal meshes can be associated with a single Skeleton asset as long as they share identical joint hierarchies. A skeletal mesh asset is signified by a purple asset type.

Unlike in your DCC, where the geometry of your character can be divided up however you want, be that in groups or a single model—Unreal divides polygon meshes up by material assignment, with each material being an individual "element" for the polygons associated with it. This is important to consider, as the more elements your character has, the more computationally expensive it is. Additionally, if any properties are required to be applied to a character, such as making a component disappear or applying cloth properties, they are required to be applied on a per-element basis—so set up your materials in your DCC appropriately.

11.2.3 Physics Asset

The physics asset is the third and optional asset that is created upon a skeletal mesh import. If you opted not to generate a physics asset, they can be manually created by **right-clicking on the Skeletal Mesh > Create > Physics Assign.** The physics asset can be used for runtime simulation behaviour; from within, you can configure the physical properties and collision volumes that can be assigned to joints in your skeletal mesh. While only a single physics asset can be assigned to the skeletal mesh, multiple physics assets can be used through alternative means, such as a cloth collision asset, or within the animation graph via a rigid body node. Physics assets are identified by an orange asset.

A common use case for a physics asset would be for run-time ragdolls, but they can also be configured for use of collision volumes for cloth or even real-time dynamics such as earrings or ponytail hair. While these assets are synonymous with "physics," their use extends beyond just that—they are used in rendering too.

11.3 Import Animation FBX

Importing an animation FBX is a very similar process; however, this time the engine will detect that our FBX file only contains joints and animation data, so we will be prompted with a different set of options.

1. **Open the Content Browser** in your Unreal project.
2. **Create a folder directory for your character's animations**.
3. **Press the IMPORT button** at the top of the Content Browser interface.
4. A dialogue window will pop up; **navigate to and select your animation FBX file** in the file browser and then press Open.
5. The FBX Import Options window will appear.
   a. **Skeleton - Choose your character's skeleton asset**
   b. **Expand the Advanced Category—**
      i. **Enable Import Attributes as Curves or Animation Attributes**
         A. Enabling this option will bring any extra float attributes that are present in the joints FBX data through into Unreal.
      ii. **Enable Delete Existing Animation Curves**
         A. This option will only affect re-imports, not newly authored files. Enabling this file will delete any pre-existing animation curves in the file prior to import so we get a clean import and only the latest data.
      iii. **Enable Delete Existing Animation Attributes**
         A. This option will only affect re-imports, not newly authored files. Enabling this file will delete any pre-existing animation attributes in the file prior to import so we get a clean import and only the latest data.
      iv. **Enable Import Bone Tracks**
         A. When enabled this option will ensure all joint animation data is imported and used. Only disable this option if you wish to have an animation containing only animation curves.
      v. **Enable Remove Redundant Keys**
         A. This option only affects the animation curves, when enabled it will remove redundant keys, such as several adjacent keys that are all the same value.
      vi. **Enable Delete Existing Morph Target Curves**
         A. This option will only affect re-imports, not newly authored files. Enabling this file will delete any pre-existing morph target data in the file prior to import so we get a clean import and only the latest data.

    vii. **Enable Do not import curves with only 0 value**

        A. If enabled this option will prevent any curves that are 0 throughout the entire animation from being imported. I recommend enabling this option as when a curve is absent the value is 0 and thus does not require the curve to be present.

   c. **Select Import**—An AnimSequence asset will be created, with a name matching the source FBX file.

11.4 Animation Assets

Inside Unreal, animation data comes in a variety of formats with various functions inside them; however, at their core, they all derive from a core animation asset. Animation assets are pure animation—it contains no mesh, no joints; it is just a series of bone transformation tracks and float curves for animation attributes or morph targets. This series of data are evaluated over time and showcased as an animation. AnimSequences are signified by a green asset colour.

AnimSequences are the asset types produced when importing an animation into Unreal and associating it with a skeleton—this will be the bread and butter of animation in Unreal, and this is the type of asset your idle, or locomotion loops would be. Additionally, an animation asset can contain additional metadata and values such as float curve values, and animation notifies at particular times. The animation data itself is stored inside animation tracks. To view all tracks contained in a sequence, navigate to the Details Panel within the AnimSequence and expand the dropdown for **Track Names** and **Compressed Track Names**. The more tracks an animation contains, the larger its disk and memory footprint, it also increases the computation expense to evaluate the animation at runtime. You can reduce the number of tracks by not including joints where necessary.

11.4.1 Animation Notifies

Animation Notifies are one of the metadata types stored inside of an animation sequence—they are in effect, an animation frame event to trigger logic. An example notify is shown in Figure 11.2. There are several different types of notify that have varying behaviour and functions; some are used for sound triggers, some for particles, but for animation, we can use skeleton notifies and sync markers to trigger events in our animation BP. We will cover how these triggers work in the animation BP section. There is an alternate type of a notify which exists over time, rather than in a single frame called a Notify State. The notify state connects to an external BP asset, where we can place logic on distinct Start, Middle and End events. The start and end events trigger at their respective times, but the middle component acts like a tick event, constantly evaluating every frame while the state is active in the animation.

Animation notifies are stored on the skeleton and can be found in the Animation Notifies window (**Skeleton Asset > Windows > Animation Notifies**).

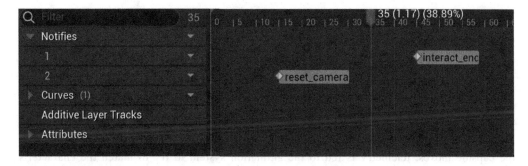

FIGURE 11.2 Animation notify track in the animation sequence asset.

FIGURE 11.3 Animation curves and their type options.

11.4.2 Animation Curves

Animation curves are additional floating-point values that reside within your animation asset—they are 2D curves with their Y-axis being the user-set value and the X-axis being time. Curves can be authored in your animation sequence, but they can also be created in your DCC with the animation and brought directly into the FBX. If a float attribute is connected to a joint, the attribute and its value will be brought into the engine for you to utilise. Animation curves are blended when animations are blended with matching curves, but if the curve is missing from the animation, it will blend to 0. Curves can be queried directly at run-time; this allows for the outputted value to be used within gameplay logic however you choose, whether that's to change the deformation of the mesh with a morph target, change a material property through a material curve or even just plug the float value into a gameplay variable. These are very useful tools.

Inside the skeleton asset, the **Anim Curves** window details each curve associated with the skeleton (**Skeleton Asset > Windows > Anim Curves**, shown in Figure 11.3). There is a Type column, which can add additional functionality to the curve. These two icons indicate whether the curves are a Morph Target curve or a Material curve; if neither of these are enabled, the curve will just evaluate as normal. Enabling the curve as a Morph Target will then directly connect the curve value to a Morph Target (blendshape) of the same name. Enabling the curve as a Material curve will allow the curve to be directly connected to a material shader, allowing for any parameter to be driven by the animation curve, such as connecting to a face material to fade in a wrinkle material when a particular expression is pulled. For optimisation purposes, curves can also be assigned to specific joints, so that when those joints are optimised to a certain level of detail, the curve stops evaluating too. To properly remove curves from your character, you must delete them from the Skeleton.

11.4.3 Root Motion

Root motion is the technique of extracting animation from the root joint of a skeleton, which can then be applied to a character to move it through the world. This is useful for gameplay if you desire an animation-driven action or movement that travels through space, utilising root motion would ensure accurate distances are travelled for the playing animation.

A common method of movement in games is physics-driven movement, where a capsule slides around the game world like an ice cube. A character is then attached to this capsule, then as the capsule moves, telemetry is fed to the animation system to try to match the character's movements with what the capsule is doing. If the capsule is static, the character will idle; if it's moving forward, it will play a run cycle. An inherent problem that occurs with this method, is that if the animations do not match the movement, it can cause issues like feet sliding where the animation doesn't correspond to the capsule movements. There are solutions to fix this problem, such as stride warping or distance matching, but these require additional configuration to set up. Root motion is an alternative way of moving a character that negates this problem entirely since the capsule is moved by the animation directly, requiring no additional matching to occur. However, this benefit comes with a trade-off, as a large granularity of data coverage is needed for every type of movement, since only movements in the root motion can be applied to the character; if it's not there—it cannot do it. This can require a vast amount of data to cover all possible orientations or movements. Since root motion can be enabled on a per-animation asset basis, you can opt to create a hybrid physics and root motion movement model that uses the best of both worlds.

It's always important to weigh up the pros and cons of root motion use, as it is not a one-size-fits-all use case for games. The fidelity trade-off comes down to responsiveness versus fidelity.

11.4.4 Additive Animation

Additive animations are animations that modify an underlying animation by adding animation instead of replacing it. Additive animations are created by subtracting one animation from another; the remainder is the additive animation that can be applied. For example, if the first animation is a static character pose and the second animation is that static pose but the character's left arm waves, the delta between those two poses is an animation that isolates just the wave on the right arm. This wave could then be added on top of any other animation—whether the character is walking, idling or jumping, the wave could be applied additively at any point. Additive animations are great for any post-process system that needs to be applied after other systems, such as a character's head looking around on top of a locomotion system or even a generic noise animation that can be applied to on everything to bring variety into animations.

You must define an AnimSequence as an additive within the asset's details panel—once it is an additive, it can no longer be used as a normal animation.

11.5 Animation Usage

With our characters and animations in the engine, how and where can we apply our characters and animations in the engine? In terms of usage, we won't "use" the skeleton asset in a typical sense, while we will do some system setup and housekeeping with the asset, the actual character is the skeletal mesh—this is the asset we will use to represent our character, whether that's placed in a level as an actor or as a component. We will then assign an animation to the skeletal mesh.

11.5.1 Skeletal Mesh Actor

Assigning animation to a skeletal mesh actor has very limited functionality, there are minimal settings we can customise without jumping into additional logic; however, this process may be suitable for simpler environment animations.

1. Add your Skeletal Mesh asset into the Level by **Dragging Skeletal Mesh Asset** from **Content Browser into the Level**.
2. **Select** the **Skeletal Mesh Actor**, and **Open** the **Details** panel.
3. **Expand** the **Animation** Category (Figure 11.4).
   a. **Set Animation Mode** to **Use Animation Asset**.

FIGURE 11.4   Animation parameters available to a skeletal mesh actor.

   b.   Additional options will appear allowing you to set an animation, whether it loops, if it
        plays at all, as well as its start position.
   c.   Expand Advanced to expose additional options such as the Playback speed.
4. With an animation set here, and playing in editor will result in the chosen animation to play
   on the Skeletal Mesh Actor.

11.5.2 Skeletal Mesh Component

While a Skeletal Mesh Actor will suffice for smaller one-shot or looping environmental animations, it is inevitable we will desire more control on how and when our animations play. We will now dive into the world of BP to poke logic at our Skeletal Mesh, but this time we will use a Skeletal Mesh Component.

   1. **Create** and Open a **Blueprint Actor**.
      a.   **Content Browser > Add > Blueprint Class**.
      b.   **Common > Actor**.
   2. Add a Skeletal Mesh Component.
      a.   **Components > Add > Skeletal Mesh**.
   3. Apply your Skeletal Mesh Asset to the Skeletal Mesh Component (Figure 11.5).
      a.   Select the Skeletal Mesh Component > Details > Mesh > Skeletal Mesh Asset.

   With our Skeletal Mesh Component setup, we can now begin to poke logic at the Component reference. Dragging from the Skeletal Mesh variable reference under the Components > Animation

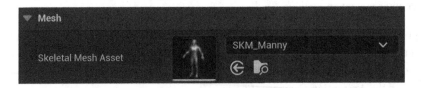

FIGURE 11.5   Skeletal mesh assignment as a blueprint component.

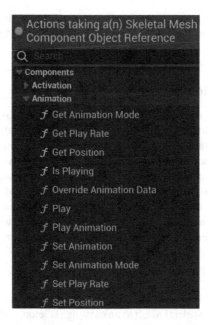

FIGURE 11.6 A sample of the animation manipulation nodes available in a blueprint.

category, we have a plethora of useful animation nodes (Figure 11.6). While there are single-use nodes for each specific function, such as "**Play**" which will play the animation, "**Set Animation**," which will set the property, there is a node labelled **Override Animation Data** which is a combination of all of these nodes in a single one—allowing you to set an animation, whether it loops, is playing, it's position and play rate all in a single node, which very useful (Figure 11.7). We can then mix and match these nodes to fire during events or functions to get the exact behaviour we want, allowing us to switch animations, which the previous method did not allow.

For basic operations, these nodes will suffice; however, for even more complex behaviour, including blending, we must use the **Animation Blueprint**—a complex state-driven graph that we can use to

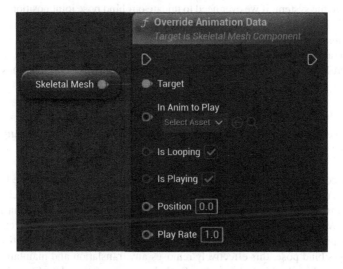

FIGURE 11.7 The override animation data node with all exposed attributes.

bring our characters to life in any way we desire. The entire BP is just dedicated to the movements and manipulation of a skeletal mesh. We have a dedicated chapter for the Animation Graph coming up.

11.6 Shareable Animation Setup

In Unreal Engine, we can set up our Skeletons to share animations across different Skeletal Meshes at runtime. We are not required to author bespoke animations or duplicate existing animation assets to get them to share across Skeletal Meshes, we can opt for a shareable animation workflow.

There are two methods we can choose from: the first workflow is via a **Retarget Source**; this workflow has multiple Skeletal Mesh assets associated with a single skeleton, and we can use the Retarget Source and Retarget Options so animations from different Skeletal Meshes can be shared with one another, but they map to compensate for the differences between character sizes. The second workflow is via the **Compatible Skeletons** workflow; this workflow allows us to have multiple Skeletal Mesh assets with multiple different Skeleton assets that can share animations with each other.

11.6.1 Retarget Source

To set up a Retarget Source workflow, we must have multiple skeletal meshes assigned to a single skeleton to continue. To add a new Skeletal Mesh to an existing skeleton, during the import process, when the FBX dialogue appears, choose the desired skeleton you wish to share. Keep in mind that the skeletons must have a matched hierarchy; this does not mean they are identical; some joints can be missing on one skeletal mesh that are on another, but this means you cannot change the hierarchy order! So if joint B is a child of joint A in one skeletal mesh, you cannot have joint A be a child of joint C!

1. When you have multiple skeletal meshes imported, open the Skeleton asset.
2. Open the Retarget Sources interface—**Window > Retarget Sources**.
3. We must now add each Skeletal Mesh as a Retarget Source.
   a. **Manage Retarget Sources > Add New > Each Skeletal Mesh**.

This system defines the bind pose for each Skeletal Mesh asset to be included in the mapping system; this allows calculations to be made between the delta of the joint transforms. Since we are setting up the bind pose in the system, if we ever need to update our bind pose joint positions, we must update the pose in the Skeleton asset. To update, **right-click the Skeletal Mesh in the Retarget Sources list and select Update**.

With our Skeletal Meshes mapped, we must now configure the bones on how we want them to map from one Skeletal Mesh to another. To do this, we must use the Retargeting Options in the Skeleton Tree.

1. **Open the Skeleton Tree** (Window > Skeleton Tree)
2. Select the **settings** icon in the **Skeleton Tree** and **enable Show Retargeting Options**. A new column will appear in the Skeleton Tree view.

From the new column, we are able to choose one of five options on a per-bone basis; this option defines the Bone Translation Retargeting Mode. We can pick from **Animation, Skeleton, Animation Scaled, Animation Relative** or **Orient and Scale**. Each option provides different mapping results between Skeletal Mesh animation data. **Animation** will use the translation data from the animation, meaning no mapping between meshes will occur. **Skeleton** will use the translation for each joint from the skeleton's bind pose; this effectively removes any translation and maintains the translation for each joint defined in the bind. Animation Scaled uses translation data from the animation but

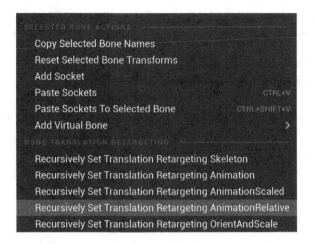

FIGURE 11.8   Right-click menu for the joints in the skeleton tree.

scales the amount of the translation based on the differences in skeleton proportions. So if a joint translates 100 units, but the difference in proportions is 10%, the joint will now move 110 units. **Animation Relative** will use relative translation data from the animation, similar to an additive animation. Finally, **Orient and Scale** does what it says on the tin and will orient and scale translation!

While each setting has benefits for different purposes, **Animation Relative** will fit most mapping cases, but often in some cases, we will not want to map any data we should leave it as **Animation**. Assigning these values to each bone at a time can be very tedious; thankfully, Unreal offers an option to Recursively Set a value to every joint below the selected joint—Right-click on a joint in the Skeleton Tree to find this option (Figure 11.8).

The final component of the setup is that we must set up the **Retarget Source** for each animation so the system knows which Skeletal Mesh the animation was authored for and can properly calculate the mappings to other Skeletal Meshes. The setting can be found in the **Asset Details for each animation sequence**, the **Retarget Source** value is found under the **Animation** Category.

With this, we can then happily share animations that will map to the differences of other characters!

11.6.2 Compatible Skeletons

An alternative approach is to use the **Compatible Skeletons** system; this too is located in the **Retarget Sources** window of the Skeleton asset. The main difference from one workflow to another is that a Compatible skeleton allows for a cleaner Skeleton asset workflow rather than all the data being stored in a single skeleton, only the necessary data is stored in each Skeleton asset.

To add a compatible Skeleton, add the Skeleton to the **Manage Compatible Skeletons** list by selecting **Add Skeleton** and choosing a Skeleton. The animations and assets associated with them are now shared with the skeletons chosen.

This compatibility is one-directional, so If you wish to have the skeletons share back and forth, we must add a compatible skeleton to each of the skeletons, not just one of them.

11.7 Remove Old Joints from the Skeleton

In your integration endeavours, you may find yourself in a situation where you have old joints in the skeleton asset which are no longer used. At some point, they may have existed in a skeletal mesh asset but no longer; however, they will still loiter in the skeleton. We will want to make sure our skeleton is always as clean as possible, so how do we clean up the skeleton and get rid of these old joints?

1. **Open** the **Skeleton** asset window.
2. **Unreal Menu > Asset > Remove Unused Bones from Skeleton**.
3. A popup window will appear; select **Yes**.
4. The old joints will be removed from your skeleton, make sure to save the asset!

12

Unreal—The Animation Blueprint

The animation blueprint (ABP) is a specific type of BP that is used to control the animation pose of a skeletal mesh. An ABP has many of the same features as a regular BP, such as the event graph where logic can be created, but it also includes the Animation Graph (AnimGraph).

12.1 Event Graph

The event graph is where you will see the most direct translation between a standard BP and an ABP. There are some minor differences, such as the ability to create Timelines being removed from an ABP, and there are several events that are unique to the ABP's event graph; these events are Initialize Animation, and Update Animation. These very similar in function to the Begin Play and Event Tick events, with the Initialize Animation being the first event fired from the ABP once it is active, and the Update Animation event is consecutively fired every frame. This is especially useful for updating the logic that the AnimGraph requires every frame.

12.2 AnimGraph

The AnimGraph is a flow-based node graph that is used to determine the pose of a skeletal mesh (Figure 12.1); this graph is updated every frame and can be setup to play different animations depending on particular logic, or even intercept the current pose to apply additive, overlay animations, or enhance our animations through procedural dynamics or even modify particular bones directly with Skeletal Control Nodes.

The start of the AnimGraph is actually at the end—The Output Pose (Figure 12.2). This node is the only default and undeletable node that will reside in your graph. The final accumulated pose that is connected to the Output Pose node is the result of all the logic from within the ABP that will then be applied to the skeletal mesh's joint transforms.

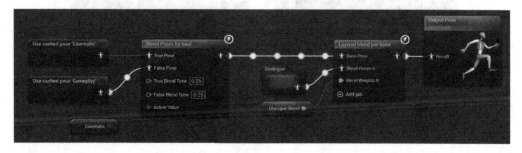

FIGURE 12.1   The AnimGraph of the Animation Blueprint.

DOI: 10.1201/9781003263258-12

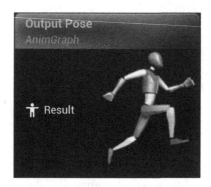

FIGURE 12.2   The end output pose of the AnimGraph.

Working backwards from the Output Pose is the execution flow. Just like the execution flow from a BP's event graph, this moves from left to right, but unlike the BP equivalent, which only denotes the execution order of nodes, the execution flow here carries a payload of information: the "current" skeletal mesh pose. This pose payload contains all transforms of all the skeletal mesh's joints as determined by the graph proceeding to a point in the execution flow. You may also notice that the execution flow is perpetually illuminated; this is because the AnimGraph is executed every frame rather than just once like a normal BP.

The graph's pose has to originate somewhere, and that is the typical animation nodes, whether that's an animation sequence player node that will play a looping animation or a blendspace player (covered shortly). All these nodes output a pose payload, which is then passed into the Output Pose via a connected execution flow.

12.2.1 Execution Flow—Branching

AnimGraphs aren't limited to having an animation plugged directly into the output pose; we can intercept the pose anywhere along its execution flow to add branching logic. There are a variety of nodes we can use to do this, such as the Blend Pose By nodes—which come in a variety of flavours (Bool, Int and Enum) (Figure 12.3).

The Blend Poses By Nodes act as a switcher in the execution flow; similar to a railroad switch for a train, as the execution flow arrives at this node logic can determine which path to split between. With the Boolean variant of this node, as the inputted value is switched between True and False, the node will switch down the True or False pose track and use the provided blend time to blend between the

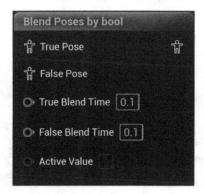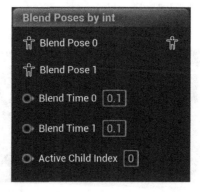

FIGURE 12.3   Blend poses by nodes.

FIGURE 12.4 The Blend node.

pose tracks. The Integer variant does the same but can utilise multiple inputs; the default node comes with two pose inputs, but more can be added by **Right Clicking The Node > Add Blend Pin**.

There is a third variant of this node, a **Blend Poses By Enumeration (ENUM)**. This node acts very similar to the Blend Poses By Integer node, except this node is computed via an enumeration variable. An enum is a list-based variable type that has a clear and readable display name that can correspond to the entry in the list. With the Blend Poses By Int, we would have Blend Pose 0, 1, 2, 3, etc. whereas a Blend Pose By Enum could have a Walk Pose, Run Pose, Crouch Pose, etc. Using an enum allows for a more comprehensible pose label compared to numbers. Enums can be created in the **Content Browser > Add New > Blueprints > Enumeration.** This will create a unique enum asset in which you can add as many entries to your list as you desire. Back in the AnimGraph, if you search for the name of your new enumeration asset you will find a corresponding Blend Poses By for that asset. Just like the Integer version, blend poses can be added by **Right Clicking The Node > Add Pin For Element**.

While the Blend Poses By Node is a track switcher, there are other nodes, such as the Blend node (Figure 12.4), that allow for multiple input poses to be active and perpetually blend with one another. The Blend node has an Alpha value input, which determines how much the node blends input pose A and B together; with Alpha 0 equally A 100% blended, Alpha 1 equally B 100% blended and Alpha 0.5 being both 50% blended. Having this option exposed allows for us to customise how the blend behaves or if it stays constantly blending the two input poses.

12.2.2 Execution Flow—Pose Space

By default, the pose payload is stored in **Local Space**, this means the transform data for each bone is stored relative to its parent bone—this is denoted by a white-coloured execution flow. While most nodes require the incoming pose to be in local space, some nodes, such as *skeletal control* nodes, require the pose to be in **Component Space.** In this space the bone's transforms are relative to the *Skeletal Mesh Component*, this is visually denoted by a blue flow (Figure 12.5). Since certain nodes

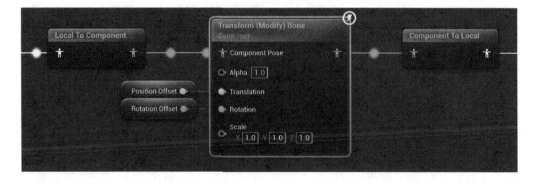

FIGURE 12.5 Local and Component space conversion nodes.

require the incoming pose to be in the appropriate space prior to the node's execution, we must convert the pose's space—the AnimGraph has a **Local to Component** and a **Component to Local** space conversion nodes that can do just this.

12.3 Animation Evaluation

When placing an AnimSequence into the AnimGraph, it will create a Sequence Player—once this is connected to an output pose, the default settings will make the animation autoplay and time will drive the animation to cycle through its frames. The sequence player node has options to customise various properties such as playback speed, whether the animation loops and the starting frame (Figure 12.6).

Animation evaluation (how it plays back) isn't limited by being driven by time; we can also manually control an animation's frame evaluation. Right-clicking on a Sequence Player will display the option to **Convert to Single Frame Animation**. This will convert the **Sequence Player** into a **Sequence Evaluator**. Instead of being evaluated by time, this node has its current frame driven by an **Explicit Time** float variable; this value can be driven by a variable to control the exact frame the animation is on. This float could be based on health or another game-dependent logic such as distance and acceleration; this use case is called Distance Matching.

12.3.1 Distance Matching

A common problem occurs with physics-based movement systems where the current animation does not cover the correct distance or acceleration that the physics capsule is performing, resulting in the character's feet appearing to slide and not contact the floor properly. To remedy this problem, distance matching can be applied—this is a form of animation evaluation where a distance metric drives the animation playback.

The basic workflow for distance matching involves a float curve inside of an animation; this float has the relevant distance metric animated across the length of the animation. For example, if a character is starting to walk from idle, the distance metric would be travel distance, and on frame 0 the distance would be 0, and each frame, the distance could increase, matching the distance covered by the animation, for example, frame 100 would have 100 units moved. This curve is then searched for the appropriate matching distance value, and it will return the relevant frame. This then keeps the distances of a physics capsule and animation 1:1, rather than relying on physics and animation playback to sync via time.

A straightforward use case for distance matching is for jumping. When you animate a jump, the animation will be authored at a fixed length. However, when in-game, the character could be jumping from different heights to the height in the animation, so the time taken to jump would be different to the authored time. If played normally; this could lead to a frozen pose once the sequence has reached the last frame. A sequence evaluator's explicit time can be driven by the character's distance to the floor, allowing them to hit the apex and landing poses at the appropriate time.

 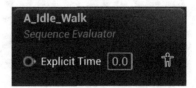

FIGURE 12.6 Sequence Player and Sequence Evaluator variants.

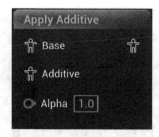

FIGURE 12.7 Additive node in the ABP.

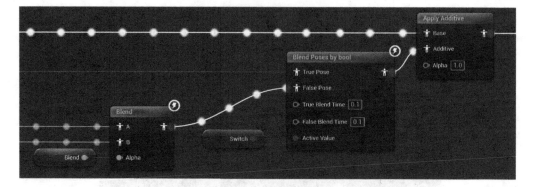

FIGURE 12.8 Branching additive data.

12.4 Additive Animation

At any point within the AnimGraph, the execution flow's pose can be enhanced with additive animations via the Apply Additive node (Figure 12.7). The Base pose input expects your typical pose, whereas the Additive pose input requires an additive animation asset, which we discussed earlier on how to set up. The outgoing pose will be the result of your incoming pose with an additive applied.

As with all of these nodes, they come with a computation cost associated with them—so it is wise to keep the number of additives to a minimum unless absolutely necessary. One method around, reducing Apply Additives nodes while maintaining a complex multilayer additive system is that, due to the fact that the Apply Additive only expects an additive pose, you are not limited by a direct additive animation connection into the node. You can use all the tools at your disposal to create complex layered, blended, or switched additive poses and apply the result of all of these at once. Maintaining complex additive behaviour, but only one Apply Additive node (Figure 12.8).

12.5 Overlay Animation

You can also overlay animation on top of your pose via the Layered Blend Per Bone node (Figure 12.9); this allows for this override on a per joint basis—meaning if you only wanted to overlay an animation's left arm animation on top of another full-body animation, you can do just that!

Just like the Blend By Int node, additional Blend Poses pins can be added by **Right Clicking the node > Add Blend Pin**. Each Blend Poses pin on the Layered Blend per Bone has an accompanying blend weight value; this is the alpha (0–1 with 1 equalling 100%) of the overlay animation.

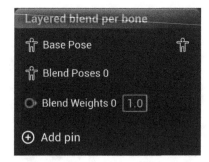

FIGURE 12.9   Layered Blend per Bone node.

Additionally, within the **Details** panel is the Config setup (Figure 12.10), where within the **Layer Setup**, we can add new entries with the matching **Bone Name** you wish to override or not. The secondary value, **Blend Depth** determines not only whether the bone from the base pose will be overwritten or not, but also the amount of blend falloff through subsequent hierarchy bones.

A **blend depth of -1**—the listed joint and subsequent children's joints **will not be overwritten**.

A **blend depth of 0**—the listed joint and subsequent child joints **will be overwritten**.

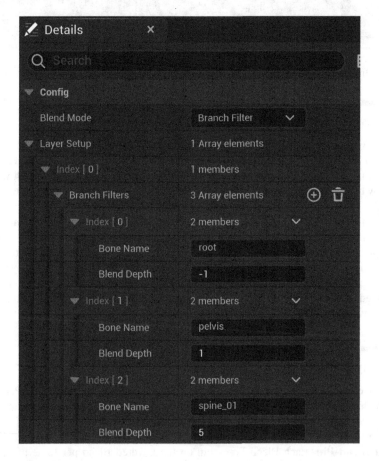

FIGURE 12.10   Layered Blend per Bone node's layer setup parameters.

A **blend depth of 1 or more**, the listed joint and subsequent child joints **will be overwritten**, BUT based on the height of the depth, the more joints will be used as a falloff for blending the data across multiple joints. For example, a blend depth of three on a three chain spine starting at spine_01, would result in spine_01 being 33% strength, spine_02 being 66% strength, spine_03 and subsequent bones being 100% strength. Essentially this allows for a smooth overlay blend over multiple bones, rather than being applied over 1.

12.6 Blendspaces

Blendspaces are an animation synthesis tool that can be used within an animation graph to create new animations based on a blend between multiple input animations. Visually, blend spaces are represented like a graph with one or two axes, which are the input values.

On the graph reside animations at specific coordinates—the final output animation is determined by where the input values currently reside on the graph, and all relevant animations around are blended to produce a new animation. Blendspaces can use one or two dimensions—the former meaning there is only a single driver axis and all animations operate on a single axis. Their use is always limited to blending between two animations at any given time, since at any given point on a straight line you can only have one animation to the left and one to the right. Two-dimensional blend spaces, on the other hand, are driven by two input axes and have the advantage of being able to blend between multiple animations at any given time due to their extra driver axis (Figure 12.11).

Unlike traditional blending methods that switch between one animation or another and only blend through a transition, a blend space allows a blend position to be held and multiple animations to be combined simultaneously to produce an output animation that is the sum of all those animations combined. The input values can even be changed at runtime, blend spaces do not have to be static.

One dimensional blend spaces are useful for a simple locomotion system where the character would require transitioning from an idle, walk and finally to a run. The driver input value starts at 0, which would have the character idle, as this number is increased, the animation will begin to blend between idle and walk until the driver value is equal to the position of the walk, then it will just play the walk animation 100%—as it continues to rise, it will then begin blending between a walk and a run until the run is 100% blended. If required, the driver value can stop and hold the number at any point, and the blend space will continue to output the blended animation at whatever point it currently is.

Two-dimensional can add an extra layer of complexity to your output pose, with an entire extra dimension offering additional blending opportunities. They can be used in a variety of ways, whether you want to improve your locomotion system from merely an idle, walk and run; the extra dimension allows you to add that as an orientation.

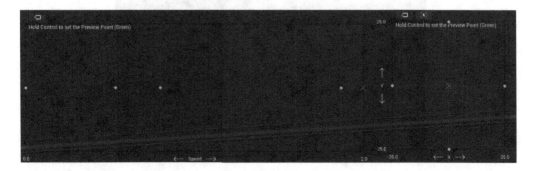

FIGURE 12.11 A one and two-dimensional blendspace variants.

12.6.1 Additive Blendspaces and Aim Offsets

Blendspaces can also exist additively; as we previously covered additive animations, their power is not limited to a single animation; they can be used in blendspaces and are perfect for additive aiming systems with the X-axis being left and right aiming, and the Y-axis being up and down aiming. When placing additive animations into a blendspace, the blendspace will then only allow assets of the same type to be used; so you cannot mix and match normal animation sequences and additive sequences in the same blendspace.

When brought into the AnimGraph, an additive blendspace will require you to place an Apply Additive node after the blendspace, just like a typical additive animation (Figure 12.12). However, Unreal also offers an Aim Offset blendspace type; this behaves exactly like an additive blendspace, but it also bundles the Apply Additive node together, like a macro to reduce the number of nodes (Figure 12.13). This is useful for most blendspace use cases where you only require the result of the blendspace, but the original example offers a little more flexibility in case you desire to intercept the pose in the additive blendspace and dynamically change it before the additive is applied.

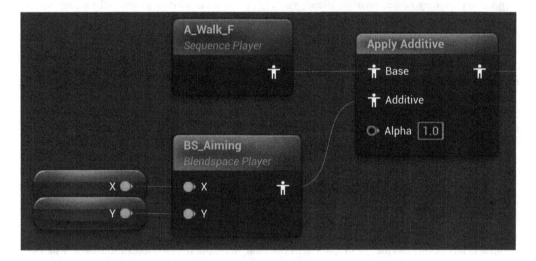

FIGURE 12.12   Additive blendspace example.

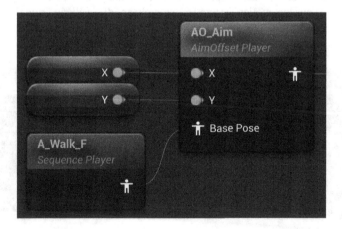

FIGURE 12.13   Aim offset player node.

FIGURE 12.14 A look at node, one of the Skeletal Control nodes.

12.7 Skeletal Control Nodes

Skeletal control nodes are tools that can be utilised to directly manipulate the behaviour of individual bones within the ABP. Many of these nodes have functionality that will be familiar to you, as they act very similarly to constraints in your DCC. The **LookAt** node is an aim constraint (Figure 12.14), the **Constraint** node is a Parent/Point/Orient/Scale constraint rolled into one, and a **Driven Controller** is very similar to a direct connection or a driven key! These nodes can be incredibly useful for getting dynamic rig-like behaviour at runtime.

To utilise skeletal control nodes, our typical **local space** pose execution must be converted into **component space**, and then converted back into local space to continue utilising non-skeletal control nodes.

One of the most powerful skeletal control nodes is the **AnimDynamics** node (Figure 12.15). This is a lightweight physics solver that can be used to add procedural secondary animation to your skeletons, particularly beneficial for danglies (ponytails, chains, wires, etc.). This node reacts to the current pose of the character at its node input and can even have world velocities influence the physics solution. Since the AnimDynamics is so lightweight, it does not have many of the features of a true simulation, such as collision interaction.

For more simplified dynamics, we can use the Spring controller (Figure 12.16), which allows us to add a spring to a joint, resulting in bouncy or swinging visuals at the joint. When using this node, it's very quick to get a bouncy character component reacting to your scene in no time at all.

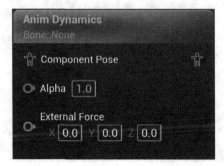

FIGURE 12.15 AnimDynamics node.

FIGURE 12.16 Spring controller node.

12.8 State Machine

As your AnimGraph becomes more complex in behaviour, managing a single layer graph can become unnecessarily complicated; to remedy this, we have another tool in the toolbelt—the State Machine (Figure 12.17). A state machine allows for the creation of a state-based animation flow, with transitional logic that defines how each state changes from one to another. Unlike a blend by node, which is a railroad switch that can alternate between any of the blend poses at any time, a state machine has functionality that defines which states can switch to specific states and which states it cannot switch to, and the conditions that must be met to transition to another state.

A state machine also adds a layer of organisation to the graph by adding levels of logic. Imagine each level of the graph being like another layer in an onion; instead of all of the AnimGraph execution logic being present on the top level of the AnimGraph, each state within the machine has its own execution flow, allowing for compartmentalisation of logic and systems into state groups.

To create a state machine, right-click in the AnimGraph's background and type "State Machine" and select it from the list. This will generate a State Machine node—double-click it to enter the graph. From within the state machine, you can add new states by right-clicking and selecting new states. By default, a state machine must always have an entry state.

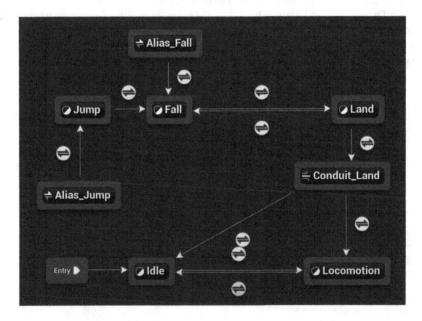

FIGURE 12.17 A state machine.

FIGURE 12.18   A transition in a state machine.

12.8.1 State Machine—Transitions/Blending

When we have multiple states prepared, we can create transitions to blend between different states; each transition includes logic criteria to trigger a blend between two animation states. To create a transition, drag from the perimeter outline of the source state to the perimeter of the destination state. A transition's direction will be noted by the arrow at the end of the transition event (Figure 12.18).

Each transition has a transition icon in the middle of the line (Figure 12.18); double-clicking it will enter the transition rules graph. This graph is where we can determine the conditions that trigger the transition. Criteria entered here can vary for each specific case, but it must output a Boolean. We could use a float value greater than X value to trigger whether a Boolean is true or an enum is set to a specific type. Once the criteria in this graph is true, the transition will activate (Figure 12.19).

Transition events come with a selection of unique nodes to aid in creating our conditional criteria. These are the Get Relevant Anim Time and Time Remaining nodes, both of which come with fractional variants (Figure 12.20). These nodes are state-specific, this is noted by state's name in brackets on the node label—this means you must create unique versions for each transition or state context. These nodes will return the current playback metrics of a state, so we could utilise the Get Relevant Anim Time Remaining node to ensure we have a specific threshold of animation remaining to trigger, for example, 0.2 remaining to trigger at the end.

Each transition has customisable properties accessible from the Details panel with the transition icon selected in the state machine. This is where you will find the duration time value for the transition. Additionally, this is where you can customise the blend type—whether you use a standard blend, custom blends or inertial blending (covered shortly).

FIGURE 12.19   Transition logic.

FIGURE 12.20   Transition logic nodes to acquire animation time.

FIGURE 12.21   Promote To Shared will allow for shareable transition logic.

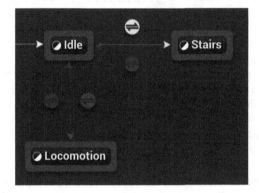

FIGURE 12.22   Coloured transitions denote shared transition logic between matching colours.

12.8.2 State Machine—Transition Logic Sharing

You may find situations in which you require duplicate logic across multiple transitions; however, do not jump to duplicating the logic between multiple transitions as this will cause you more work maintaining multiple identical transitions, which is rife for error. Instead, we can employ the use of the Transition Rule Sharing tools. In the Details panel of a transition, under Transition > Transition Rule Sharing, there is a button labelled Promote To Shared (Figure 12.21), this button will allow you to create a unique name identifier for a shareable transition.

With a shared transition created, we can set the Transition Rule Sharing value on another transition to a matching transitional name to make them share logic! With this technique, we maintain a unique transition for attributes such as blend time but with shared logic. Each shareable transition event will have matching colours to indicate which transitions match! (Figure 12.22).

12.8.3 State Machine—Standard and Custom Blends

A standard blend operates by crossfading between two animation sequences, with the transition's blend time determining the length of time the crossfade occurs over. If you enable the custom blend option from a transition's blend type, it will reveal a new graph layer accessed by the Edit Blend Graph button. From this new interface (Figure 12.23), we can determine exactly how the source state will blend into the transition state.

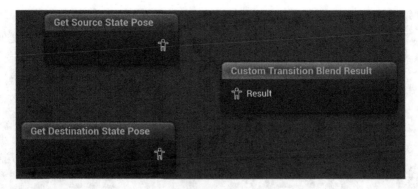

FIGURE 12.23   Custom blend graph nodes.

FIGURE 12.24   An example of a custom blend graph.

The custom blend graph also includes unique nodes to aid in the elapsed time of the transition; these can be used to drive the blend as desired. These nodes include: Get Transition Crossfade Duration, Get Transition Time Elapsed and a ratio variant.

Figure 12.24 is a custom blend graph setup to mimic a standard blend; the source and destination pose are the A/B poses of a blend, and the time of the transition drives the blend alpha from 0 to 1.

12.8.4 State Machine—Conduits and Alias States

As your state machines grow, it is inevitable you will create visual spaghetti; with multiple transitions overlapping one another, transitions connecting across dozens of states, it can become quite unreadable and a behemoth to manage (Figure 12.25). The usage of Conduits and Alias states can prevent this spaghetti by tidying up your graph, and exposing useful functionality to make your graphs easier to manage. Both of these can be created via the right click menu in the state machine graph.

First up—**conduits**. They have no state, no animation assignment, they are a way station for transitions; their utility as a transitional branching point can reduce the number of transitions used, clearing up the readability of the graph and reducing the user maintenance of many transitions. Their use can be applied in instances with several unique transitions from each and every state; you can instead centre all the transitions on a conduit (Figure 12.26).

Not only that, conduits are also useful for a branching transition state; imagine an instance where there is a state that is transitioning to several states; the logic to leave the first state is mostly identical between multiple transitions minus one criteria. Instead of duplicating this logic between multiple transitions, you can do a single transition to a conduit, then from the conduit have the only state specific logic that changes—this will remove the need to maintain duplicate logic between multiple

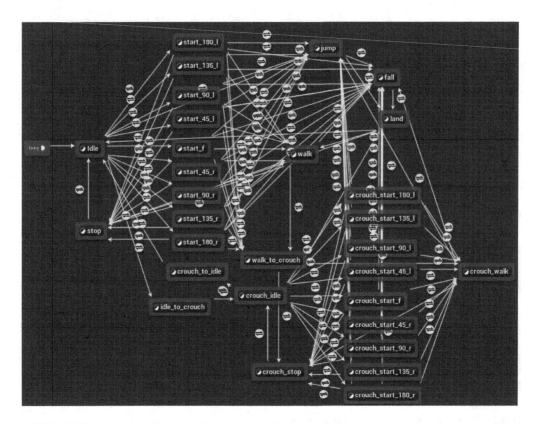

FIGURE 12.25   A disorganised state machine.

transitions. Commonly, conduits are used as an entry branch to determine a different entry state for a state machine.

Second, **Alias states**. These are states that pretend to act like another state, acting as if it is AKA sprint state, AKA walk state and AKA idle state. You are then able to create transition events from this state as if it was the state it was pretending to be. The alias states are not limited to mimicking one state; it can pretend to be every state at once, referred to as a global alias. Since an alias state can

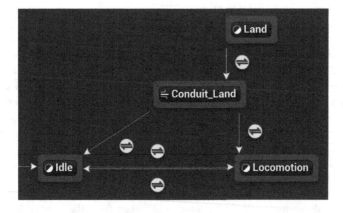

FIGURE 12.26   A state machine organised through a conduit.

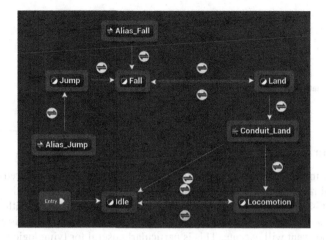

FIGURE 12.27 A state machine organised under the alias states.

be placed on the opposite side of the graph to the original state, it can be a great way to tidy up the readability of your state machine instead of having a spaghetti of transitions across the graph.

Their use can be particularly useful in instances where you have transitions from every state to a single state, as they're required to be accessed no matter which state the state machine is in. Instead of creating a spider web of transitions, we can instead use a single transition from a global alias state. This is demonstrated in Figure 12.27—the spaghetti is gone and makes your life much easier to manage one transition.

12.8.5 State Machine—Events

Within a state machine, both transitions and states have access to trigger events within the ABP under particular criteria; these can be accessed via the Details panel when a state or transition is selected (Figure 12.28). State events can be triggered under one of three circumstances: Entered State, Left State or Fully Blended State—which do exactly as they say on the tin, once entered/left/fully blended then the event will trigger. For transitions, events can be triggered under Start Transition, End Transition or Transition Interrupted. These events can be used to trigger event graph logic based on the current state of the machine's flow.

FIGURE 12.28 Triggerable state events.

FIGURE 12.29   Animation notify and its matching ABP event.

12.9 Animation Notifies

If we recall earlier in this book (refer to Section 11.4.1 in Chapter 11), we covered the functionality exposed in this animSequence assets of Notifies. After the creation of an animNotify in the anim-Sequence, an event is now available for access in the Event Graph of the ABP with a matching name but with a "AnimNotify_" notify prefix (Figure 12.29). Anytime an animation is evaluated and the notify is passed, the event will execute. This is particularly useful for tying logic to a specific frame of animation.

Another type of notify is the Sync Markers; these can be used to make different animations synchronise user-defined frames by finding a matching Sync Marker in another animation. Once a sync marker has been added to an animation, for them to begin syncing all animSequence playback nodes must be added to a matching Sync group; this option can be found in the node's details panel. The system then has a "leader" or "follower" system determining which animation should follow the match, and which should drive it. This system is particularly useful for blending between locomotion animations that may be of different lengths. A sync marker can be used to sync a foot plant so the animations match up for a better blend.

12.10 Inertial Blending (Inertialization)

Inertialization is an alternative blending technique that can be used instead of the traditional blending system. The technique was originally developed by Microsoft for Gears of War 4 and is now available to all Unreal Engine users (Figure 12.30).

One difference between traditional blending and Inertialization is the computational cost; traditional blending requires both the source animation, target animation, and the blend to be computed all simultaneously, and with a lot of blends, this can get very expensive. On the other hand, once Inertialization is activated, the source animation is no longer evaluated, and the inertia of the current pose is used to calculate a blend to the target. This evaluation is demonstrated in Figure 12.31.

The utilisation of inertialization blending has visual differences in the blend result compared to traditional blends. This is because the inertia blend utilises continued momentum through the blend, with noticeable natural inertia fall-off as one animation changes to another. On the other hand, a standard blend just crossfades two animations together.

FIGURE 12.30   The Inertialization node.

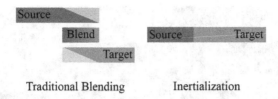

Traditional Blending   Inertialization

FIGURE 12.31   Traditional blending versus Inertialization blending.

FIGURE 12.32   The two locations to enable Inertialization.

While this all sounds amazing, inertialization blending is not a one-size-fits-all situation and, in some cases, can make some blends look worse—so give it a try and see how it looks before enabling wholesale.

12.10.1 Using Inertialization

To enable it, you must first opt-in to use it wherever blending may occur in your AnimGraph (Figure 12.32).

- **Blend Pose node > Details > Transition Type Setting > Inertialization.**
- **State Transition > Details > Blend Logic > Inertialization.**

Once enabled, you may notice your animations no longer blend—that is because we are missing an important step in the process. We are required to add an **Inertialization node** to our execution flow. Add this node at any point **after** the blend request, but it does not have to be immediately after the request; it can happen later in the graph, even as late as the final output node. However, keep in mind that overwhelming the Inertialization node with many blend requests can lead to undesirable blending results.

12.11 Anim Node Functions

Each node in the AnimGraph has evaluation functions that can trigger when the node becomes relevant, its initial update, or a function for every update of the node; essentially acting like a tick when this specific node is active. Utilising these functions can be a great way to efficiently run logic in the graph, since you can run specific functions only when necessary, or they can be employed to calculate any data that may be required of the node on its initial activation; such as determining an animation sequence's start frame based on game logic (Figure 12.33).

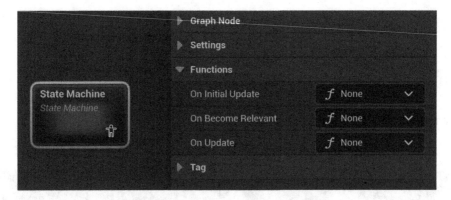

FIGURE 12.33   Anim node functions.

FIGURE 12.34   An anim node function acquires the current animation's play length.

From within the functions, we can gather or set context-sensitive information about the node that called the function. Figure 12.34 is an example of a function that was called by an animation sequence player—this function acquires the relevant node, which can be used to acquire metadata such as the sequence's play length.

12.12 Cached Pose

We are able to cache a pose—this is the process of storing a pose from our execution flow, and then we can re-use the cached pose in multiple places. Since our execution flow is limited by having 1 continuous flow and the same node can't be connected to multiple nodes, a cache pose process can be very useful for pose manipulation. We can even use the cache pose in multiple areas to share a single source of an animation, or state machine rather than duplicating systems around the graph.

To create a cached pose, add a **New Save Cache Pose** node to the graph, and then rename the cache (Figure 12.35).

Keep in mind, while a cached pose output node can be used at any level of the graph, the cache itself can only be created on the top level of an AnimGraph.

12.13 Animation Blueprint Creation

ABPs, just like animation assets, have a specific skeleton association when generated, so you must import your skeletal assets to generate a skeleton asset prior to creating and assigning an ABP.

To generate the ABP, navigate to **Content Browser > Add > Animation > Animation Blueprint.** You will then be prompted with a window to determine the target skeleton for the ABP—select the

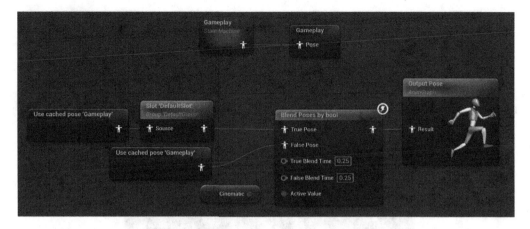

FIGURE 12.35 Cached pose usage in the AnimGraph.

relevant skeleton from the list and click **Create**. Alternatively; ABPs can be generated directly from the skeletal mesh asset by **right-clicking the asset > Create > Anim Assets > Anim Blueprint.**

12.14 Animation Blueprint Assignment

Once an ABP is created, we must assign it to a skeletal mesh to be able to operate it at runtime/ There are two areas we can assign the ABP to a skeletal mesh—the first is the Animation Mode of a Skeletal Mesh component either in the scene or on a component in a BP. The second assignment is a post-process ABP.

12.14.1 Skeletal Mesh Component Assignment

The first assignment is on the **component level**; whether you have a skeletal mesh asset in your scene, or as a component within a Blueprint asset, you are able to assign the ABP to the skeletal mesh within the **details** panel for this component. Under the category **Animation > Animation Mode > Use Animation Blueprint**, then **assign the ABP** to the **Anim Class** setting. At runtime, the ABP will execute for the ABP.

12.14.1.1 Communicating with the Component's ABP

With an ABP assigned to your skeletal mesh, it is inevitable that you will want to communicate from your BP to your ABP to drive variables or events. To do this, we must set up a Cast operation when the BP is initialised via the Begin Play event.

1. **Open the Blueprint** containing the skeletal mesh component
2. **Locate or create the BeginPlay event;** this event is executed when the BP is initialised at runtime.
3. **Drag the SkeletalMesh component from the Component List view into the Event graph**, this will spawn a variable reference to the skeletal mesh.
4. From the SkeletalMesh, **create a Get Anim Instance node**; this will return a generic ABP reference.

FIGURE 12.36   Utilisation of the Get Anim Instance node allows us to cast to the ABP and store it as a variable for later use.

FIGURE 12.37   From the ABP variable we can read and write data.

5. We must now use a **Cast** operation to the **specific ABP class name** to allow us to communicate with the unique aspects of that ABP. In this case, we are using the **Cast To ABP_Character_Master** node.
6. From the **Cast node's result,** right-click and click **Promote to Variable** so we can communicate with the ABP later instead of recasting (Figure 12.36).

With the stored ABP, we can now utilise the variable reference to communicate with the ABP however we please. We can use it to trigger events, functions or set variables (Figure 12.37).

12.14.2 Post-Process ABP

The second assignment location is as a **post-process ABP**—these differ in that they run as a post-process on a skeletal mesh! The post-process ABP will run wherever the skeletal mesh is used, and is evaluated after the Main Anim Instance for the skeletal mesh, whether that's an animation, sequencer, or even ABP, but it will evaluate before the physics calculations. Since joint data can be manipulated through the ABP like skeletal control nodes, we can use the post-process ABP to manipulate the skeletal's data for deformation or AnimDynamics. The huge benefit of utilising a post-process ABP is that we only have to apply these nodes once in the post-process ABP—now every use of the skeletal mesh will have this application. Whereas if we had multiple ABPs without using a post-process ABP, we would be required to duplicate and maintain these nodes in every single graph.

Before we assign our post-process ABP, there is an additional step we must do to our ABP to ensure it works properly. Unlike a normal ABP, which controls the source pose, our post-process ABP is not determining the source pose, and is merely acting as an intermediate process between an incoming pose and an output pose—so we must change our graph to accommodate this by adding an **Input Pose** node at the beginning of the graph, otherwise, the character will reset to bind pose! (Figure 12.38).

FIGURE 12.38   The input pose for a post-process ABP.

FIGURE 12.39 Utilisation of the Get Post Process Instance node we can acquire the Post Process ABP for communication.

12.14.2.1 Post-Process ABP Assignment

Post-process ABPs are assigned on the Skeletal Mesh. **Skeletal Mesh > Asset Details > Skeletal Mesh Category > Post Process Anim Blueprint.**

A note on performance: post-process ABPs will reinitialise whenever the Animation Mode is altered on the skeletal mesh component (SetAnimationMode; such as switching from an ABP to Animation). This Inertialisation happens on a single frame, so be careful as this could cause your frame time to exceed your budget and cause a hitch.

12.14.2.2 Communicating with the Post-Process ABP

Communication with your PP ABP may become necessary, and we can control it in a very similar way to the Skeletal Mesh component workflow, except this time instead of using the Get Anim Instance node from the Skeletal Mesh, we instead use the **Get Post Process Instance** node for the same behaviour! (Figure 12.39).

12.15 Animation Blueprint Inheritance

Similar to the inheritance offered from a typical BP, we are able to create a child ABP where we can choose to replace animations or modify behaviour. Their use is excellent for projects that require multiple characters with unique animations, but the core state machine is shared across characters. Instead of creating unique ABPs, or having a single ABP with every animation assignment in, we can simply opt for a workflow where we have a master ABP and then have children ABPs that override animations within them.

We create a child ABP in the same way as a BP one, **right-click the ABP** and choose **Create Child Blueprint Class**. The child ABP only has an Event Graph, there is no AnimGraph available—this is because we can only modify Event Graph behaviour for Events, Functions and Notifies but not for AnimGraph behaviour. For modifications to the AnimGraph, we must use the **Asset Override Editor** window (**Unreal Menu > Windows > Asset Override Editor**), shown in Figure 12.40. This interface

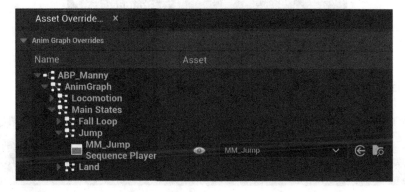

FIGURE 12.40 Child ABPs have animation overrides!

provides a list structure based on the parent ABP's state machine, from here we can access and modify references for animation sequences, blend spaces and other animation-based assignments.

12.16 AnimGraph Debugging

When our graphs are set up and operational on our skeletal meshes, we may encounter unintentional misbehaviour and errors that we must track down and fix. The ABP comes bundled with debugging tools that can make our problem-solving easier.

The first is the debug object tool, which is accessible at the top toolbar in the ABP. Play in the editor, then open your ABP and select your instance from the dropdown menu (Figure 12.41)—we will see a live preview of the ABP's execution pathways and variables 1:1 with the asset in the viewport. Each action or change will be reflected in the graph, allowing for a live preview to follow the behaviour of your graph. If the connection is successful, you will notice the animation pose execution lines pulse as shown. (Figure 12.42).

Hover over variables inside the AnimGraph to preview their current value, or alternatively right-click the variable and select Watch This Value to have a permanent floating bubble above the variable with its value (Figure 12.43).

For a further breakdown of the variables of the AnimGraph and their attributes which updates at runtime, utilise the Blueprint Debugger (Figure 12.44—found in the AnimGraph > Debug > Blueprint Debugger). This provides a high-level overview of the selected BP.

If you exhaust all your options and are still stuck, with no amount of debugging helping you, try the age of rubber ducking! Rubber ducking is the process of explaining the problem out loud (to a rubber duck) or to another person, and more often than not the solution to the problem will present itself as you explain the problem.

FIGURE 12.41   Preview instance selector in the ABP.

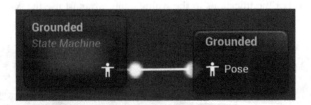

FIGURE 12.42   Live preview execution lines for runtime characters.

FIGURE 12.43   Variable watching and previewing.

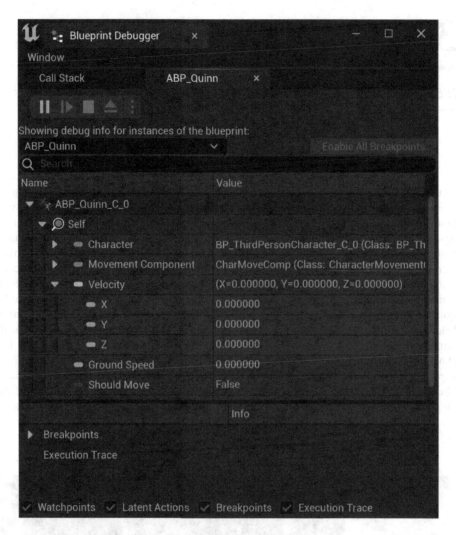

FIGURE 12.44 Blueprint Debugger User interface.

13

Unreal—The Control Rig Blueprint

The control rig BP is a new type of animation-focused BP introduced at the end of the Unreal 4 lifecycle; it is equivalent to Maya's node graph in capabilities, with a focus on being a lightweight way to manipulate skeletons (Figure 13.1). As the name suggests, the BP can be used to create control rigs in Unreal; however, its name is a bit of a misnomer, as its utility is not strictly limited to the creation of control rigs—the BP can be utilised in the animGraph and evaluated at runtime! A control rig node in the ABP can be used for many purposes, whether you want to create procedural animation, perform IK correction or even calculate deformation joints. It's an incredibly powerful tool to manipulate the skeleton's pose at runtime. The rig graph could even be utilised to rebuild all the connections from your Maya rig in the control rig blueprint—no longer will you need to bake the skeleton's deformation joints into the animations from Maya, these calculations could be done at runtime instead; moving the expense from dense animation data to computed at runtime. It's an incredibly powerful suite of tools.

Control rigs come with all the features of a regular blueprint, with functions and variable management, but this BP has an alternative to the Event Graph, it has its own graph called the **Rig Graph**. The rig graph is where you can read the current state of the skeleton and perform calculations based on it.

FIGURE 13.1 The Control Rig Blueprint.

DOI: 10.1201/9781003263258-13

13.1 Control Rig Setup

1. Enable the Control Rig Plugin (**Unreal Settings > Plugins > Control Rig Enabled**).
2. Create a Control Rig asset via the Content Browser (**Content Browser > Add > Animation > Control Rig > Control Rig** or **Right-click skeletal mesh > Create > Control Rig**).

You may notice that unlike typical animation assets; control rig blueprints are not skeleton-specific—however, we are required to import a skeleton's hierarchy to begin the manipulation of bone data. Since it is not tied to a specific skeleton asset, it can be shared across multiple skeleton assets as long as the imported hierarchy matches. To import a hierarchy, open **Window > Rig Hierarchy > Right Click > Import > Choose Skeletal Mesh**. This will allow us to begin the modification of any imported joint.

13.2 Rig Graph

13.2.1 Execution Order

A Control Rig has an execution order, so one node executes after another in a specific order; they do not run in parallel, unlike Maya. Keep this in mind when building your rig graphs to ensure an appropriate order of execution. To assist in the tracking of the graph's execution order, the Execution Stack window (Figure 13.2—**Windows > Execution Stack**) allows you to keep track of and debug the orders of your nodes.

Note that, unlike the animGraph, the control rig does not feature an output pose, the final result is after the final calculation from the execution stack.

FIGURE 13.2 The Control Rig's Execution Stack interface.

 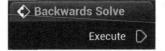

FIGURE 13.3   The Control Rig's Backwards and Forwards Solve nodes.

13.2.2 Solve Direction

While the animGraph has a single execution flow, the control rig graph's execution flow has two directions: forward and backward solve (Figure 13.3). While only one is active at any given time, it effectively creates two modes of interaction for the control rig.

The forward solve is the default solving path used for a control rig asset; this pathway is for the driving and manipulation of skeleton joints driven by constraints, controllers or other logic. This solving path is utilised when the control rig is used in an ABP or as an animation control rig. The backward solve is used when the system is used as an animation control rig and we need to put animation from a skeleton onto the controllers.

While developing your control rig asset, you are able to switch between a preview for forward or backward solving via the toolbar at the top of the window; press the three dots next to the solve to reveal a dropdown to switch between solving methods.

13.2.3 Work Preview and Debug

While developing your control rigs, it is prudent to test your work thoroughly—the control rig graph offers some additional tools that you can use to check for correct behaviour.

A basic, albeit hidden feature is that you can modify the transforms of any object, whether it's a joint or a controller, directly within the viewport. Right-click the object you wish to transform in the Rig Hierarchy and select **Control Transform**.

The control rig toolkit also has **Live Details** for each node; this is located within the Details panel with the node selected (Figure 13.4). The live details list each incoming and outgoing variable for that specific node, and as the viewport preview changes, these values will update in real-time.

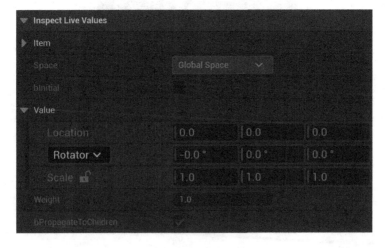

FIGURE 13.4   The Inspect Live Values interface for the Control Rig.

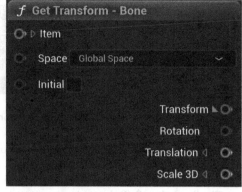

FIGURE 13.5 Set Rotation and Get Transform nodes for the Control Rig blueprint.

13.3 Control Rig Tools

The Control Rig arsenal is very comprehensive, from basic math operations to constraints and even a full-body IK system—the suite of runtime tools that Control Rig offers can support many workflows. The tools for the Control Rig work in both backward and forward solve directions. When it comes to the available tools, you don't know what you don't know, so here's a rundown of a variety of useful and common tools you can employ in your workflows.

13.3.1 Set and Get

Set and Get nodes are the basic fundamentals of the Rig Graph, the getter nodes receive information from the current scene, which we can then manipulate or change, and then the setter nodes can apply any information we provide (Figure 13.5). There are various versions of the nodes: with Set Rotation, Set Scale, Set Translation and so on. Both nodes also include an "Initial" Boolean option; this means the node will execute based on the initial state of the object, so if you got the rotation of a joint initial, it would return the bind pose value, not its current value.

13.3.2 Quaternion Rotations

When accessing rotations in the rig graph, they are in quaternion format; this is signified by a blue pin. At first, this can feel alien to those not familiar with working with them. If you would prefer to deal with Euler rotations, the rig graph offers conversion nodes to switch data between quaternion and Euler. The **To Euler** node will convert from a quaternion to an Euler, and the **From Euler** node will convert an Euler to a quaternion. Once converted into an Euler rotation, you must convert back to quaternion to apply a rotation! These conversion nodes also expose an enum to switch the rotation order of the data (Figure 13.6).

FIGURE 13.6 Quaternion to Euler and back conversion nodes.

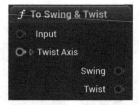

FIGURE 13.7   Rotation swing and twist isolation node for control rig.

Within quaternions, there is an understanding of the swing and twist as two different rotations; when considered as an Euler equivalent, this is akin to the swing being XY and the twist being Z, and you are able to differentiate and access the two separately while preserving the other rotation. The **To Swing & Twist** node separates these rotations for use (Figure 13.7). This could be particularly useful for isolating twist rotations, such as on a forearm twist, where we only require the twist to be isolated.

13.3.3 Math Utilities

Since the majority of the values we will be dealing with are inside the control rig number, we are provided with a plethora of math utilities to manipulate our data; from the standard arithmetic nodes for add, subtract, divide and multiply, all the way to clamping or remap nodes (Figure 13.8).

The clamp values are particularly useful for mimicking joint limits; if we get a joint's translations or rotations, we can run it through a clamp and reapply to ensure the value does not exceed a particular value (Figure 13.9).

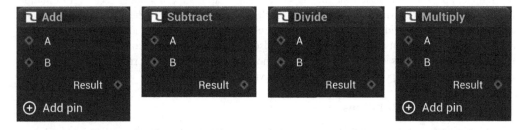

FIGURE 13.8   Basic math operations nodes.

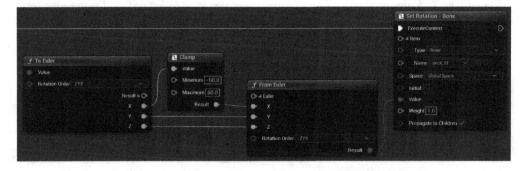

FIGURE 13.9   A utilisation of a clamp node to mimic a joint limit from Maya.

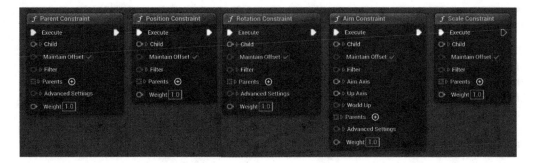

FIGURE 13.10   Various constraint nodes for the Control Rig Blueprint.

13.3.4 Constraints

The suite of common constraints is at your disposal: Parent Constraint, Position Constraint, Rotation Constraint, Scale Constraint and Aim Constraint (Figure 13.10). Each works under the principle of a Child and Parent relationship, with the Child being the destination of the constraint and the Parents being the source or driver. Each constraint has additional parameters for maintaining offset, or axis filtering—matching many of the constraint flexibility offered by Maya.

13.3.4.1 Fake Rivet Constraint

While those common constraints are offered, a useful missing constraint that is commonly used in Maya is a rivet constraint. However, we are able to "fake" a rivet within Control Rig. This technique relies on knowing the skinning information from inside Maya. We will use this information to create a Parent Constraint, allowing us to create a fake rivet that matches the skinning information.

1. **Inside Maya**, **select** a **vertex** you wish to rivet to.
2. Open the Component Editor's Smooth Skins tab (**Maya Menu > Windows > General Windows > Component Editor**).
3. Inside the Control Rig, create a **Parent Constraint** node.
4. **Copy each joint from Maya** as a **new Parent item** in Parent Constraint node, and **add the matching influence value into the Weight value**.
5. The chosen Child joint will now have a rivet matching the skinning information! *Keep in mind that this will be driven by the skinning information only, so it will not rivet to any additional simulation layers such as cloth.*

13.4 Application in AnimGraph

Applying a control rig in the animGraph is as simple as creating a **Control Rig node** and assigning a specific control rig asset within the details of the node. This empowers us to use a control rig at runtime at any point within the animGraph's execution flow.

A control rig can be used in a variety of manners from within the animGraph, since each control rig can be considered as a module, we are able to create isolated control rig modules that we can place at any point in our graph. One such use case is as an alternative skeletal control node, with the control rig BP offering many lightweight alternatives to the skeletal control nodes but at a much cheaper computation cost and without the additional need to switch to and from component space.

14

Unreal—Physics Assets

While we briefly covered physics assets in the skeleton setup chapter for Unreal, let's quickly recap. A physics asset is a type of asset associated with a skeleton that determines the collision and physics properties of the said skeleton. These assets have their own dedicated interface called the Physics Asset Editor, where you can add collision volumes to bones and define constraints between volumes to create hinges, ball joints, or even piston-like behaviour. You could even create more complex behaviour with motors and springs. The physics asset can be used to create runtime dynamics, such as hair ponytails or secondary dynamics like bags.

14.1 Physics Asset Creation and Application

To generate a physics asset for a skeletal mesh:

1. **Right-click a skeletal mesh > Create > Physics Asset > Create**.

This will create a physics asset linked to the skeletal mesh. A skeletal mesh asset can only have a single physics asset assigned to it. To assign it manually, open the skeletal mesh and navigate to the details panel's **Physics** category, there will be the **Physics Asset** variable (Figure 14.1). Alternatively, you can create and assign a physics asset at the first step, by choosing **Physics Asset > Create & Assign** instead.

While the skeletal mesh can only have a single physics asset assigned, this is merely the default—you can choose to override the physics asset on a per instance basis, such as a BP component or placed into the scene, so you are not always stuck with one physics asset for one skeletal mesh. To override the physics asset, first, **select the Skeletal Mesh component > Details Panel > Advanced > Physics Asset Override > Choose Asset** (Figure 14.2).

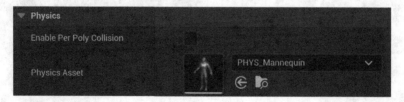

FIGURE 14.1 The assignment panel for the physics asset.

FIGURE 14.2 The assignment panel for the physics asset override within a blueprint component.

DOI: 10.1201/9781003263258-14

14.2 Physics Asset Editor

The Physics Asset Editor, formerly known as the PhAT (Physics Asset Tool), is a dedicated interface that empowers you to build the physics assets directly in the editor. Opening the physics asset, editor is as simple as double-clicking a physics asset and the editor will open (Figure 14.3).

For the most part, the physics asset interface should look very similar to the other model viewers or the most parallel to the skeletal mesh preview interface. On the left, we have the Skeleton Tree, the contextual Details panel on the right, and the physics asset-specific interfaces come in the form of the Graph and Tools windows on the bottom left and bottom right, respectively. If any of these windows are absent, they can be re-enabled via the **Toolbar > Window** dropdown.

14.2.1 Graph

The graph window (Figure 14.4) shows contextual information based on which objects you have selected at the current time, showcasing their relationships to other objects through constraints.

14.2.2 Skeleton Tree

Beyond the typical behaviour you would expect from the Skeleton Tree interface, there is additional functionality in the physics asset editor. Not only does the Skeleton Tree show bones in this interface, but it also shows physics bodies, volumes and constraints. By default, the Skeleton tree only shows bodies, this does not provide the full scope of the physics asset scene. You can change this by enabling **Show Constraints, Show Primitives,** and **Show All Bones** in the settings *(Cog icon)* for the Skeleton Tree to view the entire scene contents (Figure 14.5).

From directly in the Skeleton Tree, we can create physics bodies, by right-clicking a joint and selecting **Add/Replace Bodies** or **Add Shape.** Constraints can then be generated by selecting two or more bodies, right-clicking, then selecting **Constrain Selected Bodies.**

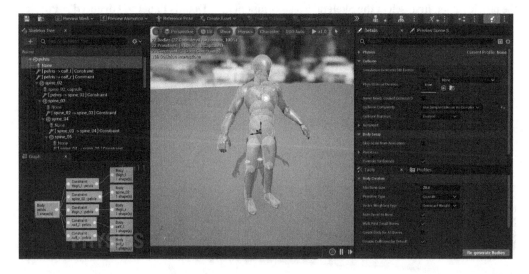

FIGURE 14.3 The Physics Asset Editor interface.

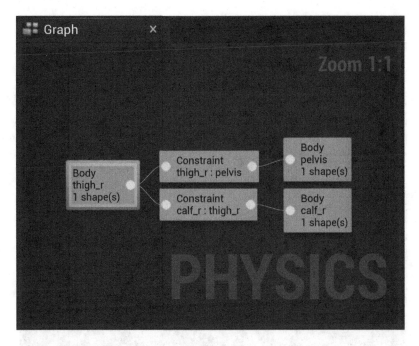

FIGURE 14.4   The graph window.

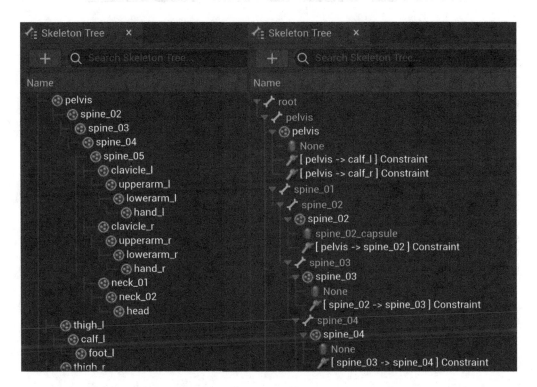

FIGURE 14.5   The Skeleton Tree view difference once constraints, primitives and bones are enabled.

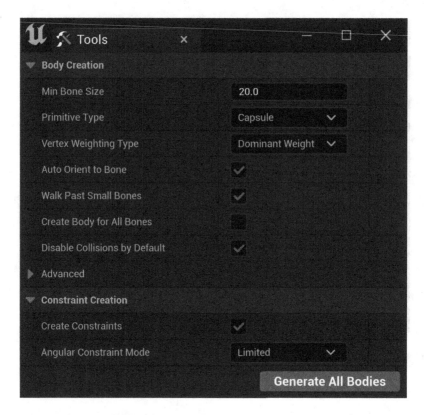

FIGURE 14.6 The physics asset Tools window.

14.2.3 Tools

The tool's interface (Figure 14.6) will be your best friend to generate new bodies with a variety of user-defined settings, whether collisions are disabled by default or generated with constraints. I recommend utilising this window for generating bodies, as it will save time applying settings manually after generation. Simply select a bone, or pre-existing body and then click generate!

14.2.4 Scene Simulation

At the top of the toolbar, you will find the Simulate button; on lower-resolution monitors, this option can be hidden away under the ≫ (Figure 14.7). The simulate button will begin the simulation of the entire physics asset scene, with gravity and forces applied. If there was a character present in the scene, they would ragdoll. The simulation also offers a Simulate Selected option under the Simulate Options, which can be used for isolated testing on specific physics assets. To disable the simulation, press the Simulate button a second time.

FIGURE 14.7 Simulate and Simulate options buttons in the physics asset window.

While the simulation is active, you are able to manipulate the physics asset for testing—**press and hold Shift**, then **right-click hold on any physics body**, then without releasing the mouse press, drag your cursor around the screen; this will begin dragging around the selected physics body around the scene. As you move the cursor around the screen, you will notice a red dot; this is your cursor movement history.

14.3 Physics Bodies

Physics bodies are used as a collision approximation of your mesh. Since games operate in real-time with a set time every frame must calculate, performing physics and collisions that are 1:1 with your mesh is incredibly expensive. This can be done offline, but until computation power catches up, we need to approximate this. In the physics asset, we attach simple primitives to our joints that will be used to collide with, instead, these primitives are held together by simple constraints to maintain the skeletal structure together; this in turn gives us a simplified character that the skinned mesh resides inside, this simplified mesh is then what is used for collisions, ragdoll, dynamics, cloth interaction and even rendering.

14.3.1 Primitives

The basic primitives used for physics assets come in the form of boxes, spheres or even capsules. You can opt to use a convex shape, but these add a considerable expense to the simulation, so the simpler the shape the better. To generate a specific shape, **right-click a joint > Add Shape** (alternatively, CTRL+1 for a sphere, CTRL+2 for a capsule, CTRL+3 for a box and CTRL+4 for a tapered capsule).

Once created, shapes can be manipulated directly in the scene with the translate, rotate and scale gizmos to align the primitive to encapsulate the mesh under it. If you desire finer tweaking for each primitive, **select the physics body**, open the **Details** panel, and under **Body Setup > Primitives,** you will find **Spheres, Boxes, Capsules** etc. which allow you to control the exact offsets, radius, length, etc. by value editing rather than eyeballing.

On top of the basic primitives, there is a primitive that is exclusive to cloth: the tapered capsule. This is a capsule that can be larger on one side than the other, making its use for cloth collisions particularly useful on character limbs such as the forearm. The capsule can be tapered via the scale gizmo with the X and Y axis, each shrinking one side; alternatively under **Body Setup > Primitives** you can control the **Tapered Capsule's Radius 1** and **Radius 2.** *On the note of cloth, capsules can be considered as two spheres, when utilising the Apex cloth system (pre-Unreal 5's chaos cloth), there is a 32-sphere limit for cloth physics asset; so keep an eye on the number of spheres used, as capsules add two not one.*

14.3.2 Physics Constraints

Physics constraints hold together the primitives in our scene, they allow us to define where one constraint attaches to another and the degrees of freedom a constrained primitive has. Without these, our physics assets would fall apart. To create a constraint between bodies, **right-click a body > Constraints > Choose a body** to constrain to.

With a constraint selected, several preset options are available to choose from on the top toolbar: **To Ball & Socket, To Hinge, To Prismatic** and **To Skeletal** (Figure 14.8). Each of these options will

FIGURE 14.8 The physics asset constraint presets on the toolbar.

configure the constraint's settings to particular presets, the hinge, for example, will limit the rotation in two out of three axes to behave like a hinge. These presets are useful for quickly getting started on a constraint, then you can configure on top.

In the Detail panel for a constraint, we are able to apply translation and rotational limits to the body, similar to the limits you can apply to a joint in Maya. With a constraint selected, the translation limits are found in the **Detail panel's Linear Limits** category, and the rotation limits are found in the **Angular Limits** category. Both systems allow for each axis to be set in one of three states, free, limited or locked. Free allows that axis to be in any position or rotation and is not clamped, limited on the other hand, allows for a user-defined range the axis can be within; and locked means it is static. Rotational axes can have a per-axis defined limit range, whereas positional has a singular value that applies to each axis. These limits are crucial for mimicking real-life counterpart limits, such as a knee rotation that would require two locked axis and one limited rotation to provide realistic behaviour.

When it comes to defining the limits, you may notice that unlike Maya, where you can define a specific value for the minimum and maximum, this system only takes in a single value. For example, if you have a value of 25 degrees, it will only apply 12.5 degrees in each direction. You can alter this so the constraint's starting point is not directly in the centre of the range; to do this, select the constraint in the viewport and **press and hold ALT while rotating the constraint**; notice how the constraint does not rotate but the limit range does. The Simulate Selected tool is particularly useful for testing if a constraint's limits are working appropriately; use this to your advantage!

Hidden under the **Advanced** dropdown in each **Limits** category are additional options (Figure 14.9) to customise the **Soft Constraint** settings, which are springs. Springs are enabled by default, and they provide a bounce to the body when it hits a limit instead of stopping dead. Enabled this can provide a more organic feeling with limited constraints, whereas you can get more robotic limits with the springs disabled.

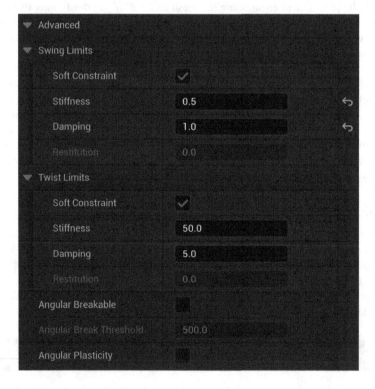

FIGURE 14.9 The advanced options for the soft constraint.

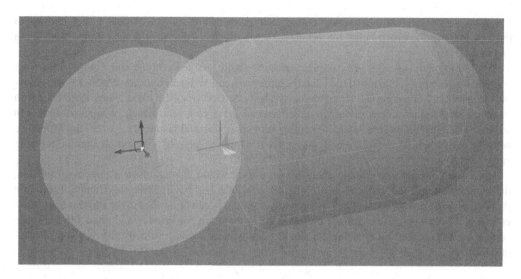

FIGURE 14.10 An example of overlapping capsules that will benefit from the disable collision option.

A useful setting to **disable** for each constraint is the **Disable Collision** Boolean; this does not, in fact, disable collision entirely; it only disables collision between the bodies connected by the constraint (Figure 14.10). This is important to disable if you have areas where two bodies intersect; they could still collide with one another unless collision between the bodies is disabled specifically; simply keep this checkbox on and it will solve the issue.

14.3.3 Body Collision

Collisions between bodies can be customised on a per-body basis, so if you had three bodies, you could have one collide with all three, but two only collide with one each. This granular control allows you to create more complex behaviour in your physics assets. An example of this would be for a character, you could have the upper arm bodies not collide with the spine bodies to allow for a much wider range of motion, but then the forearm could collide with everything.

Collision can be set on a body by right-clicking it, and under the **Collision** sub-menu, there are a variety of options. From this list, select **Enable Collision All (Ctrl + Left Bracket)**, this option will enable this body to collide with each body currently in the scene. For more granular control, select two or more bodies and return to the same menu for additional options to **Enable Collision (Left Bracket)** or **Disable Collision (Right Bracket)** between the bodies. Alternatively, when the bodies are selected, an **Enable Collision** or **Disable Collision** button will be on the toolbar.

14.3.4 Physics Properties

Physics bodies have one of two types: simulated or kinematic. Simulated means the body will use physics, whereas kinematic means they will not be affected by physics, utilising their animation input pose; however, they can collide with simulated bodies. If a body is set to simulated, its behaviour under physics can be modified by the physics properties found in the Details panel with the body selected.

The mass of an object heavily determines how it behaves, primitives will automatically allocate a specific mass depending on the primitive's size, with multiple primitives all adding to the automatic value. Each primitive can be opted for with the Contribute To Mass Boolean in the Body Setup window. The mass value allows you to override the automatic value with your own on a per-body basis.

If you notice any jittering on chains of bodies, consider reducing the mass value on each body, with the first body in the chain being the heaviest, then halve the value for the next body, halve again and so on.

Exposed to physics bodies are damping values for both Linear Damping and Angular Damping, with the former applying to translation and the latter for rotation. Damping adds drag to a body, reducing the sensitivity of the physics simulation to the body. Small values can make a huge difference with damping, with higher values giving an underwater or gravityless feel, which can be undesirable in some cases. When modifying, try incrementing very small decimal values of 0.1 to see the difference between each level. By default, a body has a linear damping value of 0.01 and an angular damping value of 0.

When you consider what would change how a body would change under a physics simulation, the biggest factor is the material itself - the material of a body can define the friction, restitution (bounciness) and density of an object. For physics bodies, this can be defined in the **Physics Material** - an external asset that can be utilised project wide to maintain consistency and allow for wholesale edits, these parameters can be defined in the Physics asset that will drastically change the properties of the body.

14.3.5 Physics Body Mirroring

Save yourself the trouble of matching physics bodies across symmetrical characters by utilising the mirror tool. **Right-click any physics body and press Mirror (or press M)** to mirror the physics body, primitives, and even the constraint to the opposite limb. This tool has some expectations of a mirrored joint name, such as a R/L suffix or prefix to match to—so if it does not mirror, check your joint names.

14.4 Skeletal Mesh Bounds

Physics assets are not only used for collisions and physics, they are also used for bounds calculations. A bound is a simplified volume that an object takes up in 3D space; this is used to calculate whether an object is on screen or not. A bound preview can be enabled in the viewport by enabling **Show > Advanced > Bounds** (Figure 14.11). For skeletal meshes, since their skeletons can deform and move in their object space, we are required to use physics assets to more accurately check if an object is on screen or not. Each primitive in the physics asset is included in the bounds of the skeleton mesh, this can be opted out on a per-primitive basis with the **Consider For Bounds** Boolean in the physics asset. The utilisation of physics assets for bounds checks can also be disabled wholesale on the skeletal mesh component, by enabling the **Component Use Fixed Skel Bounds** option under the **Optimisation** category. While it is cheaper to enable it, you may experience issues where the character will stop rendering even if it is on screen.

14.5 Ragdoll Trigger

Utilising your physics asset as a ragdoll is a common request, so let's walk through the process of triggering a ragdoll in-game. The prerequisites for this require that you have a skeletal mesh inside of a BP already, whether that's your player character's skeletal mesh in your BP pawn or just a skeletal mesh in an actor. Additionally, make sure you've set up and assigned a physics asset for that skeletal mesh.

1. Select the desired skeletal mesh in the components panel of the BP, and navigate to the Collision category in the details panel.
2. Set the Collision Presets option to Ragdoll.

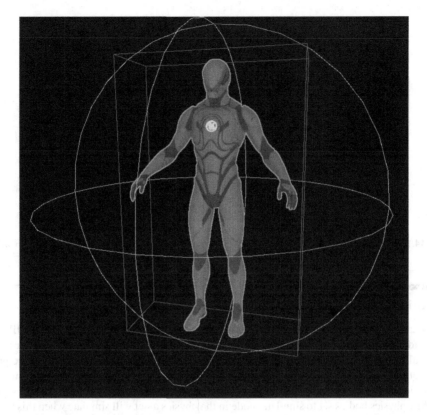

FIGURE 14.11 The bounds of a skeletal mesh.

3. Create a 'Set Simulate Physics' node in the event graph.
4. Assign the skeletal mesh as the Target input in the Set Simulate Physics node.
5. Enable the simulate Boolean option (Figure 14.12).

The Set Simulate Physics node is the primary node for enabling and disabling the ragdoll state on the skeletal mesh. Next, we need to trigger this node—if a pawn is being used, we could simply use an input trigger to drive it, or we could alternatively use a trigger volume. Any form of trigger or event will do (Figure 14.13); simply connect to the Set Simulate Physics node, which will activate ragdoll on your skeletal mesh!

FIGURE 14.12 Example blueprint nodes to enable a physics simulation for a skeletal mesh.

FIGURE 14.13 Example nodes to trigger the physics asset, player input "F" on the left, and a trigger box overlap on the right.

14.6 AnimGraph RigidBody

Not only can we apply a physics asset on the skeletal mesh level, but we are also able to utilise these assets inside the animGraph via the RigidBody node (Figure 14.14). This node allows for a physics asset simulation to take place at a specific point in the animGraph flow influenced by the previous input's motions, coupled with all the features of the graph to enhance your physics assets with state-like behaviour, it's an incredibly useful and powerful tool to add secondary animations to your characters. Any physics bodies set to simulate mode in the physics asset will simulate when this rigidbody node is active. The RigidBody node resides in component space like a skeletal control node, so you will be required to convert your local space pose to a component pose to operate.

Not only will the rigidBody node accept the default physics asset for the skeletal mesh, but you can also override it with any physics asset that can be utilised to create an animGraph-specific physics asset that could focus exclusively on dynamics, for example, whether that's a ponytail or a chain.

The node also comes bundled with a ton of customisable options to control and manipulate the input and output of the simulation; I won't go into detail as the tooltips for each option have a comprehensive breakdown in the editor, so be sure to hover over each one to see exactly what they do!

FIGURE 14.14 The RigidBody node in the animation graph.

15

Unreal—Sequencer Cinematics

Sequencer is Unreal's animation toolkit, commonly used to create cinematic animations or in-editor animations without leaving the package. The sequencer acts similarly to video editing software, but for all things 3D; you can animate, apply sound, spawn visual effects, trigger gameplay logic or events and even animate cameras. Sequencer can not only be used to create runtime cinematics, but it can also be used as an offline renderer—meaning you can prerender any sequences into a video file, utilising Unreal as a renderer if you wanted to make an animated movie.

You can make your own Level Sequencers via the **Content Browser > Add > Cinematics > Level Sequence**. Opening the Level Sequence will open the track-based Sequencer interface.

15.1 Keyframing and Animation

Sequencers' bread and butter is animation, and this workflow comes packed with all you would expect from a track-based animation workflow (Figure 15.1). Each sequencer track can be expanded to reveal animateable attributes, which can be easily keyed with the appropriate + icon for each take row, with the arrow keys jumping to the previous or next key for that track. We are not limited to viewing our animations on this linear timeline track; there is also a curve editor accessible from the Sequencer Curves toolbar button ( ). The curve editor can provide a more traditional view that many animators are familiar with and prefer to work with (Figure 15.2).

When skeletal mesh actors are placed in the sequencer, they will not only have access to transform attributes, but they will also include a track for animation; from this track, we can apply any animation for the appropriate skeleton. This allows a clip-based workflow to stitch animations together to build strings of sequences.

15.2 Pre/Post Roll Frames

When utilising animation sequences, you may encounter situations as demonstrated in the image below: we have a run animation, but in frames 0–9 we have no animation data, which causes the mesh to default to the bind pose. Unreal offers Pre-Roll and Post-Roll frames as an exposed attribute that will hold the first frame for an X amount of frames in the past or the last frame for an N amount of frames in the future. **This can be accessed by right-clicking the animation > properties > pre-roll frames/post-roll frames.** Once entered, you will notice a striped arrow before or after the animation sequence, denoting the number of frames you have chosen (Figure 15.3).

15.3 Keep State

When the sequencer has finished playback in-game, any possessed actor will revert to its original state prior to the sequencer property modifications. This is the default behaviour of level

DOI: 10.1201/9781003263258-15

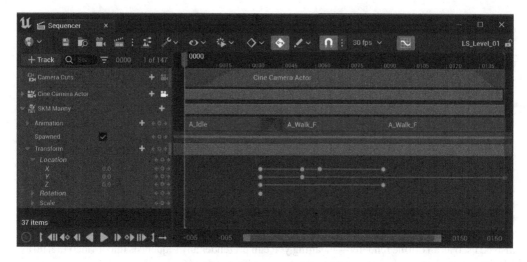

FIGURE 15.1   The sequencer timeline interface.

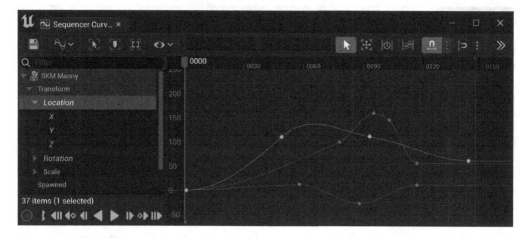

FIGURE 15.2   The sequencer curve editor.

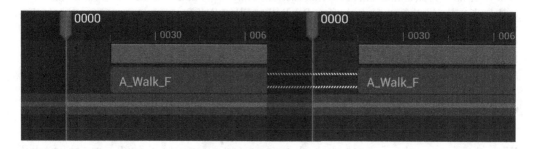

FIGURE 15.3   Pre-roll frames before and after in the timeline.

sequencers in Unreal; however, it can be changed to keep its state. Each sequencer track has the option to Keep State; this is accessible by **right-clicking the track > Edit Section > When Finished > Keep State.** This per-track option allows for flexibility, so some tracks can reset and others cannot.

You may notice the default option for the When Finished property is Project Default—This is because there is a project setting we can modify if we desire to set it to Keep State by default. However, this option is not exposed to the editor's UI; we must add a preference to the **DefaultEngine.ini** located in **/Unreal Project Folder/Config.**

```
[/Script/LevelSequence.LevelSequence]
DefaultCompletionMode=KeepState
```

15.4 Possessable and Spawnable

Actors within a sequencer exist in one of two states; possessable or spawnable. Possessable means the actor already exists within the current level, and the Sequencer is "possessing" that actor to manipulate and modify its properties. Spawnable, on the other hand, is an actor that is created with the Sequencer and can be chosen to destroy when the Sequencer ends or persist after the Sequencer has ended. This state is useful to note when building gameplay cinematics for objects you want to add or possess, as you may wish to possess objects from the scene to modify and not always spawn in unique assets. The only issue that must be noted with possessables is that if you are not at the correct level with the correct possessable items, the binding to that actor will break in the sequencer and be missing until you preview the sequencer in the correct level. Spawnable objects do not have this issue.

Pre-existing actors can simply be dragged from the Scene Outliner into the Sequencer interface to become possessable, and actors you wish to be spawnable require to be dragged from the Content Browser to the Sequencer interface or added via the +Track button in Sequencer. Actors can also be switched between possessable and spawnable states by right-clicking the actor within Sequencer and selecting **Convert To Spawnable/Possessable.**

15.5 Cameras

Unreal is equipped with a Cine Camera Actor, which will empower you to bring all your film creations to life; this actor is a virtual camera with properties that emulate real-world counterparts. Included functionality allows for film back and depth of field options, among many other lens properties. Each of these settings can be accessed from the Details panel with a camera selected. For those familiar with cameras, these settings may be second nature, but let's do a quick summary to get everyone on the same page.

15.5.1 Film Back and Focal Length

The film back refers to the width and height dimension of the camera's sensor (measured in mm), Unreal provides several preset dimensions, such as 16:9 DSLR, Super 35mm or IMAX 70mm— each switches sensor width and heights to give different visual looks to the camera. The film back is paired with the camera's focal length to dictate the visual coverage of the camera, the camera's field of view. The focal length value is a real-world distance (measured in mm) between the point of convergence on a lens and the camera's sensor, changing this value can give the visual effect of a zoom (Figure 15.4).

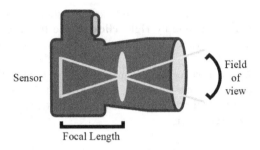

FIGURE 15.4   Camera diagram for film back and focal length.

15.5.2 Depth of Field

The depth of field (abbreviated DOF) is a series of parameters that control the focus and blur of a camera's view (Figure 15.5). While film back and focal length influence the DOF, it's primarily driven by the **aperture** and the **focus distance**. While we won't get too deep into how camera lenses' operate, the summary is that the aperture controls how big the opening that lets light into the camera is; this, in turn, will change how out of focus the view will become. The focus distance

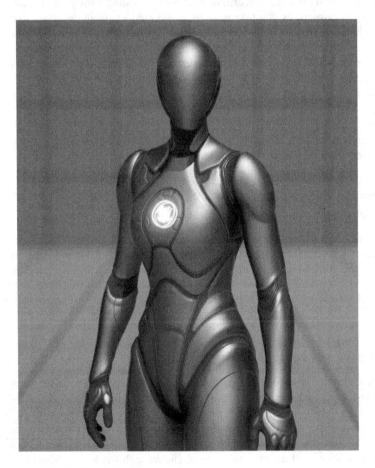

FIGURE 15.5   Depth of field in Unreal Engine 5.

FIGURE 15.6 Focus settings available for cine cameras.

is a distance metric from the camera to the point we desire to be in focus. With the focus distance set on our subject and a small aperture value, we can create a view where our subject is in focus and the front and behind are blurred. This is a fantastic cinematic technique to help focus the viewer's attention on a specific subject.

Within the details of a camera, you will find the focus settings category; this dropdown contains controls for the focus distance parameter (Figure 15.6). The focus method has three options: Disabled, Manual or Tracking. Manual allows for a user-driven input to control the focus distance value; this can be set as a static value or animated through Sequencer. Tracking will utilise an additional actor to automatically calculate a focus distance value, the distance between the camera and the assigned actor will be used for the focus distance. The focus distance can then be smoothed with the Interp Speed value or even have a fixed offset applied (Figure 15.7).

The Draw Debug Focus Plane option will enable a handy debug visualisation of where the focus distance plane is from the camera. It is visualised by a bright purple plane that will intersect forward into the scene.

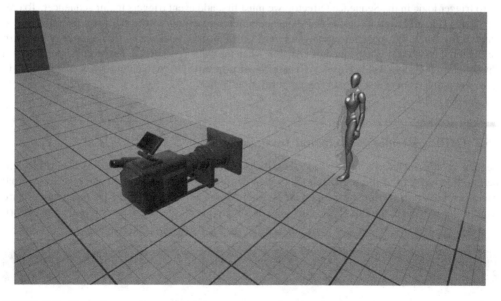

FIGURE 15.7 Focus distance plane to aid in visualising where the focus plane is.

FIGURE 15.8   Camera cut track in the sequencer timeline.

15.5.3 Camera Cut Track

Cameras can be placed into your scene as an actor from the Place Actors window, but they can also be animated from within a sequencer to make cutscenes. Pressing the camera icon (▦) from the sequencer's toolbar will create not only a Cine Camera Actor but also a Camera Cuts track. The camera cut track is used to designate which camera is active and which sequencer should be used. The camera cut track allows for multiple cameras to be present in the sequencer file, and the camera cut track can be used to switch between different cameras. Add new cameras to the track via the + icon on the track (Figure 15.8).

A hidden feature of the camera cut track is the ability to blend. This will blend a camera cut in, out or crossfade between two different cameras. This can be enabled by **right-clicking the Camera Cuts Track > Enable Can Blend.** Once enabled, you are able to **drag from the top left/right corner** of any camera cut segment, and it will create a blend in/out or crossfade. The blend curve can be customised by right-clicking the blend area and hovering over Options (Figure 15.9).

15.6 Events and Sequencer Director

The sequencer is not only limited to animation; we can trigger BP events with accompanied logic directly within the sequencer. Each sequencer has its own unique event graph called the Sequence Director. This is accessible via the Sequencer Director toolbar button (▦).

To trigger logic in the Sequence Director, we must first add event triggers to our sequencer. To create events, add an **Event Track** to the sequencer, then **add events to the track by pressing the + icon on the track**. We must now create an **Event End Point** for that event—this is the node that will be triggered from inside the Sequencer Director when the event is activated. **Right-click the event on the timeline > Properties > Event > Create New Endpoint**. This will create a new custom node in the event graph from which we can trigger our desired logic!

15.7 Offline Render to External Image/Video

Sequencer also includes a render to external file feature to utilise the engine as an offline renderer—this will export the sequencer as a video or image sequence that you can take to external packages. To export, we must first open the **Render Movie Settings** interface via the clapper board icon in the sequencer toolbar (▦). This interface includes all the parameters required to export,

FIGURE 15.9   Camera blending in the camera cut track.

including the file type (video or image sequence), framerate, compression and export paths. If you want to export to a video sequence, select the Video Sequence (AVI) option from the Image Output Format selection or any of the Image Sequence options (PNG/JPG) to render each frame as an image.

15.8 Runtime Sequencer Trigger

Sequencers can be triggered at runtime either automatically at the beginning of a level, or via a triggered event. If you add a sequencer asset to your scene, navigate to the Details panel, under the Playback tab is a variable labelled Auto Play. If enabled, the sequencer will automatically play on game start (Figure 15.10).

15.8.1 Trigger Volume

We may prefer to use trigger volumes that activate playback of our cutscene, which can be utilised if a player enters a specific room/area to trigger a specific cutscene.

Let's create a generic cutscene trigger BP that we can utilise throughout our project.

1. **Create a blueprint** via the **Content Browser > Add > Blueprint Class > Actor > Pick Parent Class**.
2. Expand the **All Classes** dropdown, search and select **TriggerBox**.
   a. We are utilising the TriggerBox class, rather than a standard actor class to piggyback on pre-existing trigger box behaviour and logic.
3. Rename the blueprint accordingly; for example **BP_Sequencer_Trigger**.
4. **Open the blueprint**.
5. Since we are inheriting from the TriggerBox class, we have some preset components. The Collision Component is the trigger volume we want to use to activate behaviour. Let's create our logic by **right-clicking the component > Add Event > Add OnComponentBeginOverlap.** This will create an event that will trigger when any actor overlaps with this component (Figure 15.11).
6. Since the event will trigger for any actor, we need to filter to see if our player character was the actor that overlapped. Let's **add a Branch node**, and **connect the Other Actor pin** to an **Equals node** and compare with the **Get Player Pawn output pin** (Figure 15.12).

FIGURE 15.10 Assignment of a sequencer.

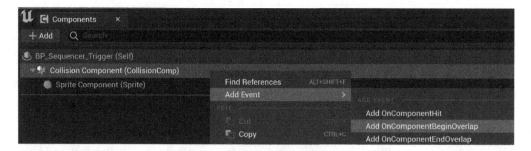

FIGURE 15.11   OnComponentBeginOverlap event for a collision component.

FIGURE 15.12   OnComponentBeginOverlap events connected to blueprint nodes.

7. To make this system generic, we need to create a public level sequence variable that can be modified on a per-instance basis so we can reuse it across our project. Let's create a new variable via the **My Blueprint > Variables > +** interface.

    a. Name the variable **Level_Sequence**.
    b. Select the variable and navigate to the **Details** panel.
    c. Change the variable type to **Level Sequence Actor.**
    d. **Enable Instance Editable** Boolean—this will make the variable public.

8. Drag the Level_Sequence variable into the event graph and select **Get**.

9. Drag from the Level_Sequence variable and **search & choose the Play node**.

10. **Connect** the **Play node** to the **Branch node**. Our BP logic is now complete! (Figure 15.13).

11. Let's use this! Add both your **BP_Sequencer_Trigger** and a chosen **Sequencer** asset into a scene. Feel free to customise the volume size of the trigger to fit your environment.

12. **Select** the **BP_Sequencer_Trigger** in the scene and open the **Details** panel.

13. **Set the Level_Sequence variable** to your chosen Sequencer asset.

14. **Play the game and enter the volume**—the sequencer will successfully trigger! This BP can now be reused for different cinematic triggers, just add duplicate BP and point the level sequence variable to a different actor! It's that simple!

FIGURE 15.13   Blueprint nodes to trigger the level sequence to play.

15.9 Function Trigger on Variable Change

One neat and relatively unknown feature of Sequencer is that you can attach a sequencer variable to trigger a function when the variable is modified instead of creating separate logic that checks for the variable's state changing. To do this, we merely require one variable and one function.

The setup is as simple as having a variable, and then having a function that matches the name of the variable but with the **Set** keyword before the variable name. So if we have a Boolean called "**Trigger**", our function would be called "**SetTrigger**". The next step is to enable a property on the variable and on the function; in the details panel of the variable you need to enable the "**Expose to Cinematics**" property. As for the function, it requires the "**Call in Editor**" to be enabled.

With both options enabled and the name matching, modifying the variable in Sequencer will cause the function to fire, even when scrubbing the sequencer timeline!

15.10 Sequencer to AnimGraph

A neat feature in the toolkit is the functionality to inject a sequencer animation into the animGraph—this is particularly useful for playing cinematic animations on gameplay characters from within the sequencer. It's super straightforward to set up with the Slot node in the ABP.

1. Open the **ABP's AnimGraph**.
2. **Add a Slot node**—the default node is labelled **Slot 'DefaultSlot'** (Figure 15.14).
3. **Insert the node into the AnimGraph's execution flow**; while the slot is not active, the node will not do anything.
4. Create a Sequencer asset that contains the character's skeletal mesh with an animation sequence assigned.
5. **Right-click the Animation sequence on the timeline > Properties > Animation > Slot Name.**
   a. The Slot Name setting is what is used to match the Sequencer animation with the Slot node in the ABP.
6. With both options at the DefaultSlot value, the animation will inject successfully into the ABP.

By default, every skeleton only has a single slot, DefaultSlot, but we can make and customise our own slots. To do so, open the Skeleton asset or the ABP and Window > Anim Slot Manager. From this interface, we can add more slots for use with our systems.

FIGURE 15.14 The Slot node in the ABP.

16

Unreal—Cloth Dynamics

Built directly into the Unreal editor are the tools to create run-time cloth simulations to bring your assets to life with procedural animation. Currently, this can only be applied to skeletal meshes, so any static meshes that we require cloth on must convert to a skeletal mesh. The system can be utilised to add animation to loose clothing items such as straps, skirts and long coats or even for in-world items such as flags.

The clothing tools rely on a series of masks that define how much vertices can move away from their skinned position when simulated, with a series of cloth properties that define how those vertices move within those limits. The properties range from being able to reduce the flexibility of the surface, the weight of it, or even how stretchy it is. While the simulation is designed for cloth, its application is not limited to cloth—we can apply these vertex simulations to any component we may want vertex movement on, such as skin slide, loose flesh or even hair!

Within UE5, the clothing tools utilise Epic's proprietary Chaos physics to simulate the cloth, while in older versions of the engine, NVidia's APEX is utilised. These two differ very little in the engine-side workflow, excluding the cloth property values that are completely revamped between the two, more on this shortly.

16.1 Cloth Creation Part 1—Prerequisites

When the cloth is assigned to a skeletal mesh, it is applied to an element—an element is defined by material assignment, so all polygons of a mesh with a single material assignment are one element. Since we are limited to assigning a cloth to a single material element, any polygons we want to assign cloth to must have a consistent material assignment per piece of cloth. So if we wanted multiple pieces of cloth, they can exist on multiple materials, but if we wanted a single piece of cloth, it must exist on one material. Our skeletal mesh must adhere to this prerequisite—if it does not, the art must change.

Since an element could encompass a much larger area than just the area we want to apply the cloth to, this could result in an unnecessary computation cost for our cloth. Since the cloth is assigned to all vertices of the element, there could be a large unnecessary area to which we do not need to apply the cloth. To remedy this, consider having a duplicate material in your DCC and assigning the duplicate only to the area desired to have cloth applied - as this will reduce the number of vertices the cloth is applied to.

16.2 Cloth Creation Part 2—Data Creation

1. Open the Skeletal Mesh asset you wish to apply the cloth to.
2. Open the Clothing interface via **Window > Clothing.** This is where we will customise our clothing, but first, we must create a clothing profile!

DOI: 10.1201/9781003263258-16

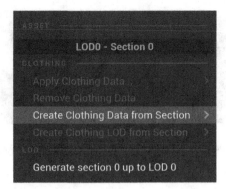

FIGURE 16.1 User interface to create clothing data from a section in Unreal.

3. In the viewport, select the element which you desire to create the cloth for, then **Right-Click > Clothing > Create Clothing Data from Section > Create** (Figure 16.1). This will create a new cloth profile, visible in the Clothing window's data list.

   a. Except for a new profile in the clothing data list, there will be no change in the scene. This is because the clothing tool has to create clothing data and then assign it separately. This is so you could have a different mesh for the simulation to the render mesh, such as using a lower poly simulation mesh for the clothing data and then applying the data to a higher poly element.

4. **Clothing can be applied in one of two ways:**

   a. Apply the data to the element via **Right-Click > Clothing > Apply Clothing Data > choose the relevant cloth profile**.

   b. **Details Panel > LOD 0 > Sections > Clothing dropdown** (Figure 16.2).

16.3 Cloth Creation Part 3—Painting Masks

With our data created and assigned, you may still notice nothing happens; that's because we're missing our cloth masks. The clothing simulation is performed by a variety of masks that define particular properties, with each mask performing a different function. These masks can be painted directly in the editor. Masks are shown under the Masks category in the Clothing window; new masks can be added via the + icon, and the target column details the type of mask they are; this can be switched by

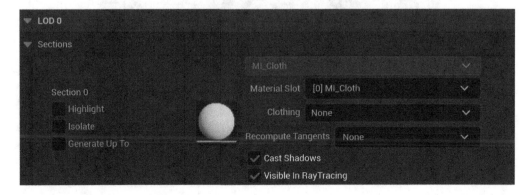

FIGURE 16.2 LOD panel for assigning cloth to a skeletal mesh element.

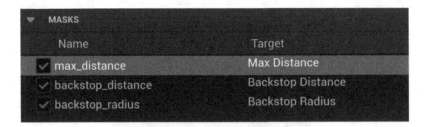

FIGURE 16.3 Examples of the paint masks available for the clothing tool.

right-clicking the mask and changing the target. With each clothing asset comes a default mask, the Max Distance mask (Figure 16.3).

The function of the Mask Distance mask is to define, on a per-vertex basis, how far that vertex can move away from its skinned position. Meaning that if a vertex has a painted value of 100, that vertex, when simulated, can move up to 100 units away from where that vertex would be if it was only skinned. There are over a dozen masks that perform a range of functions to control the cloth to your exact liking.

Let's begin by painting our Max Distance mask. Select the mask from the Masks list, then press the **Activate Cloth Paint** button on the top of the Skeletal Mesh window's toolbar. This will update the Clothing panel with several paint-focused parameters, and the viewport will change to a painting mode. The painting mode is identified by a green brush that will follow your cursor, and your cloth mesh will have turned a bright pink and the edges will be visible (Figure 16.4).

FIGURE 16.4 Painting with a brush in the Unreal Editor.

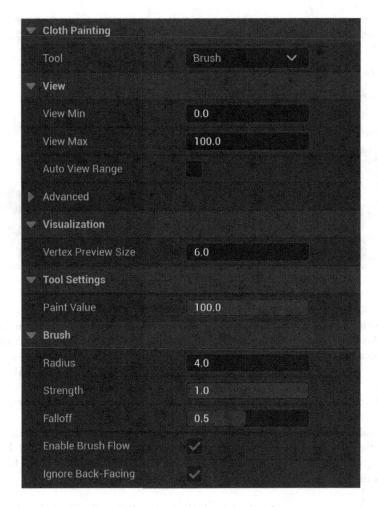

FIGURE 16.5   The paint brush tools available under the Cloth Painting interface.

The clothing panel will now have a series of painting options; these options allow for the customisation of brush behaviour and viewport display settings (Figure 16.5). The first option, the tool, changes the paint brush mode we are in: Brush, Fill, Smooth and Gradient. Changing the selected tool changes the mode and behaviour of the brush and exposes different settings.

The **brush tool** is the standard tool; this is similar to a brush in any other package, the user can paint a value on the cloth mesh. The brush category includes options for the radius, which will increase the size of the brush, strength, which modifies how much of the paint value applies (think of it like a multiplier of the paint value); and falloff which controls the decrease of paint value applied at the outer edges of the brush, allowing for a softer brush stroke (this can be left at 1 to make all vertices under the brush apply the full paint value).

The **fill tool** is similar to Maya's flood tool, except the tool has a **threshold** value that can be controlled. With a threshold of 100, the fill tool acts exactly like the flood tool and will replace the entire mask's value; however, the threshold can be used only to replace the paint value of similar paint values to the vertex selected, allowing for greater control of what is filled.

The **smooth tool** will cause the brush to blur existing values in the masks to have a nice smooth value change; this can be used to reduce any harsh value changes and get a smooth gradient blend between mask values.

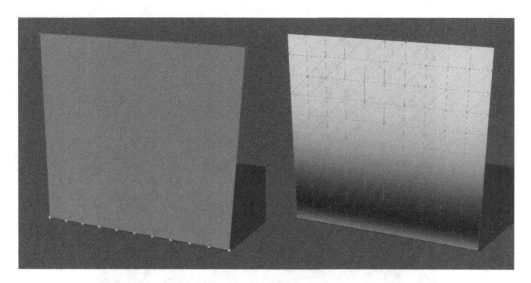

FIGURE 16.6   An example demonstration of the gradient paint brush tool.

If the smooth tool isn't cutting it for your gradient needs, then the dedicated **gradient tool** may be for you; this can create gradient blends between two user-determined values across your cloth mesh. You must first set your **Gradient Start & End** values, then define the start and end of the gradient in the viewport; **Left Mouse-Click** to highlight your starting area, this will highlight the vertices green. Then define your end area by pressing **Ctrl + Left Mouse-Click** on vertices; this will highlight the vertices in red (Figure 16.6). When you are happy to activate the gradient—press the **Enter** key. Done!

The **paint value** is our main overarching value; this determines the value the brush applies to the mask. While the UI slider is limited to 0–100, it can exceed 100 if manually entered. Depending on the mask, the paint value performs differently, but as previously explained for a Max Distance mask, it controls the distance the cloth can move from the skinned position.

16.3.1 Cloth Properties

The cloth properties can be found under the **Config > Cloth Config** portion of the **Clothing** interface. These are a series of parameters that can define how your cloth moves, and how it interacts with collisions. These properties can cause cloth to behave like fine silk or even heavy leather. Since Unreal has had two different solutions for cloth, that being Apex and Chaos cloth, they each have their own unique set of properties. However, it is important to note that Apex cloth is deprecated and can only be found in older versions of Unreal.

While I won't cover the full extent of each unique property, as there are a lot of configuration options and more are added in updates, I will cover a handful of some of the most useful properties I use to get the best-looking cloth. If you are ever in doubt about an option, hover over the setting for comprehensive tooltips of what the option does! (Figure 16.7). If you do not fully understand an option even after these descriptions, the best course of action is to experiment with the value, change it and see how it modifies your cloth!

- **Mass Properties**:
  - **Density** - This value can easily modify the type of cloth. Unreal provides a handful of examples, **0.1 Silk, 0.2 Cotton, Light Leather 0.3, 0.4 Denim, 0.6 Heavy Leather and 0.7 Melton Wool**.

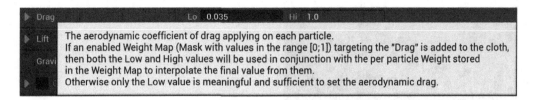

FIGURE 16.7 The clothing properties feature descriptive tooltips for each option.

- **Collision Properties**:
  - **Collision Thickness**—Modifies the padded distance between cloth and collision shapes.
  - **Friction Coefficient**—Value defines the friction of the cloth when colliding with collision shapes.
  - **Use Self Collisions**—Enables the cloth to collide with itself.
  - **Self Collision Friction**—Value defines friction for self-collisions.
- **Environmental Properties**:
  - **Damping Coefficient**—Smoothens out the stability of the cloth simulation, however high values give an underwater effect, so it is best to keep to low values.

16.3.2 Updating Cloth Profile Mesh

You may inevitably find yourself in need of updating your cloth simulation mesh after you have already painted and set your cloth properties; do not fret, as there is a procedure to do just this while preserving all of the work you have done so far.

1. Ensure you are happy with your new cloth mesh inside your DCC, then **re-export your skeletal mesh** while ensuring the updated cloth mesh has skinning data!
2. Inside the editor, open your skeletal mesh and press the **Reimport Base Mesh** button on the top toolbar. This will update all meshes, bones while and skinning data for the asset.
3. **Select the updated element in the viewport and right-click to open up the menu.**
4. Previously, we had selected Create Clothing Data from Section. To update a cloth mesh, we must now use the option called **Create Clothing LOD from Section** (Figure 16.8).
5. Expand the options—for **Target Asset** choose your cloth profile, **LOD index** select **Replace LOD0** to replace the current data. Enable the **Remap Parameters**—this will transfer your paint weighting from the previous mesh to your new mesh.
6. Press Create—complete.

16.3.3 Collision

Since runtime cloth is expensive to compute, Unreal's cloth by default only interacts with its "local" collision; this local collision is defined by the physics asset that can be assigned in the cloth's profile. Cloth can be opted in to interact with the world around it; this is limited to objects that are marked as static, so dynamic objects, including player characters will not be able to interact with it. However, enabling this option makes the cloth considerably more expensive.

16.3.3.1 Local Collision

Within the Config section, you will find a **Physics Asset** assignment; this references an external asset that will be used for the "local" collisions since the Physics asset is relative to the skeletal mesh component and has no understanding of the world to interact with (Figure 16.9).

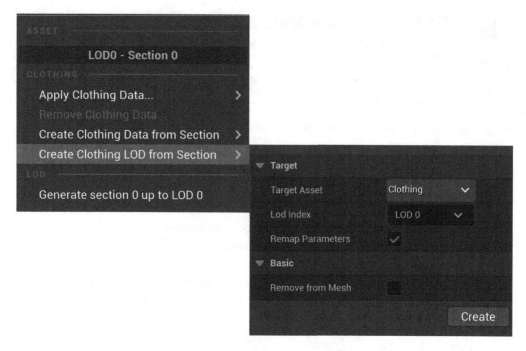

FIGURE 16.8 Method to create a LOD or replace an existing cloth simulation mesh.

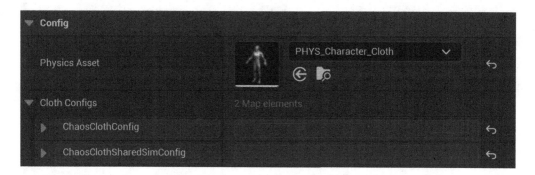

FIGURE 16.9 The location of the cloth physics asset assignment in the Config window.

Utilise the knowledge covered in a previous chapter to build a unique physics asset for your cloth profile to prevent any clipping or layering. When building the asset, be sure to make use of the **Tapered Capsules**; these are cloth-specific capsules that one end can be smaller than the other, making them particularly useful for the limbs of a human (Figure 16.10).

WARNING: A limitation to note if you are utilising the Apex cloth solution is that the physics asset has a **limit of 32 spheres or 5 boxes**; any and all shapes added beyond this limit will be ignored by the cloth simulation. Often users can misinterpret this as a bug, as their collision shapes can stop interacting with the cloth—this is not a bug, it's a limitation of apex! Keep in mind that capsules and tapered capsules count towards the limit as two spheres, not one! So keep an eye on the total sphere count!

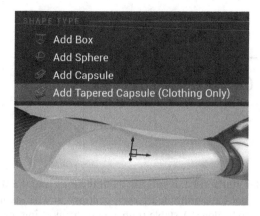

FIGURE 16.10   A tapered capsule, a capsule specifically for cloth collision that is useful for character limbs.

16.3.3.2 *World Collision (Collide with Environment)*

To enable world collision, you must enable the **Collide With Environment** Boolean found in the **Skeletal Mesh Component's detail** panel, under the **Clothing** category. Once enabled, the cloth will begin to interact with objects in the world that are marked as **Static**, so unfortunately, we cannot get our cloth to interact with other dynamic objects (such as a player or vehicles) with a simple setup.

This does come with some caveats, excluding the fact that it is more expensive, the maximum number of environment collisions is set to 32 shapes by default, and Unreal adds an extra volume padding to collisions of two. Fortunately, these can both be edited in the **Engine/Config/BaseEngine.ini** file under the [ClothSettings] category. If you have the computational expense to spare, you could increase the EnvironmentCollisionMaxShapes value, or if you're looking to optimise then drop this value!

```
[ClothSettings]
EnvironmentCollisionPadding = 2.f
EnvironmentCollisionThickness = 2.f
EnvironmentCollisionMaxShapes = 32
```

16.3.4 Wind

Wind Directional Source actors can be found in the **Place Actors Window > All Classes > Wind Directional Source**. When added to the scene, they will begin to influence all clothing simulations by adding wind, whether that's small subtle gusts or heavy storm winds—this is entirely customisable. The use of wind can prevent your clothing simulations from appearing static when the component is at a standstill; a small breeze can add much-needed life to a clothing simulation.

From within the Details panel for the Wind Directional Source actor, you will find the Wind Directional Source Component category, which displays a variety of options to customise the wind to your liking. By default, the wind affects the entire level universally; no matter if you have walls or are underground, the wind affects the cloth, except when the Point Wind option is enabled. This makes the wind switch from a global influence behaviour to a proximity behaviour; the proximity is scaled by the radius value. The strength, speed, minimum and maximum gust amount control how the frequency and amplitude of the wind, with the min and max gust amount adding variance to the gust.

Keep in mind that the options in the Wind Directional Source Component are not the only parameters that change the wind's behaviour; we must also define the rotation or forward direction of the wind actor, as this will dictate the direction the wind blows!

17

Unreal—The Optimisation

While hardware gets better all the time, it still has its limitations, and the sky is not the limit. Next-generation hardware does not have unlimited power, contrary to what its marketing may portray - optimisations always have to be done. A stable framerate is the most important aspect of a game and sacrifices must be made to ensure a consistent framerate. If you are targeting 60 frames per second, the entire render time of each frame is 16.6666666667 milliseconds—that is not a lot of time to calculate every component of the game from logic, animation, lighting, VFX and sound. Whether the optimisations are in the quality of assets, or in clever approaches to reduce computation workload, such as a reduction of fidelity at distances, the quality impact is less noticeable but still efficient.

Optimisation isn't anyone in particular's problem; it is everyone's problem at all times. It should not be left till the last minute, and all produced work should be consistently optimally produced. High-quality work does not just mean high fidelity, it means it fits its purpose of efficiency, practical and ultimately, usable. Creating messy, computationally expensive work and cleaning it up later are awful practices, and a fix-it-later mentality can lead to enormous technical debt, which will cause you to suffer later. However, premature optimisation for micro-savings is just as bad, as they waste valuable development time. Keep in mind that there is a difference between aggressive early optimisation that will detriment the product you make and general optimisation of acting on good, clean and efficient practices to make your work have optimal performance. Common sense should prevail here; do not reduce the quality of your work unnecessarily—only reduce fidelity when it's the only path.

Let's dive into a few practices you can do as a TA to keep your department optimised!

17.1 Game Content Size Optimisation

The storage size footprint of your data is an imperative consideration. For those who are developing a physical product that needs to be burnt to a disc, disc sizes are not infinite; while the current standard of Blu-Ray disc comes in several storage sizes, the larger the Blu-Ray disc costs more to use—meaning larger production costs. Even if the product is digital-only, you should strive for consumer-friendly sizes—players with internet bandwidth caps or limited storage space will appreciate it. Everyone on the team can do their part to reduce file sizes, while there is no silver bullet to this, lots of small savings will add up to a greater overall saving.

17.1.1 The Size Map Tool

The size map tool in Unreal allows you to view the total footprint of an asset or folder. The size map can be accessed by right-clicking an asset in the content browser and selecting size map (alternatively, Alt+Shift+M with the asset selected). The size map will display an asset and all its hard references; these are assets that need to be loaded to make this asset function. This can be used to identify the problem files, as the sizes of the assets in the size map are proportionate to their actual storage size, so if you notice an unnecessarily large texture or animation, there could be something wrong with the asset (Figure 17.1).

DOI: 10.1201/9781003263258-17

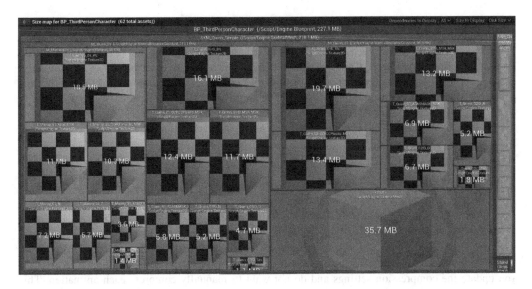

FIGURE 17.1 The size map tool in Unreal.

17.1.2 Animation File Size Reduction

Animation files are no doubt the most common asset used for a character, as games can contain thousands of animation assets. There are several ways to reduce the file size of an animation content asset.

17.1.2.1 Animation Track Reduction

Within the Details panel of an animation sequence asset, you will find the Animation Track Names property (Figure 17.2). This array is a list of every animated joint that will be evaluated when this animation plays back. The more tracks, the larger the file size, and the more expensive this animation will be to evaluate and playback. Diving into these tracks allows you to ascertain whether some animations have unnecessary joint data in them, as not all the joints of a skeleton are necessary to be present in animation at all times. For example, if we have a character with a face, we could exclude face joints from animations that are body only.

There is currently no way to remove tracks directly in the editor; you will need to delete the unnecessary joints from the FBX file directly prior to importing. Performing this across your suite of animations can help reduce your file size and computation use.

17.1.2.2 Animation Compression

While data compression may seem like the most obvious pathway to file size reduction, its use in animations can come with detrimental effects on the fidelity of animation for stronger compression, so the cost-effectiveness must be weighed up: is the sacrifice of file size, worth the gain of higher quality animations? There could even be a trade-off where cinematic animations are compressed less than

FIGURE 17.2 Animation Track Names in the Animation Sequence asset.

gameplay animations, for example. Each animation sequence has a variety of compression settings we can customise in the details panel.

While you can hover over each option for a detailed tooltip, the options that make the most difference are the **Bone** and **Curve Compression Settings**, which require external uassets. These assets detail an array of codecs and compression settings that can be applied to your animations. Since the codec parameter is an array, multiple codecs can be applied to a single compression.

- **Least Destructive**—No compression, this uses the raw animation data.
- **Remove Every Second Key**—Simply removes every other frame.
- **Remove Linear Keys**—Remove keys that are linear to the adjacent keys.
- **Remove Trivial Keys**—Constant keys across the entire animation are removed.
- **Bitwise Compress Only**—Compresses data, instead of reducing keys, comes in various precisions *(Float 96, Fixed 48, Interval Fixed 32, Fixed 32, Identity)*.
- **Per Track Compression**—Remove Linear Keys + Bitwise Compress codecs.

The compression assets include a function to re-compress all associated animation assets in case you update the compression settings and do not want to manually compress each animation. This function can be accessed by right-clicking the compression asset and clicking Compress, or via the Compress button on the toolbar with the asset open.

If you do create your very own compression, the default compression assets for new animations can be customised in**Engine\Config\BaseEngine.ini** - insert your new compression asset paths here so you do not need to reapply each time.

```
[Animation.DefaultObjectSettings]
BoneCompressionSettings="/Engine/Animation/
DefaultAnimBoneCompressionSettings"
AnimationRecorderBoneCompressionSettings="/Engine/Animation/
DefaultRecorderBoneCompression"
CurveCompressionSettings="/Engine/Animation/
DefaultAnimCurveCompressionSettings"
```

17.1.3 Texture Size Reduction

Texture assets will often be the culprits for the largest footprint; there are several steps we can take to reduce the file size, some of which will reduce the fidelity.

17.1.3.1 DXT5 versus DXT1

In the Compression category of your texture, you will find the Compression Settings value (Figure 17.3); the base value will be **Default (DXT1/5, BC1/3 on DX11)**. *For simplicity, when the engine is running on DirectX11 or later DXT1 = BC1, and DXT5 = BC3, these are the newer labels for the same compression.* When importing a texture, the engine will dynamically try to choose which is the best compression for you: DXT5 includes all RGB channels and an alpha channel totaling RGBA, whereas DXT1 omits the alpha channel, leaving only RGB. If the imported texture has an alpha present, the engine will opt for DXT5; if not, it will choose DXT1.

To switch between DXT5/DXT1, toggle the **Compress Without Alpha** option in the texture settings. You will quickly notice that when switching between DXT1 and DXT5, the resource size will nearly double when utilising DXT5 to include an alpha channel when compared to DXT1. So while the engine will try to pick the appropriate compression for you, some textures may slip through with an alpha present and potentially double your texture sizes! So be sure to verify all your textures, as these savings will soon add up!

FIGURE 17.3   Compression settings for texture assets in Unreal.

17.1.3.2 Engine-Wide Texture Size Limit

The resolution of each texture can have a huge difference in the file size, especially when you consider the resolution jumps from 1024×1024 to 2k, and 4k. These jumps do not double in pixel count, they quadruple each time—2k is 4 times 1k, and 4k is 4 times 2k. This can be detrimental not only to the storage size of your textures but also to their impact on runtime memory.

One solution to this is to set an engine-wide hard limit on texture sizes; this can be determined by the assigned texture group, allowing for environments to have a different limit than that of characters or vehicles. The texture group of an asset can be assigned inside the texture asset in the details panel's level of detail category (Figure 17.4).

To set the maximum texture size, we must navigate to the engine's config folder from File Explorer and open the BaseDeviceProfiles ini. This currently cannot be modified in the editor.

```
Location - Engine\Config\BaseDeviceProfiles.ini
[GlobalDefaults DeviceProfile]
+TextureLODGroups=(Group=TEXTUREGROUP_Character, MinLODSize=1,
MaxLODSize=2048…
+TextureLODGroups=(Group=TEXTUREGROUP_CharacterNormalMap, MinLODSize=1,
MaxLODSize=2048…
+TextureLODGroups=(Group=TEXTUREGROUP_CharacterSpecular, MinLODSize=1,
MaxLODSize=2048…
```

Under the MaxLODSize flag, we can determine the forced maximum resolution of each texture group utilised in the project - this would not affect the originally imported assets if they exceed your max size, they are merely sampled down to adhere to this limit. Ensure the value you set here is divisible by 2 - so 2, 4, 6, 8, 16, 32, 64, 128, 256, 512, 1024, 2048, 4096 and so on.

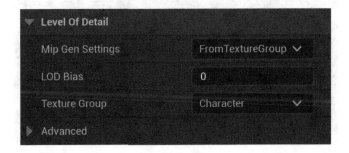

FIGURE 17.4   Level of detail settings for texture assets in Unreal.

17.2 Level of Detail (LOD)

Level of detail, or LODs, are variants of an asset that drop in their fidelity as we drop through levels. The first LOD, LOD 00, would be the most high quality with the highest polycount and all the bells and whistles. As we iterate through levels of details to 01, 02, 03 and so on, we gradually reduce the fidelity of the asset, removing polygons, joints, removing cloth simulations, lowering max skinned influences or even reducing material counts to simplify the asset through each level. At runtime, we can then measure the asset's metrics screen real estate to drive a switch of an asset's LODs.

When we are right next to an object, we should see the asset in its best form, which is LOD00, but when an asset is far away from the camera we only require a simplified asset, so we can use a lower LOD to reduce the computation of an asset. As an asset moves between being right next to the camera and on the horizon, we can gradually reduce the asset through the level of detail increments to reduce the noticeability of the asset being switched out for a lower-quality one.

LODs can be applied to both static meshes and skeletal meshes. The level of details for an asset can automatically be generated inside of Unreal, and they have some fantastic tools that can save valuable production time, which we will cover. We will also cover the manual integration of the level of details. Utilising nanite workflow for static meshes does currently replace the requirement for LODs, but LODs are still required for any static meshes that require transparencies or skeletal mesh assets; at the time of writing this book this is true, maybe one day this sentence will be redundant.

17.2.1 LOD Auto-Generation

The auto-generation of LODs has never been easier, and Unreal adds better and better tools with every update to enhance and supplement your workflow so you can focus time on more creative endeavours.

17.2.1.1 Static Mesh

To generate LODs for a static mesh, open the static mesh actor and navigate to the details panel. Under the LOD Settings category (Figure 17.5), you will find an attribute for the Number of LODs.

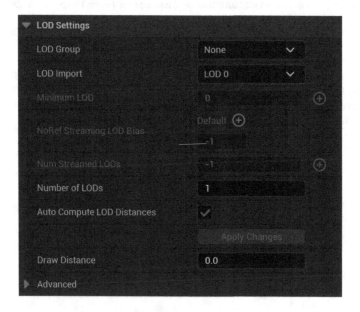

FIGURE 17.5 LOD Settings interface for static meshes.

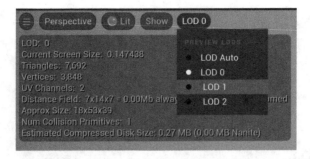

FIGURE 17.6 Viewport LOD switching tool.

This number can be modified to your desired count of LODs; between 4 and 6 is a good number of levels. Once entered, the Apply Changes button will appear—press it. This will generate the number of entered LODs with default settings, reducing the triangle count of the mesh by 50% with each level (50%, 25%, 12.5% and so on). Switching between the LODs can be performed by selecting the LOD button at the top of the viewport and then selecting a level of detail (Figure 17.6).

If you desire further fine tweaking of the LOD settings, you can customise how the mesh has been auto-LOD'd through the Reduction Settings category, found under LOD0. The primary driver of the reduction is driven by the Percent Triangles value however, you can opt to reduce by vertices instead of triangles via the Termination value. Change these values to your heart's content, then press Apply Changes to modify this LOD.

17.2.1.2 Skeletal Mesh

For skeletal meshes, the process for adding LODs is identical; simply increase the value of the number of LODs, then press Apply Changes. However, in the Reduction Settings where the skeletal mesh is a lot more comprehensive compared to a static mesh, the percentage reduction of triangles/vertices is still the primary driver of reduction, but since there is a lot more data that is necessary to preserve on a skeletal mesh, such as skinning information, morph targets, bone edges or even vertex colour boundaries, there are additional options to preserve this data at the cost of more triangles.

- **Max Bone Influences**—This controls the maximum count of skinned bone influences per vertex for this current LOD; you may remember this setting from when we skinned in Maya. Maintain a similar max influence for closer LODs and a lower for distant LODs.
- **Volumetric Correction**—Multiplier to control the 3D space the LOD exhibits compared to its original LOD. Lower values will cause flattened shapes to spherical objects, whereas higher values will maintain spherical shapes.
- **Remap Morph Targets**—This will convert morph targets from LOD0 to work with this LOD. Disable morph targets for distant LODs.
- **Enforce Bone Boundaries**—This will reduce edge reduction in areas between bones to ensure additional topology for deformation. I'd recommend keeping this on.
- **Merge Coincident Vertices Bones**—This will ensure vertices that are located at the same position have identical skin weighting. This is useful for meshes that are built in pieces, to prevent holes from appearing in the gaps between pieces.
- **Lock Mesh Edges**—On generated LODs, sometimes visual errors may occur with chunks of vertices floating away from the model. To fix these, enable this value to lock the edges in place and not simplify them.
- **Lock Vertex Colour Boundaries**—Similar to the bone boundaries, this ensures preservation between multiple vertex colours. I'd recommend keeping this on if using vertex colours.

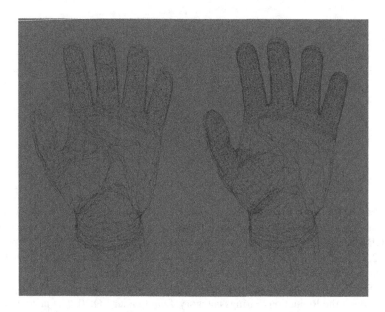

FIGURE 17.7   A mesh before and after finger prioritisation.

While not in the Reduction Settings category, the **Bones to Prioritise** value found in the LOD Info category can severely change the reduction result. This parameter takes an array of bones and utilises them in the reduction process to maintain their integrity and not compromise the silhouette of a model too much. This can make a big difference in areas where the automatic reduction is destroying information, such as in the hands, where we need to preserve finger shape for articulation. Figure 17.7 demonstrates a before and after prioritisation of finger joints for the Unreal Mannequin character, as you can see a much deeper priority on maintaining geometric shapes for deformation around that area.

17.2.2 LOD Manual Integration

We may opt for manually authored LODs by artists, as when it comes to hero assets, having user-defined control over the silhouette, shape and deformation at all levels of detail is often necessary. The auto-LODs can help if production is tight, but if the artists have the time and resources, it's better to give it a human touch. To manually set up LODs, we must take a step back into our DCC as we need to prepare our FBX. We will start this section assuming you already have the level of detail art prepared; since the reduction of triangle counts is an art task, we will jump over that part of the tutorial and just focus on setting up the LODs to operate in the engine.

We can begin by creating a LOD Group in Maya (**Edit > LOD (Level of Detail) > Create LOD Group**); see Figure 17.8.

FIGURE 17.8   The create level of detail group option.

FIGURE 17.9   Each group below the LOD group is a LOD entry.

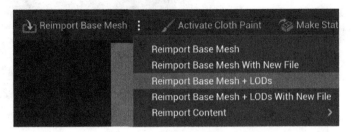

FIGURE 17.10   The reimport base mesh + LODs option in Unreal.

This will add a new type of group to the outliner (Figure 17.9). This group acts as a holder for all LODs, with each subsequent group being a new level of detail. To add a new LOD, simply add a new child group.

Move the relevant geometry for each of your skeleton's LODs into the LOD group. Make sure all the geometry in each LOD is skinned to your skeleton too! To speed this process up, use the Copy Skin Weights tool to copy from higher to lower LODs.

In the channel box for the LOD group, you will find extra attributes that control the LOD's visibility inside of Maya. The display attribute can toggle visibility, or you can use these parameters to operate LODs in Maya.

When you are happy, export the skeleton as previously covered. When the FBX is prepared, we need to import the LODs into Unreal. If your skeleton has already been imported and you have a pre-existing skeletal mesh that you desire to import LODs for, you must first enable the **Import Mesh LODs** checkbox option found in the asset's detail panel, under **Import Settings > Mesh**. Next, we can press the Reimport Base Mesh options button, and select Reimport Base Mesh + LODs; this will then begin the import process (Figure 17.10).

After this is complete, verify all LODs have been imported properly. Use the LOD switcher button at the top of the viewport to ensure the correct number of LODs are present.

17.2.3 LOD Info—Screen Size

For each level of detail, we have a customisable Screen Size float value which corresponds to the screen percentage the asset must take up of the viewport to switch between specific LODs. For skeletal meshes, this is found within Asset Details > LOD > LOD info, whereas for static meshes, it is Asset Details > LOD (*To enable customisation for static meshes, you must first disable Auto Compute LOD Distances in LOD settings*).

For example, if a LOD is set to 0.5, it will use that LOD when the asset takes up 50% or more of the screen, whereas 0.25 is 25% or more and so on. Each level should reduce this value, ensuring the next LOD is smaller than the previous, such as LOD0 at 0.5, LOD1 at 0.25, LOD2 at 0.125 and LOD3 at 0.0625. Refer to Figure 17.11 for a screen percentage breakdown.

Confirming your LOD screen percentage values can be hard to eyeball, but luckily Unreal provides a nice debug command to visualise the current LOD level for skeletal meshes in your scene. In the Console (*accessible at the bottom left of the Unreal Editor or press ` at runtime*) enter the **a.VizualizeLODs 1** command to enable, and **a.VizualizeLODs 0** to disable (Figure 17.12).

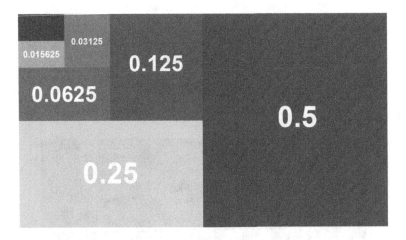

FIGURE 17.11   A screen percentage breakdown.

FIGURE 17.12   a.VizualizeLODs command for debugging.

17.2.4 LOD Info—Hysteresis

During the transition between LODs, the meshes will switch over a single frame, which can cause a noticeable pop to the viewer. Sometimes the camera view can hover at the threshold of this switch and continuously switch back and forth, bringing this pop to the forefront of the viewer's attention due to the LOD switching repeatedly causing visual flicker. To counteract this, within the LOD Info for each LOD, you will find the **Hysteresis** value, this controls an offset to screen size for the current LOD to switch back to the previous LOD. This effectively changes the value of the LOD threshold depending on the direction (whether lower to higher or higher to lower). This can be visualised by a hysteresis

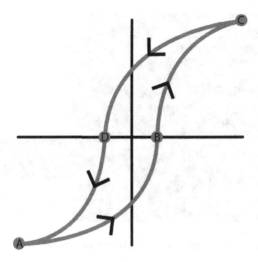

FIGURE 17.13 Hysteresis diagram.

loop curve in Figure 17.13, with points B and D being the threshold values, which are different for increasing and decreasing.

Imagine a situation where the LOD switch is at 0.5. And the camera moves between 0.49 and 0.50, in any non-hysteresis situation, this would just pop back and forth. If you add a 0.05 hysteresis value, when the value moves from 0.49 to 0.5, the LOD will no longer switch, instead, the screen size to trigger the switch has been shifted by the hysteresis value, so once the screen size equals the threshold plus the hysteresis (in this case 0.55) then the LOD will switch; then, between 0.5 and 0.55, the LOD will be present, then as it reduces to 0.49, the LOD will switch back. This essentially reduces the flicker capability by adding a delayed screen size entry, so the switch-back values differ.

17.2.5 LOD Info—Remove Joints from LODs

Removing joints from your LODs can be an additional step to decrease the runtime evaluation cost of your skeletons; the fewer joints the skeleton needs to update the transforms for, the less computation needs to be performed. At a distant level of detail, smaller joints such as fingers or toes are not necessary to be updated as they will not change the silhouette of your skeleton, so these are ideal candidates to remove.

From within the LOD Info for each LOD, there is a Bones to Remove array that allows you to add new entries for each joint you wish to remove from the current LOD (Figure 17.14). This interface can

FIGURE 17.14 Bones to remove setting in the skeletal mesh LOD settings.

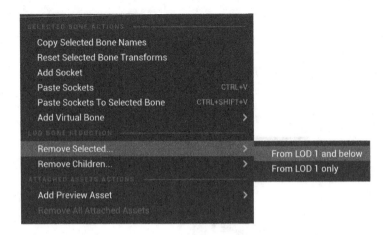

FIGURE 17.15   Remove selected bones option from the right-click menu in the skeleton tree.

be quite laborious to enter dozens of joint names one by one; luckily, there is an alternative method to remove joints from the LOD.

Alternatively, you can select joints from the Skeleton Tree window, right click and select remove from LOD and below (Figure 17.15). This will apply to not only this current LOD but also remove from all preceding LODs. This is useful to remove a joint from LOD2-4 in one operation instead of removing it from each LOD individually.

To view the remaining joints for the currently previewed LOD, you can select Show LOD Bones from the Skeleton Tree's settings icon (Figure 17.16). Switching between LODs in the previewer will update the Skeleton Tree window with the relevant joints.

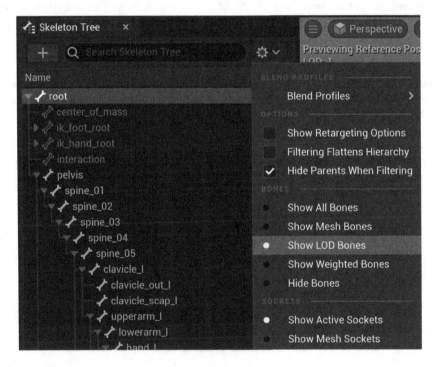

FIGURE 17.16   Skeleton Tree settings to view all LOD bones.

If you do make a mistake and accidentally remove a joint that you want back, simply remove the joint from the Bones to Remove array list.

17.3 ABP—State Machine Optimisations

There are a variety of optimisations and efficient practices we can employ to squeeze the most performance out of our ABP!

17.3.1 Multi-Threaded Animation Update

First, enabling multi-threaded animation updates for our ABPs allows for the native update, montages, players, blend trees, etc. to run on a worker thread instead of the game thread, where the computation workload is lighter. To do this, we must change a project setting and enable the setting on a per ABP basis.
Project Settings > General Settings > Anim Blueprints > Allow Multi Threaded Animation Update and **ABP Class Settings > Use Multi Threaded Animation Update.**

Keep in mind that if the ABP's root motion mode is set to Root Motion From Everything, then multi-threaded criteria will not be met, as character movement runs on the game thread. So ensure that any ABPs that do not require root motion from everything have this option disabled to utilise multi-threading updates!

17.3.2 Animation Fast Path

The animation fast path allows nodes within the animGraph to optimally access variables directly rather than require the execution of Blueprint code to acquire the value, which can cause an unnecessary call to the Blueprint Virtual Machine, adding expense to your graph every frame. The fast path is denoted by a white lightning symbol on the top right of an animGraph node—if this symbol is missing, the fast path has been exited for that node (Figure 17.17).

The animation fast path can be invalidated when a node's input variables are not a 1:1 access and the value has been unsafely modified or changed prior to being accessed, such as by performing maths alterations to the value, conversion between variable types or even daisy chaining nodes to access nested variables can all cause invalidation of the fast path.

To enable the use of the fast path in your project, ensure the Optimise Anim Blueprint Member Variable Access project setting is enabled (**Project Settings > General Settings > Anim Blueprints**). Then, node by node, check for the lightning symbol in the animGraph to identify whether the fast path has been successfully applied or not.

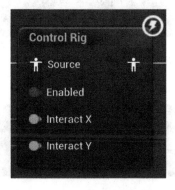

FIGURE 17.17 An animation node with the fast path lightning bolt.

17.3.2.1 Do's and Don'ts

- **Do**—access variables directly is the best method to ensure a fast path; this is a simple 1:1 connection that will not cause any problems. "NOT" Booleans are safe too (Figure 17.18).
- **Don't**—access variables via references, such as in the example demonstrated in Figure 17.19; this will cause the fast path to be exited. Instead, we should use the **Property Access** node to access directly to acquire the same functionality but maintain the fast path shown in Figure 17.20.
- **Don't**—use "AND" or "OR" nodes, these also cause the fast path to being exited (Figure 17.21). To resolve this issue, consider restructuring your variables into a combined value, or have an additional variable that is the end result of this criteria and connect that new variable instead.
- **Do**—accessing struct variables via split, or break nodes is a safe practice! (Figure 17.22).
- **Don't**—use any maths modes to alter a variable prior to connection; this will break fast path! (Figure 17.23).

FIGURE 17.18   Fast path safe practices of Boolean and not Booleans.

FIGURE 17.19   Fast path unsafe practice of reference variable access.

FIGURE 17.20   Fast path safe alternative of Property Access.

FIGURE 17.21   Fast path unsafe AND or OR nodes.

FIGURE 17.22　Fast path safe break or split struct variables.

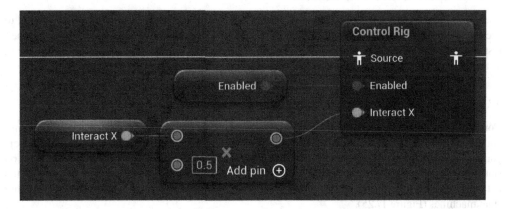

FIGURE 17.23　Fast path unsafe of math or logic alterations.

17.3.2.2 Fast Path Warnings

For the most optimal graph, we must ensure all our nodes adhere to the fast path. Look out for that lightning bolt; it will make all the difference! If you are having difficulty identifying all of the fast path issues in your ABP, you are in luck—Unreal also offers a tool to identify and warn you about any Blueprint logic being executed in the animGraph.

To enable, access the **Class Settings** inside each **ABP** on the top toolbar, and enable the **"Warn About Blueprint Usage"** option. Once enabled, all Blueprint usage will be flagged in the compiler log at the bottom of the window! Hope that helps!

17.3.3 AnimGraph LODs

When it comes to most "pass-through" nodes in the ABP (Nodes that have input and output)—each includes a **LOD Threshold** value. To use this system, LODs must be set up for the skeletal mesh that the ABP is assigned. This value customises at which LOD level the node stops working, and the graph will simply pass through it as if it were not there.

Setting a LOD value of 2 will ensure the node works until the skeletal mesh's LOD equals this value, then once it exceeds the threshold, the node will turn off. This can be useful for what would be classified as cosmetic nodes, nodes that change the visuals but not the function of what the ABP is performing, such as skeletal mesh control nodes that can be turned off at a distance and not noticed.

FIGURE 17.24 Local and Component space conversion nodes.

17.3.4 Additional Efficient AnimGraph Practices

On top of the multi-threaded update, animation fast path and animGraph LODs optimisations, here are a handful of efficient practices to ensure your graph is as optimal as possible.

17.3.4.1 Space Conversion Bundles

Since animGraph conversion nodes have expenses associated with the space change, it is advised to use these nodes sparingly and try to bundle as many of your component space operations together, instead of having multiple points in the graph that you convert to component space and back to local, as this conversion cost will add up with each conversion! (Figure 17.24).

17.3.4.2 Nested State Machine Reduction

Consider your animGraph's state machine structure and reduce the number of nested state machines you have since each state machine has an additional cost, so if you are six sub-state machines deep, you are running the computation cost of all of these even though the primary focus is the logic on state machine 6. Instead, structure your graph as flat as possible with a blend poses nodes that switch between state machines on the top level rather than relying on a state machine to switch between other state machines (Figure 17.25).

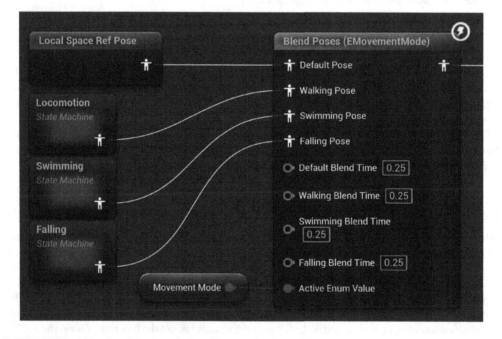

FIGURE 17.25 Alternate to nested states, the utilisation of a blend poses node.

Additionally, you can take advantage of the caching system to reduce the nesting of machines; by creating all state machines on the top level, you can cache their poses and then use them in a deeper layer of the graph.

17.3.4.3 State Machine Max Transition per Frame

In the details panel of the State Machine nodes, there is a value for **Max Transitions Per Frame**; this value determines the maximum number of transitions that the state machine can perform on the same frame. By default, this value is 3; however, reducing this value can improve performance but can cause frame delays in transition reactions.

17.3.4.4 Event Graph Animation Update Misuse

While it can be tempting to place lots of logic on the ABP's Animation Update event, try to keep it to a minimum. Take advantage of the functions that can be run on an active node, which will only execute when relevant, saving valuable computation.

17.4 Skeletal Mesh—Skeleton Pose Update

If left to their own devices, skeletal meshes will update their pose every frame, even if the pose has not changed or if it's not even rendered. While this can be fine for playable characters, some skeletal mesh use cases in environments can unnecessarily update when not required, eating into your computation resources.

We are able to manually control when a skeletal mesh component's update occurs via the **No Skeleton Update** bool available in Blueprints, allowing for full flexibility to control the update of this component (Figure 17.26). However, if you prefer a more automated method that does not require manual logic, the **Visibility Based Anim Tick Option** in a skeletal mesh component's detail panel will provide just that. There are four options to choose from.

1. **Always Tick Pose and Refresh Bones**—This is the default setting; the ABP and skeleton joints will perpetually update.
2. **Always Tick Pose**—The pose will update, but the skeleton's joints will not reflect the pose updates until the skeletal mesh is rendered.
3. **Only Tick Pose when Rendered**—Both pose and skeleton joints will not be updated until the skeletal mesh is rendered. (This is the most similar to No Skeleton Update, but will automatically toggle True/False based on if it is rendered).
4. **Only Tick Montages when Not Rendered**—Similar to option 3, but Montages will be updated when not rendered.

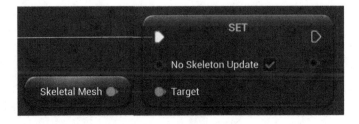

FIGURE 17.26 The No Skeleton Update option available for Skeletal Mesh components.

Since setting every instance of a skeletal mesh's visibility-based anim tick option can be a laborious and tedious process rife with errors, we are able to set a project-wide default that will affect all skeletal mesh components in the editor. There is currently no interface for this, and this must be set in DefaultEngine.ini (Project\Config\DefaultEngine.ini).

```
[/Script/Engine.SkeletalMeshComponent]
VisibilityBasedAnimTickOption=OnlyTickPoseWhenRendered
```

At the time of writing, this currently only modifies the default for skeletal mesh components, not skeletal mesh actors in the scene. However, for those who are comfortable diving into the engine's source code, we are able to modify the defaults directly in the files.

```
Instance 1: SkeletalMeshComponent.cpp
"\Engine\Source\Runtime\Engine\Private\Components\SkeletalMeshComponent.
cpp" on Line 214 (in 5.1)
VisibilityBasedAnimTickOption = EVisibilityBasedAnimTickOption::AlwaysTick
PoseAndRefreshBones;

Instance 2: SkeletalMeshActor.cpp
"\Engine\Source\Runtime\Engine\Private\Animation\SkeletalMeshActor.cpp" on
Line 24 (in 5.1)
SkeletalMeshComponent->VisibilityBasedAnimTickOption = EVisibilityBasedAnim
TickOption::AlwaysTickPose;
```

Modify the **EVisibilityBasedAnimTickOption** to **OnlyTickPoseWhenRendered.**

17.5 Blueprint—Tick

The event tick node (Figure 17.27) is often looked upon as evil incarnate, and I'm here to tell you it's not—if used correctly! The event tick node executes on every single frame, and when you have dozens of blueprints all ticking every single frame, it can be very easy to abuse, often leading to a seriously detrimental impact on performance, which is understandable given its bad reputation. Here are a handful of preventative steps we can take to get the most out of our event tick.

17.5.1 Enable and Disable Tick

Often many blueprints and their components do not require ticking all the time, or sometimes never, so let's get some control over when our blueprint will tick to prevent unnecessary calculations where not required.

On a Blueprint level, we can disable tick by default in the **Blueprint Class Defaults** with the **Start With Tick Enabled** Boolean option. This option defines whether the tick event should automatically begin executing when the game starts. This is useful if you do not require the tick to begin operating

FIGURE 17.27   The Event Tick function.

FIGURE 17.28   The Set Actor Ticked Enabled node.

immediately and require it at a later date. Not only does the BP tick, but each component can also independently tick; we can disable this by selecting a component in the **Components** window and disabling **Start With Tick Enabled** in the Details panel.

We now need to enable our tick at will; this can be done via the **Set Actor Tick Enabled** or **Set Component Tick Enabled** blueprint function nodes (Figure 17.28), which accept a Boolean to toggle the tick. This function could be connected to an event to begin ticking, then disabled when you no longer need the tick.

I would recommend in most cases to have **Start With Tick Enabled** set to **False** on both the Blueprint and Component level, then manually control when the tick happens unless it's input driven, such as a player character blueprint that requires to tick.

For those more comfortable with diving into the world of building Unreal from source code (a topic we will not be covering in this book), you can modify the **Actor.cpp** and **ActorComponent.cpp** code to ensure all actors and their components default to starting with tick disabled in the following files and lines.

```
Engine\Source\Runtime\Engine\Private\Actor.cpp
PrimaryActorTick.bStartWithTickEnabled = false;
Engine\Source\Runtime\Engine\Private\Components\ActorComponent.cpp
PrimaryComponentTick.bStartWithTickEnabled = false;
```

17.5.2 Finding Ticking Objects

At runtime, you can utilise the command "**DumpTicks**" in the output log (Window > Output Log) to print a to output a list of not only the ticking actors and components in your scene, but also every "registered" tick, so ticks that are disabled but ready to enable. This can be useful for tracking down exactly what has been activated and is executing at runtime. (Figure 17.29).

FIGURE 17.29   DumpTicks Logs into the Output Log.

17.5.3 Tick Interval Reduction

The rate of each Blueprint tick execution is fully customisable, both offline and at runtime. In a **Blueprint's Class Defaults,** there is the **Tick Interval** float value; by default, this is set to 0, this means every single tick or frame, the Tick Event will execute. As we increase this number, we increase the time between tick executions, resulting in fewer ticks.

By default, 0 means every frame will execute the tick, which would result in 60 times a second if it were a 60FPS game, 120FPS 120 times—you can probably see why this can easily become an issue across dozens of blueprints. Once the Tick Interval value is modified to a non-0 value, it now utilises real time (in seconds) as the time interval between executions. So simply, a value of 1 will tick every 1 second, 0.5 every half second, 0.25 will be four times in a second. As this number gets lower, we will eventually find ourselves at the frame time required for 30, 60 or even 120 FPS—0.333˙, 0.01666˙, 0.00833˙ seconds, respectively. *To calculate this frame time, simply divide 1 by the desired frame rate.* Customising this value allows you to run a logic tick independent of your frame rate; you may target a 120 FPS game but only want 30 calculations a second, for example.

The tick interval is not only customisable in the class defaults, but you can also modify it at runtime using the **Set Actor Tick Interval** blueprint function node, exposing further control on the frequency of tick at runtime. You could use this to your advantage to reduce tick when not in focus, for example.

17.6 Blueprint—References and Casts

In blueprinting logic, if you have a variable reference to another asset, or perform a cast, this will result in what is called a **hard reference** (Figure 17.30). A hard reference causes the associated assets to always be loaded into memory with the asset that references them; this can cause all sorts of detrimental effects to your project if there are chains and chains of references that entangle gigabytes of data into memory. It's even more nefarious, as the asset will be brought into memory regardless if it is used or not.

All of the references for an asset are available to view in the **Size Map**; once opened, in the top right corner there is a dropdown. The default value shows the disc size of the asset; however, if you select **Memory Size** instead, it will showcase the runtime footprint of this asset and all of its dependencies and hard references.

Now, while casts and hard references do have some potential for development issues if misused or abused, their use is absolutely warranted and practical in many cases, such as a BP casting to its own component's ABP, as they will always be loaded together, for example.

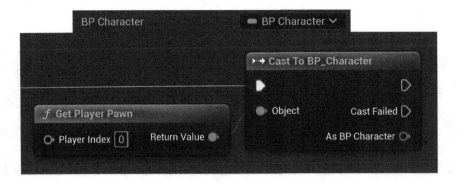

FIGURE 17.30 Blueprint cast or variables held are hard references.

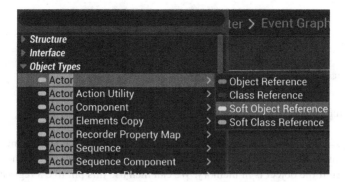

FIGURE 17.31 The option to switch reference types for variables.

17.6.1 Hard References and Soft References

So what can we do about our entangled hard references, and what are the best practices to reduce the memory footprint? The anti-thesis of hard references is soft references! Where a hard reference will force the asset into memory at all times, a soft reference does not; it will maintain a reference to the asset, but you must manually manage the asset's loaded state, checking and loading it into memory when it is desired to be accessed and unloaded it when you are done. Both soft and hard references have their place in development, and one is not inherently better than the other; they are both tools to get results.

When assigning a variable type, you can define which reference type to use—choosing between a hard reference (**Object Reference**), which is the default, or a soft reference (**Soft Object Reference**). Hard references are denoted by a dark blue icon, while soft references have a light blue icon (Figure 17.31).

17.6.1.1 Soft Reference Workflow

Working with soft references requires a slightly different workflow than the straightforward workflow of hard references. You will notice immediately that when trying to find functions or variables for a soft reference, there are very few you can access (Figure 17.32). This is because we must first

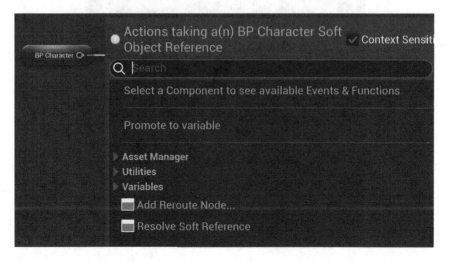

FIGURE 17.32 A soft reference does not have the same access as a hard reference.

FIGURE 17.33   A resolve soft reference node.

resolve our soft reference to check if the asset is in memory to access; if it is not, then we will load it into memory.

First, we must utilise a **Resolve Soft Reference** node from our soft reference variable (Figure 17.33). This will attempt to acquire the class or object the variable is referencing, and this will successfully return if the object is in memory. We can then use this pin like a regular hard reference and access variables, functions, etc. However, if the object is not in memory, the node will return None and fail to work.

We have two methods of loading assets into memory. The **Load Asset Blocking** node will load references into memory if you require the asset immediately with no delay, but this can lead to hitches in your project, especially when loading assets with a larger footprint. The alternative is the **ASync Load Asset** node, which will instead load the asset asynchronously instead of stalling, which can take some time to load the asset into memory. This is why the node includes a Completed execution pathway for us to utilise once the asset is in memory (Figure 17.34).

The async variant is a safer and less destructive method to use, but it comes with some inflexibility, such as load times, and the node cannot be used in functions while the Load Asset Blocking can. For both nodes, you do not need to validate whether the node is already in memory or not; the nodes have internal checks, and if the asset is already loaded, it will just return the loaded asset.

All hard references that make sense should be replaced with this workflow, use common sense here as there exists a level of diminishing returns, such as wasted resources converting an ABP that is inside a BP, as they will always be loaded together regardless.

17.6.1.2 Soft References Stuck in Memory

In the same way variables and casts can cause a hard reference to keep assets in memory perpetually, there is a point of concern that must be addressed with the Load Asset nodes—that their resolved

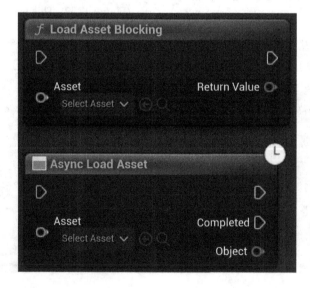

FIGURE 17.34   Load Asset Blocking and Async Load Asset nodes.

FIGURE 17.35 Clearing an Async Load Class Asset node with the Set Object Class Reference (by ref) node.

pins will keep their loaded asset in memory—forever. Unless the blueprint performing the action is destroyed, it will behave just like a hard reference, which is not good!

This is easily resolved for the **Load Asset Blocking** nodes as if they are used within a function, as values are not maintained after a function, so the values can be neatly cleared up. However, this is an issue for the asynchronous nodes that cannot be run in a function.

A solution to remedy this for the Async nodes is to utilise the **Set By - Ref Var** from the load node to reset the pin's value to **None**. This will not unload the asset from memory but will disconnect the pin from the asset so that when the asset is no longer needed, it can be cleaned up by Unreal (Figure 17.35).

17.6.2 Casts

Endeavour to reduce the casts in areas that make sense—for example, we should remove all casts from unrelated blueprints, or in instances where a blueprint is casting to another blueprint for one situation. Since a cast operates like a hard reference, causing the casted asset becomes entangled and loaded into memory with the caster asset, taking up precious memory resources unnecessarily.

It is not worthwhile removing casts in instances such as a Blueprint casting to an internal component's ABP, as both the ABP and BP will exist together, so it is not worthwhile removing this type of cast.

17.6.2.1 Cast Repetition

If a cast has to happen in a blueprint; do not then cast again to the same actor from the exact blueprint—this is bad. As noted, casts are an expensive operation that can entangle blueprints into memory together—so while performing this operation once can be necessary to acquire the asset reference, repeatedly performing the cast to acquire the same actor reference is a pointless expense.

Instead, perform the cast once—then store the result as a variable and reuse it (Figure 17.36).

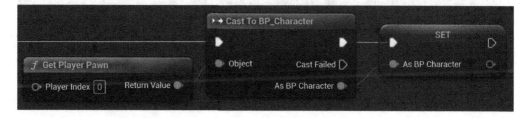

FIGURE 17.36 Storing a cast as a variable to re-use later instead of recasting.

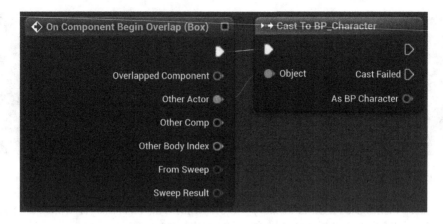

FIGURE 17.37   A common unnecessary cast to check for an actor overlap.

17.6.2.2 Cast Alternatives

Often developers will utilise a cast after an ActorBeginOverlap to validate that the overlapping actor is the correct actor (Figure 17.37), this is often an unnecessary cast as alternative methods of performing the same check can be done.

An alternative would be to check the class of the overlapping actor to validate if it's the correct class we are looking for—this is a cleaner check than a cast! (Figure 17.38).

Another alternative would be to compare the Other Actor against the Get Player Pawn result—this confirms the overlap actor is the player blueprint without the cast operation (Figure 17.39).

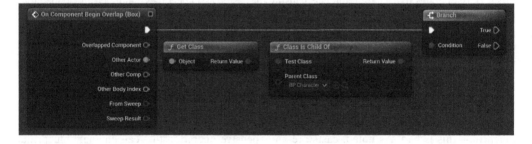

FIGURE 17.38   Alternate check if the actor is of a particular class.

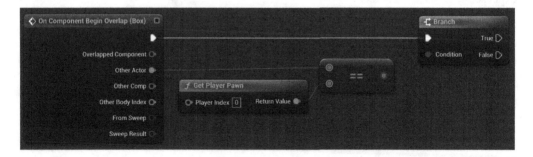

FIGURE 17.39   Alternate check if the actor is equal to the player pawn.

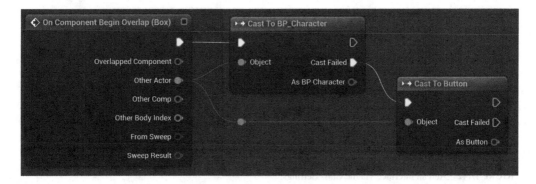

FIGURE 17.40   A bad practice of stack casts to check if the actor is one of many different classes.

This check can be worse if it requires checking for multiple class types; daisy chains of cast failure connections to casts to validate if the overlap is one of many classes is a poor workflow (Figure 17.40), as there is a better solution for this: interfaces!

17.7 Blueprint—Interfaces

An interface is a blueprint implementable system that allows you to share functions across any blueprint class and utilise them to call a function in another class with an interface without the need for a cast. Their utility for calling functions in other classes without a cast makes their proper use a very efficient practice to ensure assets are not tangled together as hard references. When calling functions in other blueprints, interfaces still require a reference to the blueprint but not its specific type, acting like a blind cast—shouting the function into the dark in the hope there is a receiver on the other side. Interfaces and casts can live together in perpetuity, and one is not the replacement for the other; they are another tool, use each for their best purpose.

Blueprint interfaces can be created from the **Content Browser > Add New > Blueprints > Blueprint Interface** (Figure 17.41). Upon opening, you will notice an immediate difference from a

FIGURE 17.41   A blueprint interface asset.

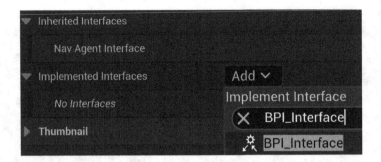

FIGURE 17.42   Add an interface via the Class Settings.

regular blueprint: no event graph, no construction script, only a list of functions and the graph view is read-only, meaning you cannot place blueprint nodes into them. Adding functions to the My Blueprint window will add shareable functions to the interface.

To implement an interface into our blueprint assets, we must open the **Class Settings** for the target blueprint, where you will find a category called **Interfaces**. Press the **Add** button and then choose your interface (Figure 17.42).

A new category will appear in the **My Blueprint** window called **Interfaces** (Figure 17.43). This will populate a list of every function on the interface. To add these to your blueprint, **right click** a function and press **Implement Event**. Alternatively, you can add the event via the right click menu in the event graph. This event will be triggered when the function is called via an interface.

Now you will notice the interface functions can be called from any asset reference, regardless of the type. This means you can call a function without the need for a cast (Figure 17.44).

Let's clean this up further by validating if the other actor contains the interface prior to calling via the **Does Implement Interface** node (Figure 17.45). This is an optimal check instead of the multiple casts problem we covered earlier. This is expandable by merely adding the interface to additional classes, rather than stringing more casts together.

FIGURE 17.43   Interface functions are now accessible in the blueprint.

FIGURE 17.44 Executing a function on another actor with the need for the cast.

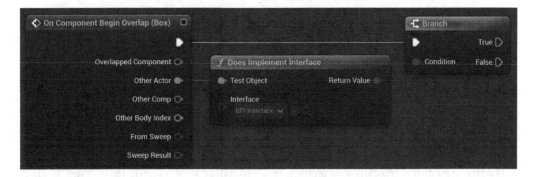

FIGURE 17.45 An alternative check to the multiple casts is the utilisation of the Does Implement Interface node.

17.8 Profiling

While we can do everything we can to create content and pipelines in the most optimal way, we still inevitably have to go further with our optimisation, and the only way we can do that is with targeted fixes identified via profiling. Profiling is the process of getting into the weeds and measuring how long a frame takes to compute and exactly what is going on in that frame. By dissecting a frame, we can see exactly what is taking up too much of our frame time and then apply targeted fixes to reduce that.

17.8.1 Stats

Firstly, one easy way to begin dissecting the frame on a high level is to utilise the **Stat FPS** (ctrl+shift+h) and **Stat Unit** (shift+l) commands (Figure 17.46). These can both be enabled in the output log, and they toggle a HUD overlay that breaks down various statistics about the game. Stat FPS details the current frame rate in FPS and the current milliseconds it took to render the frame. Stat Unit, on the other hand, breaks down how long each component of the frame took to compute (refer to Table 17.1 for a description of each stat unit counter). Keep note of the ms for each component, as if they exceed your frame time budget, then you are not running at frame rate! (*60FPS = 16.66, 30FPS = 33.33*).

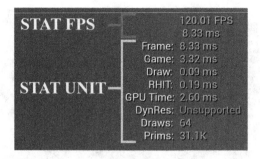

FIGURE 17.46   STAT FPS and STAT UNIT displayed in-engine.

TABLE 17.1

Title and Description for Each STAT FPS and UNIT Counter.

Label	Description
Frame	Total time to compute current frame
Game	CPU Game Thread Time *(C++ & BP Logic, Physics, Spawning, etc.)*
Draw	CPU Render Thread Time
GPU	GPU Render Time
RHIT	Render Hardware Interface Thread Time *(DirectX, OpenGL, Vulkan, etc.)*
DynRes	If dynamic resolution is used, this will show the current resolution.
Draws	Total draw primitive calls
Prims	Total triangle count being drawn

Notice how the total frame time is not equal to the game time + draw time + gpu time. These calculate in parallel not consecutively!

The largest number is typically your problem area, and will be what is referred to as being "bound." If you are bottlenecked by CPU performance, then you are CPU bound, or if the GPU is your problem, then you are GPU bound. This means that the calculations required for that component are taking longer than the allocated frame time, so targeted optimisations must be made. Keep in mind that, while you will be bound to GPU or CPU at any given time and will target optimisations for one area, this does not mean that both areas will not require work, nor does it mean to ignore any efficiencies with the non-bound area. The less intensive your game is to run, the wider audience you could have on PC with lower end hardware, or you could potentially bump up your overall framerate if you get it to hit another lower FPS target threshold!

It is important for you to profile in context; try not to profile in the editor as it will give inaccurate results. Test on your target platform or in a standalone build for the more reliable results! Let's cover some profiling techniques we can perform to analyse our frame time, and what exactly is causing us issues!

Additionally, if you are interested in viewing these stats over time, you are able to use the **Stat UnitGraph** command to visualise a history of the unit stats. This can be useful for identifying hitches or spikes in your game.

17.8.2 Statistics Window

Starting off with the Statistics window, this is accessible via **Tools > Audit > Statistics** (Figure 17.47). This is a viewable data table featuring data about the current scene. The dropdown in the top left allows switching between different modes, such as statistics about your textures or primitives.

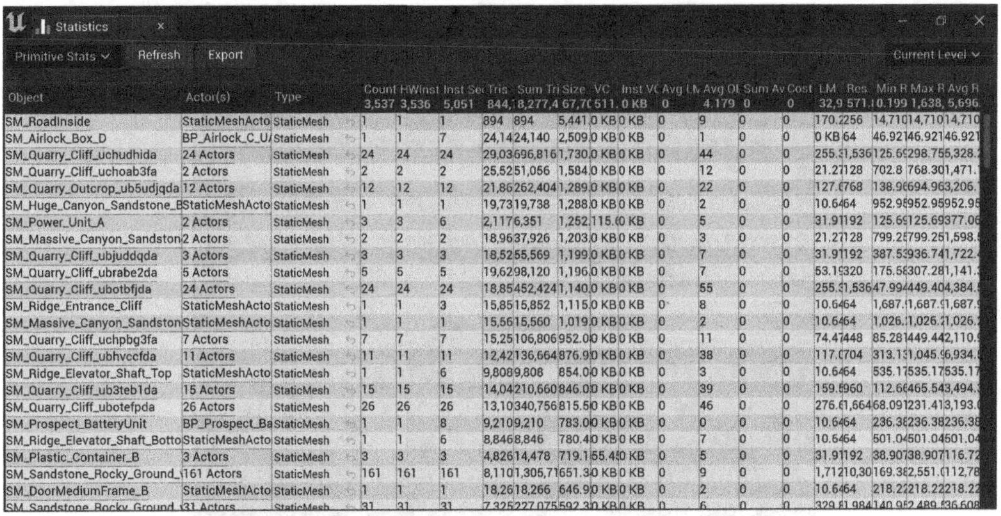

FIGURE 17.47 The statistics window in engine.

This data table structure is incredibly useful since you can organise by each column from high to low, with this ability, it's very easy to find the largest texture present in the scene, or the highest polygon asset—this makes it a breeze to find problem assets that may stand leagues above the rest.

17.8.3 Profiling GPU

To begin GPU profiling, you can grab a snapshot of your current frame by pressing **Ctrl + Shift + Comma** while playing your game. This will open the **GPU Visualiser window** (Figure 17.48) with a breakdown of every piece of computation performed by the GPU on the frame on which you pressed the shortcut. The interface is split into two primary parts: the top section breaks down the frame in bar graph format, featuring a block colour for each significant portion of the frame, while the bottom section has the frame time in a dropdown table format. In the bottom table, you are able to organise the list to sort from most expensive to least expensive by pressing the duration row.

Expanding the scene category details a thorough breakdown of how the scene time is being used; every component that is GPU-orientated from your lights, nanite or post-processing will be listed here. Diving into each category, we have to find the biggest culprits for poor performance, again we are looking to ensure our total duration is less than our frame budget, so any big standouts should be flagged and investigated. Some processes are just inevitably expensive, but worth the cost.

17.8.4 Unreal Insights (CPU, GPU and Memory)

Unreal Insights is an incredibly powerful tool that can be used to analyse all hardware component calculations of your game, from CPU, GPU to even memory allocation. This not only records singular frames of capture for analysis, but we are also able to capture and measure over a period of time—allowing us to capture any stuttering or hitches we may experience to be able to easily diagnose. Unreal Insights has an intuitive and informative user interface that can be utilised to clearly diagnose and break down each and every component of your scene to identify efficiencies or problem areas.

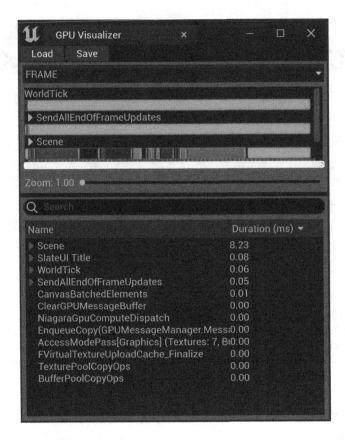

FIGURE 17.48   The GPU visualiser.

17.8.4.1 Tracing with Unreal Insights

To profile, we need to do a trace. A trace allows us to record a snapshot of telemetry data as our game runs; this is stored in an external file for use with the Unreal Insights tool. To start a trace, **press tilde (`)** or **in the output log** enter the command **Trace.File**. This will begin capturing to an external file—play your game, perform some actions and get a good sample size. Once you are happy to stop, utilise the command Trace.Stop. This will then export the trace to the**Project\ Saved\Profiling**folder.

With our trace ready, we can now dive into the Unreal Insights toolkit. From the top toolbar of Unreal, we can access the insights tool via Tools > Run Unreal Insights. This will load a standalone programme interface (Figure 17.49). The landing page you will see first is the Session Browser—from here, you can navigate between all the captured traces that the engine detects. Select the relevant trace and press Open Trace. If you find your trace not listed here, press the arrow in the bottom right corner and use the Open function to navigate to your project's saved folder, and you will find your traces inside Profiling.

The interface may appear overwhelming, but don't fret, let's break it down.

The interface is split into three main sections:

1. The **Frames** window is a timeline of all the captured frames from the trace. Visually, the graph details the time in milliseconds each frame took to calculate, making frames that hitch easy to spot.

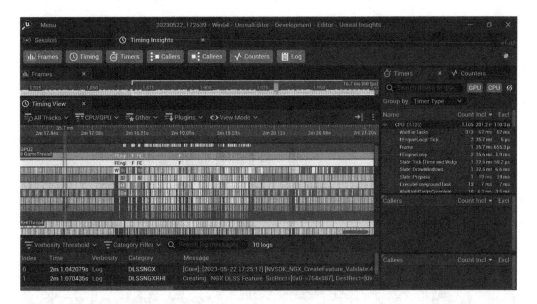

FIGURE 17.49 Unreal insights.

2. The **Timing View** window is a thorough breakdown of every computation event that was executed over the sampled trace, and how long each individual event took. This is where we will dive into identifying problem areas.

3. The **Timers & Counters** windows shows similar information to the timing view but in a sortable data table structure with total counts of event instances too, allowing for easy high to low sorting to find your most expensive areas.

Selecting a frame from the Frames window and zooming into the Timing View will enlighten you to the computation taking place on your frame. Each block signifies a specific computation; they each feature a label so you can be notified what that chunk is (Figure 17.50).This snapshot is a great example of why you should profile in context, such as standalone builds for accurate results, as you can see a large chunk for "Slate Tick" at 4ms is taking up a good chunk of the time there; this would be absent in context! Examining this information, whether that's on a normal frame or diagnosing a hitch frame, you can find exactly "what" is causing the problem, now we can move on to what we can do about it.

Now that we have these tools, we can identify problematic areas. The next step is to investigate and identify why they are expensive. Too often in development, people can identify a problem area, and instead of finding out why it's problematic, they result to the easiest solution to get rid of it. This is a bad process and should only be used as a last resort if there are no other options available. There is often a reason why it is expensive associated with a problem, often it is not set up correctly, or it is not LODing, and the list goes on. We must identify why they are a problem, and even then, we should compromise on quality before we perform the final resort of cutting.

17.9 Dropping Fidelity

In the ultimate worst case, where we have debugged and made our work as efficient as possible, exhausting all our options and are still not hitting our frame budget, we can compromise on fidelity. If we are releasing on multiple platforms, we may not need to laterally reduce fidelity across the board,

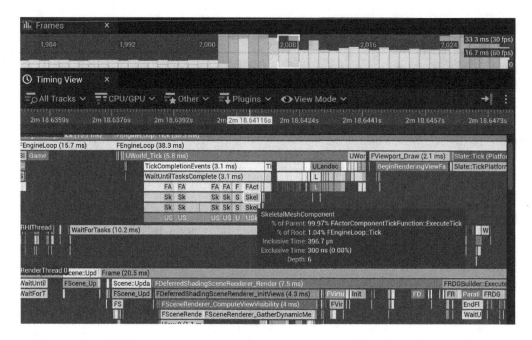

FIGURE 17.50   Unreal insights.

with one platform having optimisations that another may not. Let's tailor our experience for each specific platform to get the most out of them.

To control our per platform settings, we can use the Device Profiles interface, which can be found under **Tools > Platforms > Device Profiles**. This is a user-friendly interface for modifying the **DefaultDeviceProfiles.ini** file located in your project's config folder. The left side of the window will display platforms that are supported by the default engine settings. You are able to add new platforms in the **BaseDeviceProfiles.ini** found in your **Engine/Config** folder. Any adjustments will be reflected in this interface.

To begin modifying a platform's specific settings, press the **...** button on the right of your target platform. The newly opened interface is where we can begin to customise our project's platform settings.

The parent device profile allows you to select a parent profile, providing an inheritance-based structure. For example, the WindowsEditor and WindowsClient profiles are all children of the Windows profile, so any modification made to Windows will trickle down to the children.

The Texture LOD settings you will be familiar with already, as we previously discussed the manual ini version of this in the texture optimisation section; this interface allows for a per platform texture optimisations without the need to edit the ini directly.

The console variables section allows us to customise the console parameters utilised in the project; these are split into categories for organisational purposes. While these can be daunting to understand, there is a handy resource built into Unreal to educate you on what every single command does—let me introduce the Console Variables tool (Figure 17.51—**Help > Console Variables**). This will generate searchable help documentation for a list of all commands in the editor and what they do. Looking for all the commands related to animation? Shadows? Nanite? Lumen? It's all here for you.

The console commands can drastically change your game, performance and visual look, so be careful when modifying any and make sure you test them extensively! We do not want to negatively impact the game beyond your intentions.

Unreal Engine 5 Console Variables and Commands

FIGURE 17.51 Unreal Engine 5 console variables and commands.

18

Evaluation

Now you've come to a close on your project or piece of work, what's next? Well first congratulate yourself on the work produced, game development can be hard and stressful, and coupled with the fact when you are too close to a piece of work for too long you sometimes cannot see the forest for the trees—so take a step back, be proud of the work you and your team have done, celebrate! At least for a moment.

After every major milestone, piece of work or game project, try to take the time to reflect on your process, the work made, what went right and what went wrong. This is often referred to as a post-mortem. These can be done to self-analyse yourself or your team's practices to ensure you are self-aware and critical to identifying areas of improvement, whether that's in the process or the outputted work itself. The day you think you've got nothing to improve on is the day there's something wrong. As the old saying goes, art is never finished, it is let go.

A big component of these post-mortems, when you determine what you did right, it isn't to merely pat yourself on the back; it's to find out **why** that went right—did you apply a good working practice such as automating a piece of work so it takes less time in the long run? Did you have a cross-department collaboration that worked well because of transparent communication? Perform this same analysis on what went wrong; find the weaknesses and why it went wrong, and make notes—make sure it doesn't happen again next time. Learn from the mistakes made project-wide and don't do them again.

I would recommend creating a list of improvements to make for next time, whether you keep this to yourself or share it with your team or colleagues, you can refer back to this cheat sheet at a later date to make sure no issues are slipping back into your workflow.

18.1 Looking Forward

As part of your evaluation, I recommend looking forward to the future; your next task or project—and endeavouring to investigate any new technologies, tools, or practices that you and your team could employ to make the game and your work better. Always keep an eye out for new technologies emerging that could speed up your workflow tremendously. At the time of writing this book, the biggest technologies coming forward right now are machine learning and artificial intelligence to help with the development, creation and automation of tasks. Whether these will be the biggest new technologies in five or ten years is yet to be seen.

The Unreal Engine development team is on the cutting edge, providing state-of-the-art technologies ready to ship in your games, make the most of these industry-leading tools right at your doorstep! The very talented folks at Epic are pouring incredible resources into Unreal to improve all aspects of development, not just the end product but also changes to workflow to allow for more flexibility and quicker iteration. I can see a situation in the near future where Unreal removes the need for external packages and all work produced, whether that's animations, rigging, modelling, texturing or even code, is all encapsulated within the engine, so you never have to leave it to an external DCC. The

DOI: 10.1201/9781003263258-18

beginnings of this for character work are beginning to happen with tools such as Control Rig, and there are even some skinning and skeleton tools created for the editor. Historically, there have been a few external plugins that were essential in the past, but now Unreal offers this functionality built-in, slowly becoming a one-stop shop for everything game and film. The future looks bright for this field and the Unreal Engine toolkit.

18.1.1 Continued Learning

As we stated right at the beginning, learning never stops, and every day will be a school day. Keep learning and keep growing your knowledge base; this industry just keeps getting better and better technology, so keep up with it and it'll allow you to bring your wildest creations to life and get easier with each passing year.

18.1.1.1 Recommended Reading

- GameAnim, Jonathan Cooper (2019).
- Digital Creature Rigging, Stewart Jones (2012).
- MoCap for Artists, Midori Kitagawa (2008).
- Stop Staring, Jason Osipa (2010).
- Acting for Animators, Ed Hooks (2003).
- The Illusion of Life, Frank Thomas and Ollie Johnston (1981).
- Animator's Survival Kit, Richard Williams (2001).

Continue learning with me on my YouTube channel: **www.youtube.com/MattLakeTA**
Reach out on X (formerly Twitter): **https://twitter.com/MattLakeTA**
Good luck with your projects☺

References

Maxwell, J.C. (2000). Failing Forward. Thomas Nelson Publishers.
Williams, R. (2009). The Animator's Survival Kit. Faber and Faber.

Index

Printed in the United States
by Baker & Taylor Publisher Services